FIELD INSTRUCTION IN SOCIAL WORK EDUCATION

A comprehensive guide to social work praxis, this book provides a clear conceptual understanding of fieldwork supervision in India. It elaborates on the dynamic components of fieldwork instruction – the methodologies and effective strategies, the supervisor–student–agency triad, challenges and the future.

The volume underlines the importance of student mentoring and the imperative need to develop creative and competent strategies to make fieldwork education more responsive and effective. It also emphasises the need for the inclusion of social justice-oriented perspectives and approaches in fieldwork training in India. Instructive and anecdotal, the chapters in this volume reflect on the challenges which students and supervisors face on a regular basis in different environments while dealing with critical circumstances. The focus of the book is to delineate strategies and approaches which promote skill building and the ability in students to understand sociocultural contexts of the field and engage with them effectively.

This volume will be an essential resource for social work educators, field practitioners and students of social work, law, public policy, sociology and social entrepreneurship.

Roshni Nair is Assistant Professor at the Centre for Criminology and Justice, School of Social Work, Tata Institute of Social Sciences, Deonar, Mumbai.

Srilatha Juvva is Professor at the Centre for Disability Studies and Action, School of Social Work, Tata Institute of Social Sciences, Deonar, Mumbai.

Vimla V. Nadkarni is a former president of the International Association of Schools of Social Work (IASSW) and the retired Dean and Professor of the School of Social Work, Tata Institute of Social Sciences, Deonar, Mumbai.

FIELD INSTRUCTION IN SOCIAL WORK EDUCATION

The Indian Experience

Edited by Roshni Nair, Srilatha Juvva and Vimla V. Nadkarni

LONDON AND NEW YORK

First published 2020
by Routledge
2 Park Square, Milton Park, Abingdon, Oxon OX14 4RN

and by Routledge
52 Vanderbilt Avenue, New York, NY 10017

Routledge is an imprint of the Taylor & Francis Group, an informa business

© 2020 selection and editorial matter, Roshni Nair, Srilatha Juvva and Vimla V. Nadkarni; individual chapters, the contributors

The right of Roshni Nair, Srilatha Juvva and Vimla V. Nadkarni to be identified as the authors of the editorial material, and of the authors for their individual chapters, has been asserted in accordance with sections 77 and 78 of the Copyright, Designs and Patents Act 1988.

All rights reserved. No part of this book may be reprinted or reproduced or utilised in any form or by any electronic, mechanical, or other means, now known or hereafter invented, including photocopying and recording, or in any information storage or retrieval system, without permission in writing from the publishers.

Trademark notice: Product or corporate names may be trademarks or registered trademarks, and are used only for identification and explanation without intent to infringe.

British Library Cataloguing-in-Publication Data
A catalogue record for this book is available from the British Library

Library of Congress Cataloging-in-Publication Data
Names: Nair, Roshni, editor. | Juvva, Srilatha, editor. |
    Nadkarni, Vimla V., editor.
Title: Field instruction in social work education : a guide to research in
    India / edited by Roshni Nair, Srilatha Juvva, And Vimla V Nadkarni.
Description: First Edition. | New York : Routledge, 2019. | Includes
    bibliographical references and index.
Identifiers: LCCN 2019033856 |
Subjects: LCSH: Social service—India. | Social workers—Training of—India.
Classification: LCC HV393 .F54 2019 | DDC 361.3071/55—dc23
LC record available at https://lccn.loc.gov/2019033856

ISBN: 978-0-8153-8387-1 (hbk)
ISBN: 978-0-367-42456-5 (pbk)
ISBN: 978-0-367-81032-0 (ebk)

Typeset in Bembo
by Apex CoVantage, LLC

CONTENTS

List of figures   *vii*
List of tables   *viii*
List of contributors   *ix*
Foreword by Armaity S. Desai   *x*
Acknowledgements   *xv*

    Introduction: changing nature of fieldwork   1
    Vimla V. Nadkarni, Srilatha Juvva and Roshni Nair

1   Facilitating learning of social work values through student supervision   9
    Lata Narayan

2   Fieldwork and contemporary realities: convergence and complexities   29
    Nagmani Rao

3   Coordinating fieldwork: challenges and learning   49
    Pamela Singla

4   Fieldwork supervision: from vigilantism to nurturance   68
    Neelam Sukhramani

5	The conscious use of theory in social work practice: illustrations from fieldwork *Sandra Joseph*	87
6	Recording and documentation in fieldwork *Mohua Nigudkar*	105
7	Supervision using conferences in social work practicum *Kalyani Talvelkar*	127
8	Concurrent fieldwork training and supervision in social work: challenges and solutions in the context of Barak Valley, Assam *Kaivalya T. Desai*	153
9	The adaptive supervisor *Helen Joseph*	179
	Conclusion: issues for the future of field instruction in social work education *Srilatha Juvva, Vimla V. Nadkarni and Roshni Nair*	196
	Index	*211*

FIGURES

1.1	Core values of the *Samagratā* framework	11
3.1	Stakeholders in the fieldwork department	50
5.1	Input, transformation and output in the systems framework	96
5.2	Mapping the four basic systems	97
5.3	Mapping the four systems in the larger eco-system	98
5.4	Integrating theory and practice mapping an 'Empowerment-Based Eco-Systems Model' in the '*Mahalir Thittam*' project	99
6.1	Multiple contexts and factors that impinge upon fieldwork	110
6.2	Purpose of fieldwork recording	122
7.1	Components of fieldwork planning	137
7.2	Models/theories that guide group supervision and group conference	143
9.1	Facilitation matrix	187
10.1	The BSD praxis framework for field instruction	208

TABLES

2.1	Specialisation-based field assignments	37
3.1	A proposed pattern for fieldwork	65
8.1	Expected semester-wise learning outcomes at graduate level	156
8.2	Expected year-wise learning outcomes at post graduate level	157
8.3	Ethnic composition of communities	160
8.4	BSW 1st semester: contents for paper on fieldwork	171
8.5	Framework for concurrent fieldwork reports	174
8.6	Criteria for internal assessment of concurrent fieldwork placements	175

CONTRIBUTORS

Kaivalya T. Desai is an assistant professor at the Department of Social Work, Assam University, Silchar, Assam.

Helen Joseph is a retired professor; she taught at the College of Social Work, Nirmala Niketan, University of Mumbai, Mumbai.

Sandra Joseph is an associate professor, Former Head of Social Work, and currently the IQAC Co-coordinator at the Stella Maris College (Autonomous), Chennai.

Lata Narayan is a retired professor; she taught at the Centre for Lifelong Learning, Tata Institute of Social Sciences, Mumbai.

Mohua Nigudkar is an assistant professor at the Centre for Equity and Justice for Children and Families, School of Social Work, Tata Institute of Social Sciences, Mumbai.

Nagmani Rao is a retired associate professor; she taught at the Karve Institute of Social Service, Pune.

Pamela Singla, is a professor at the Department of Social Work, University of Delhi.

Neelam Sukhramani is an associate professor at the Department of Social Work, Jamia Millia Islamia, New Delhi.

Kalyani Talvelkar is an assistant professor at the College of Social Work, Nirmala Niketan, Mumbai.

FOREWORD

I take great pleasure in writing this foreword for the book *Field Instruction in Social Work Education: The Indian Experience*. The book is very welcome as it brings out the various facets of being a fieldwork instructor and also the components of participants and process, in field instruction. Moreover, it updates the concerns and issues affecting field instruction in the present-day context of university education. As the authors of the various chapters come from and work in different parts of a pluralistic and diverse country like India, they also raise concerns and, at times, solutions in their respective contexts. Additionally, their location in large metropoles with innumerable NGOs as well as locations in the northeast with sparse services further accentuates the differences and demands made on the fieldwork instructor to provide adequate learning experiences by the institutions for social work education. Some chapters have raised the issue of using the term "supervisor" and observed that the process is more as enabler or facilitator than one merely overseeing the student's work and, therefore, questioned its use. Since we describe the classroom teacher as instructor, I have settled for the words fieldwork instructor. That does not mean that she/he instructs but uses a variety of techniques in the learning process of which enabling or facilitating might be one, just as teachers also use a variety of techniques in the classroom to assist in the student's learning process.

Fieldwork in social work education is equivalent to laboratory work by students of science. It is a living laboratory for students to understand the complexity of human behaviour, interpersonal and social interaction, society, social structure and mechanisms of inequality and oppression and several such topics. It is also an opportunity to learn the skills of intervention and change through working with individuals and families, groups and communities, as well as with management of organisations and utilising data to bring about social change. Hence, it is a very vital aspect for the development of professional skills and to build the professional self for social work as a profession.

Because of the importance of fieldwork as a learning tool, the role of the fieldwork instructor becomes vital. Much of the professional outcome depends on the nature of field experience and the role of the fieldwork instructor. While trained social workers in organisations, where students are placed, are recognised and take the responsibility of fieldwork instructors, inevitably not all such organisations have a trained social worker, or have one who may be trained but not sufficiently competent to be a fieldwork instructor. Hence, many of the social work faculty have to also become both fieldwork and classroom instructors. It is also advisable that students under the fieldwork instructor of the agency have a faculty advisor who can take group conferences of her/his students and help integrate classroom learning with field learning. Such academic inputs are essential to help students integrate classroom theories with their observations and practice in the field. Hence, it is necessary that a faculty member have only five students for direct fieldwork instruction and, possibly, another three to whom she/he is advisor. Fieldwork instructors and faculty advisors have to make periodic trips to the organisation and many have to negotiate distances and transport problems. Each week, they have to read the recordings of the work of their five students and use the feedback with each individual student once a week and also as a basis with the whole group for student conferences. Additionally, they have classroom teaching, student's research projects to guide for MA and PhD scholars, preparation for classes keeping up with the latest literature, and their own research for which they barely have enough time. Hence, the UGC Second Review Committee for Social Work Education (1976) had suggested five students and optimally eight students for fieldwork instruction. Beyond that it will not yield suitable results. This norm was reiterated, I understand, by the UGC Third Review Committee (2001) and was practiced in several institutions. In Maharashtra the grant giving body, Department of Social Justice and Empowerment, had adopted it for norms and faculty appointments. These should be brought to the notice of all grant giving bodies. With the lapse of time and new personnel such details are forgotten. Several institutions had an inordinate number of students per faculty, which made individual conferences as a learning tool impossible. It is no wonder then that some authors have written about disruptive rules introduced by their respective universities or the University Grants Commission. In many cases, hours of work on fieldwork instruction are not taken into consideration as a part of the teaching load. These inputs are also not part of the points for Career Advancement. Research and publishing are given stress for which overloaded social work faculty do not find the time. These are genuine difficulties which the UGC needs to solve through its Panel on Social Work Education or with a special committee of social work educators set up by it.

The chapter describing problems of fieldwork in locations where there are few non-government organisations working at the grassroots, entitled "Concurrent fieldwork training and supervision in social work: challenges and solutions in the context of Barrack Valley, Assam", reminded me of my own days of fieldwork in Mumbai as a student (1955–1957) of the Tata Institute of Social Sciences. Not only were organisations fewer, they did not even have adequate funds for activities for the students with children such as paper and crayons, clay for modelling, trips with clients to the hospital, or an outing for a group or activities with women's groups. So that students are not frustrated, a modest effort was started to raise some money with a charity show. The proceeds were used by the students for fieldwork activities. Later it raised sufficient funds to assist organisations to recruit professional social workers by giving 100 per cent funding to them for the first year and then gradually tapering it off by 25 per cent till the fifth year. This gave the opportunity for them to experience the use of trained professional personnel and an incentive to gradually take over the full financing. This was the brainchild of Prof. (Ms.) Manu Desai, starting the initiative with her specialisation batch of Family and Child Welfare. By the late eighties, this practice was discontinued as, by then, most of the organisations had trained social workers. Locations that do not have suitable trained social workers may try this method.

Moreover, often the faculty are frustrated as agencies are available, but many of them function in the old mould and are averse to any change. Hence, organising projects in the field, in areas identified as requiring intervention, is one strategy that is used by several institutions for social work education. It allows students the opportunity to participate in management and influencing policy, aside from skills in intervention. Usually financed by public charity trusts for a limited period, it requires putting up an appropriate proposal and financial requirements over a three year or five year period agreed to by the Trust. This is also an opportunity for faculty to be closer to the field to test out the theories taught and to bring field experiences in classroom teaching. It is especially useful for young faculty who may have an MPhil or PhD, another requirement of the UGC but do not have the required field experience for integrating field realities with classroom teaching. It was an issue pointed out in one of the chapters. Trying to train students for largely rural communities in the state from an urban situated institution is a difficult proposition because of travel time required and the local community finding it difficult to identify with visiting students. It is necessary for institutions to locate closer to the rural communities and, in fact, make it a hub for attracting the villagers for assistance by the social work education institution. The location of the Tata Institute Rural Campus in Tuljapur could achieve this end.

Moreover, there is nothing sacrosanct about keeping fieldwork days on Tuesdays and Thursdays as seems to be the prevailing norm mentioned by several authors. For students, it is almost a 'schizophrenic' existence between class days following fieldwork days and vice versa. It is best to join the two days to a weekend such as Thursday, Friday and Saturday (half day) constituting 15 hours so that the students can have an opportunity to work on projects and, on special occasions as needed, also include Sunday. This kind of block fieldwork in the week has been found to be useful in providing various learning experiences to students. It will especially help students to travel and stay in the local community and learn its problems and cultural practices. It has been done in both the College of Social Work, Nirmala Niketan and the TISS. Interestingly, while urban located institutions for social work education do not face the problems of scarcity of good organisations for placement of students, they have the unique issue of several institutions for social work education located in metropoles competing for placement of their students. However, change of fieldwork days may avoid overcrowding.

It is also very necessary to build a fieldwork curriculum, a problem identified by some authors. The classroom teacher has a detailed outline of the subject to be taught and the expected outcome from the input, tested by examinations. On the other hand, the fieldwork instructor does not have any such guidelines. If she/he is a field instructor from the placement organisation, she/he may not be even aware of what is being taught in the classroom, especially in the methods subjects of casework, group work, community organisation and administration for correlating theory with practice appropriately to enhance the students' learning. For this reason a detailed exercise was undertaken by the faculty of the College of Social Work, Nirmala Niketan, to identify the tasks. Based on the objectives, which were identified as knowledge, skills and attitudes, a corresponding input of fieldwork task was identified and its outcome noted, which provided an easier method of evaluating the student at the end of the semester. For example, a beginning student in fieldwork, who is a Master's student from another discipline, needs to be given very concrete tasks that are to be carried out with the client system, whether an individual or a family, a group or a community. All faculty were involved in evolving the system. A meeting was called for briefing all fieldwork instructors and even those under whom students were placed but were not their instructors, because it was they who identified the various activities for the student and gave on-the-spot help to the student. It made more clear to them what needed to be done at each stage of learning. Such exercises should be tried in other institutions. It can be exhausting but rewarding.

It was very interesting to read of experiments tried by faculty to increase learning experiences for students. A very significant method was discussed in the chapter on "The conscious use of theory in social work practice: Illustration from fieldwork". It utilises systems theory and an integrated social work practice approach by identifying client system, target system, action system and change agent system. It was very refreshing to find the author using this approach to the client system whether individual or family, group or community. Though restricted to application to a group, that the author has used this theory in its application gives a very important message to the reader. I have believed in this approach and have developed and taught a course on "Integrated Social Work Practice" at the College of Social Work, Nirmala Niketan and then later at the Tata Institute of Social Sciences. I have used it even in my own situations such as when moving from one institution to another in my career. It helped me to understand the organisation, identify the problems and strategise the intervention. It is my hope that someday, many institutions will teach this theory for social work practice as students need to intervene at various levels and focus on different client systems in their practice and not necessarily exclusively only as case workers, group workers or community workers in the Indian Context.

Facilitating students' learning of social work values through field instruction identifies a new perspective, "*Samagratā*", and a framework for social work practice.

While the author states the core values of social work practice are applied both in the curriculum and field practice, the chapter contextualises Indian core values that also guide practice. It is an interesting evolution of value-based social work focused on the three aspects of the person: Spirituality, society and environment. It provides an expansion of our perspective on values to be integrated into social work practice and is a significant contribution to social work.

The many issues in field instruction that this document has brought out, aside from the past experience shared by the authors, suggest a need for an organisation to speak on behalf of the profession, a Council on Social Work Education, which the Governments have come and gone but not established. Professional bodies of social work education and social workers in India should make very sustained efforts to set up such a council. In its absence they should be the spokesperson on behalf of the profession, taking up issues such as academic policies inappropriate for the profession. Individual institutions cannot succeed as well. It would also be useful if, under Refresher Courses of Universities, courses would be provided to young faculty and fieldwork instructors and also train trainers in each institution, at least in their region who, in turn, could train faculty and agency-based field instructors. Many years ago based on similar courses in the University of Chicago, School of Social Service Administration, I had developed a course in Fieldwork Instruction in Social Work Education and another on Teaching/Training in Social Work Education and taught them at the College of Social Work, Nirmala Niketan, and the Tata Institute of Social Sciences to the second year Master's degree students in preparation for the role they are likely to play on graduating, because of the lack of experienced social workers in the field. The presence and participation of fieldwork instructors and classroom educators auditing these courses made for an extremely useful learning experience for students because of the interactions between them.

This book has invited authors from various parts of the country and the varying ecological and socio-cultural contexts in which the profession is practiced. This makes very interesting reading and various aspects of fieldwork instruction are brought out and discussed. Several bring out issues which need to be addressed. As one who has been a fieldwork instructor for most of her years as a social work educator, I could not but share my experiences which addressed some of the issues raised. Several chapters bring in new approaches and practices which would not have been known but for the sharing by the authors. Dr Roshni Nair, Dr Srilatha Juvva and Dr Vimla V. Nadkarni are to be congratulated for bringing out this publication and I hope that it impacts fieldwork instruction in social work education.

Armaity S. Desai[1]

Note

1 Principal, College of Social Work Nirmala Niketan (affiliated to the University of Mumbai). Director, Tata Institute of Social Sciences, Mumbai, Chairperson, University Grants Commission, New Delhi.

ACKNOWLEDGEMENTS

A book such as this is a collaborative adventure involving several social work educators, all of whom generously shared their rich experience in field instruction. Given the demanding deadlines, we have tried our best to be as wide-ranging as possible in terms of coverage, context and content. And we wish to thank all those who unhesitatingly accepted our request and participated in this venture under strict time pressure.

First and foremost, we would like to thank Dr Armaity S. Desai, former Chairperson of University Grants Commission and former Director of TISS for agreeing to write the foreword. She has been our guiding light and a philosopher, friend and mentor who has always been most enthusiastic and has motivated us unstintingly towards the growing need to provide high-quality training to students and supervisors in social work supervision.

We would also like to thank our colleague Dr Sandhya Limaye for her encouragement right from the day the three of us first talked about producing this book and persisting till we managed to finalise the manuscript.

We are of course grateful to our families for their tolerance and cheerful support throughout the gestation of this.

Our gratitude and respects to our teachers in formal education and our mentors who inspired us through their care and nurturing guidance and supervision.

Last and not the least, we would like to thank Shoma Choudhury and her team at Routledge India Publishing for accepting the idea and guiding us through the process of review of the manuscript. We are also grateful to the reviewers for their useful suggestions, which improved the work qualitatively.

INTRODUCTION

Changing nature of fieldwork

Vimla V. Nadkarni, Srilatha Juvva and Roshni Nair

Fieldwork is accepted as integral in the teaching of professional social work, which is both an academic discipline and practice-based profession (IASSW/IFSW, 2014). Being a practice-based profession; social work without fieldwork is like learning medicine without internship and 'dirtying one's hands' in the field. It has been described as the 'signature pedagogy' of the profession (Wayne, Riskin, & Bogo, 2010). Only through fieldwork placements supervised by experienced social workers are social work students[1] able to understand the context for practice, advocacy, research, administration and the varied range of roles that social workers play.

Fieldwork supervision or field instruction refers to the process whereby social work students learn to apply their classroom learning in the field under the close guidance of a social worker. The social worker is generally a post-graduate who works in an organisation and has the capacity to teach (train or mentor or nurture) social work students. There are various methods and tools which have over the years been proven to be effective in imparting knowledge, skills and values to the students. These are individual and group conferences, fieldwork orientation visits, study tours, rural camps, fieldwork seminars and so on. These have been discussed in detail in the various chapters in this book.

With the growing social problems in the country and changing realities in India, there has been an increasing need for social work education programs. While social inequalities and poverty have increased in the era of globalisation, there are also newly emerging issues which are gaining greater attention in social work education that embraces a human rights, social equality and social change perspective. These issues continue to negatively affect the quality of life of the most disadvantaged, poor and oppressed populations in the country.

Diversity in the population based in class, caste, gender, ethnicity, geographical distribution and many other features makes working with people for protection of their rights, equality and social justice a great challenge for social work. The social work college in Silchar, for example, identifies the migrant populations as partners in social work interventions as they are the poorest and live difficult lives with lack of basic income and infrastructure. They are exploited and oppressed by their employers with little hope for a bondage-free existence (see Kaivalya T. Desai's chapter). The physical environment itself further aggravates problems of reaching out to these people through fieldwork and field action projects by social work students, faculty and fieldwork supervisors.

However, despite these seemingly insurmountable barriers, from the inception of professional social work in India, institutions of social work education (social work colleges) around the country have been responsive to social and development issues and challenges arising from the changing contexts. To illustrate, disaster intervention has continued to evoke spontaneous responses from colleges and departments since the early years of their establishment. Some take leadership to organise a collective response of bringing together students and faculty from different colleges/departments to work on disaster relief. For example, colleges from Mumbai, Delhi and Uttarakhand collaborated to intervene during the Himalayan Tsunami in 2013. Based on these experiences over several years, courses have been developed and are being taught in the social work degree programs. These inform social work practice in disaster affected areas. Development work here would also include collaborating with other professionals for dealing with housing, health, education, status of women and children, provision of drinking water and sanitation facilities, as well as partnering with the people for better preparation for future disasters. The adult literacy movement is another example of social work involvement in the field of education in the 70s. The impetus was provided by the government of that time to universalise education through literacy. While social work students were trained to be volunteers to conduct literacy classes in the neighbourhood slum communities, it also stimulated teaching of non-formal education or adult education through non-formal methods. These and other platforms for intervention evolved into significant fieldwork placements for social work students.

Problems of housing for the poor, malnutrition, lack of access to water and sanitation, lack of infrastructure like roads and other forms of communication continue to affect the majority of Indians in rural areas and particularly the economically and socially backward populations across the country. The looming dangers of climate change with the degradation of forests and changing ecology have also to be addressed.

India has a long history of charity and philanthropic work. Civil society organisations have been active and collaborated in development programs with the government through all the five-year plans. Social services and social work organisations, including non-government organisations NGOs, have been participating actively in implementation of various social development schemes initiated by the central and state governments and have provided new ideas and strategies in strengthening community development (Nadkarni, Balakrishnan, & Yesudhas, 2016). These organisations are important partners in facilitating practice oriented learning for social work.

The current context of social work requires the linking of the 2030 Agenda for Sustainable Development with 17 goals and 169 targets (however complex and ambitious they seem). The Agenda reiterates the need to realise "human rights for all", to "leave no one behind" and "to reach the furthest behind first", by opening several opportunities to advance the realisation of human rights for people everywhere, without discrimination. (www.ohchr.org/en/issues/SDGS/pages/the2030agenda.aspx).

The profession faces multiple challenges not only in relation to the old and new social and developmental problems to be addressed but also the rapidity of growth of the profession. This includes a spurt in social work degree programs across the country and the inadequacy of fieldwork placements in terms of numbers and urban and rural distribution. According to Bhatt, there are 526 colleges/departments of social work (Bhatt & Phukon, 2015). There are several more that are unlisted. Fresh social work graduates without fieldwork experience are being appointed as faculty in the departments and colleges of social work.

There is a dearth of professional social workers working at the grassroots in rural and urban communities through non-government organisations, and a preference seems to exist for work in industries adopting corporate social responsibility. This entails another challenge for adapting to new fieldwork and supervision spaces. In these contexts, the role of the field instructor or fieldwork supervisor with field-based experience thus becomes critical to impart appropriate knowledge, skills, values and attitudes to the students to become effective social workers. As the chapters in this book demonstrate, field instruction or supervision in any context reflects a collaborative relationship between the supervisor, the field and the social work college. It is through the intertwining processes of theory-practice-reflection (or praxis) that social work learning takes place.

The following section outlines the purpose of the book and provides a summary of each chapter in the book.

Purpose of this book

Need for field-based student supervisors

With the increase in the number of new programs and in the number of students, we need more social workers in the field to play the role of field instructors. Also, many members of the faculty in the social work institutions need comprehensive texts to guide them in the methods of field instruction. Often fieldwork remains the first or only experience students have of direct work with people and thus field instructors have to assume a bigger responsibility to ensure that they receive appropriate and relevant guidance in the field.

Need to critically examine field instruction in changing contexts

Though it is often stated that fieldwork is a critical component of social work education, there have been few attempts to critically examine field instruction in the changing context. This becomes essential if social work education has to address the new problems and issues facing our country. There is no comprehensive treatise which covers the range of needs of field instructors, which this book will provide through coverage of the gamut of methods and innovations.

Aim and contents of the book

This book aims to educate the social work supervisors about the importance of quality fieldwork supervision and the effective strategies to provide field instruction to students. This is critical in professional social work education where a social work student completes the degree with minimum hours of work in the field. 'In the field' refers to direct work with people at various levels — social work interventions at the macro, meso and micro levels including social policy and social research. This book will start with the context of social work practice and a conceptual understanding of fieldwork supervision or field instruction, go on to elaborate its components and facets, the methodology and effective strategies, supervisor–student–agency triad, challenges and the future. While it is intended for the social work educator, it will also be a resource for agency personnel, researchers, student learners, volunteers or anyone interested in engaging with the field of social work. As the book focuses on the Indian context, the increasing number of foreign universities sending their social work students for field practice in India will also find the book useful.

Highlighting the changing context of fieldwork across various regions and programs of social work in this book, the authors have discussed and bring forth what have emerged as strategies for effective field instruction. This drawing from their own experiences based in different geographies and cultural contexts also gives scope for academicians, curricular developers and field practitioners to strengthen the curriculum and hold as sacrosanct core elements within fieldwork and yet factor in the diversity the field demands. They also document reflections by supervisors of various challenges that the latter have encountered vis a vis the supervisor-agency-student triad and how they have tried to respond to them. These reflections and writings become an important resource for various stakeholders in the Indian context to refer to and learn from. The crucial element of developing skills of cultural competence can then be acknowledged and built on. The narratives give an overview of what is happening in different parts of the country as well as become an important document of indigenised field instruction.

Some parts of this book will focus on the preparation of the self as a student social worker to be able to undertake tasks pertaining to fieldwork. The student is exposed to complex challenges that s/he should deal with and in the process be able to skillfully navigate himself or herself through the systems they encounter, modifying or altering them in the process and producing the desired results for impact and scale.

Organisation of the book

The book is organised in the following way: The introductory chapter, Changing nature of fieldwork gives an overview of some contexts that are changing in field instruction today and related challenges.

Chapter one titled 'Facilitating learning of social work values through student supervision' by Lata Narayan contextualises the practice of ethical social work by emphasising the values embedded in the profession and the way in which they guide the teaching-learning-practice process. She highlights the complexities, challenges and contradictions that the context poses to the profession and its practice and suggests the use of an ethical framework to address them. The author argues for the need for alignment of values of the self, supervisor and the profession in order to practice effectively and navigate the incongruence that professional dilemmas pose. She introduces a framework to locate this drawing from values that are both culturally and spiritually specific to the Indian context.

Chapter two titled 'Fieldwork and contemporary realities: convergence and complexities' by Nagmani Rao gives an overview of how changing curriculum and field realities have placed additional responsibilities before academicians who often are also supervising fieldwork and how these need to be reviewed to make fieldwork effective and meaningful for both supervisors and students. She describes the challenging complex set of factors involving the nexus between the social work student, supervisor and the fieldwork agency in creating learning opportunities. She argues that there is no one universally applicable learning model. The curriculum is expected to go beyond the demands of the field and provide interlinkages. To illustrate, the agency is challenged to prioritise to suit the learning needs of the student and yet adhere to its own goals. The student is expected to contend with the diversity of the changing contexts, shape attitudes and deal with the challenges of becoming a social work professional. Finally, the supervisor through transparency, convergence, accountability and agreement is expected to foster the growth of all stakeholders, namely, the student, the agency, the profession and the college which they represent. Rao encourages us to work towards convergence of both fieldwork and contemporary realities.

Chapter three titled, 'Coordinating fieldwork: challenges and learning' by Pamela Singla is based on her experience of the Delhi School of Social Work. It documents a trajectory of how the curriculum was initially planned and administered and over time how and why a few changes were made in the pedagogy of fieldwork itself. She also focuses on challenges in coordinating fieldwork and describes the components and array of tasks involved in fieldwork and preparation for fieldwork. She traces the curricular changes that altered the ways in which these components were transacted. The ability to hold the 'old' and welcome and embrace the 'new' in order to find a common ground and design a structure for fieldwork is described. She highlights the significant and important role of the fieldwork coordinator.

In chapter four titled 'Fieldwork supervision: from vigilantism to nurturance', Neelam Sukhramani discusses the changing demands on the supervisor and how the concept of supervision itself in fieldwork needs to move on from a traditional monitoring to a more nurturing and mentoring role. She traces the nurturance that is required of the supervisor through the learning process of the student. This calls for introspection and self-awareness at all times. The effort to build the capacity of fieldwork supervisors is inadequate. The disciplinary uniqueness of social work is not taken into account while addressing issues of supervision. Further, competing commitments of supervisors affect the quality of supervision. Another challenge that social work educators face is related to creating an alignment between diverse backgrounds, educational disciplines and competencies of the students with comprehension of the ever changing social contexts in the professional journey of students. The supervisors are constantly challenged to facilitate learning, build perspectives and reflective thinking and foster inquiry and self-awareness. The supervisor is not only a mentor and a motivator but also a learner with openness to learn from the student. She stresses that supervisors should have both the skills of social work and the ability to teach them.

Chapter five by Sandra Joseph titled 'The conscious use of theory in social work practice: illustrations from fieldwork', brings to light the theory-practice connect. She elucidates this by linking a few theories to a site of fieldwork practice involving the empowerment of women as an example, thus making the application of theory easy to comprehend. She highlights the lack of a unifying model that can hold multiple and intersecting perspectives for theory, practice, policy and research. The input-process-output model influences the outcomes that lead to a shift in systems, thus making right what is not working. She elucidates the use of theory/concepts to inform 'reflective practice' in social work education.

In chapter six, 'Recording and documentation in fieldwork', Mohua Nigudkar details the process of documentation and record keeping in field instruction as it enhances the writing and analytical skills and in structuring work and building clarity regarding social issues in students. She provides a very structured discussion with excellent illustrations of recording and documentation of different types. To begin with she explains the difference between recording and documentation and their importance in their own right. She provides specific guidelines for recordings, outlining objectives and purpose and how students can excel in writing. She also highlights the importance of documentation and record keeping as a way of ensuring that incremental and continued learning is sustained throughout the field instruction. In their writing the students are expected to relate to the context and this forms the basis for analysis and reflection. This is the only document where each student is expected to think critically, reflect, synthesise and perform an action and therefore is very crucial to praxis in student learning.

Chapter seven titled 'Supervision using conferences in social work practicum' by Kalyani Talvelkar discusses the supervisor-student relationship with a special focus on conferences and draws attention to the logistics, content, planning and value that they play in contributing to the relationship and learning journey. She describes the process related to supervision through conferences such as getting to know the field, immersion, planning, feedback, learning, analysis and praxis. The role of diverse stakeholders in supervisory conferences is explicated. She highlights the unique selling point of supervision in fieldwork, namely individual and group conferences and their modalities of implementation. While this is one site of relating theory to practice, it is also the window for bridging and providing closure and answers to questions and concerns that students experience in the process of engaging with the clients and their contexts. Conferences challenge the skills and competencies of the supervisor in being able to create an enabling learning environment for the student. She encourages supervisors to explore the use of technology to make supervision an enriching and meaningful process. In order to unleash the full potential of the student, it is imperative the potential of the supervisor is also harnessed and brought into action.

Kaivalya T. Desai, in chapter eight, 'Concurrent fieldwork training and supervision in social work: challenges and solutions in the context of barak valley, assam', highlights the context-specific challenges that have emerged due to expansion of social work education in India to remote areas within a five-year integrated BSW and MSW program. The students are a homogeneous group and hence fieldwork is structured as a linear exposure from rural community to urban agency; thus all students have a similar exposure and learning experience. The nuances related to the region, diversity of ethnicity, migration, affiliation to tribe, non-tribe groups and the geographical location of the tea estates are the unique contexts to which the students are exposed. The disconnection between ground realities and social work education challenges the adjustment and competencies of the students. Fieldwork is not often recognised in the criteria for the Academic Performance Index and this deters the motivation of supervisors. He advocates the need to have course work in fieldwork and fieldwork seminars.

The subsequent chapter nine, titled 'The adaptive supervisor', by Helen Joseph discusses how supervision itself needs to respond to both the changing profile of students and adult learners. She narrates the need for the supervisor to be flexible and adaptive to the needs of the student and yet accomplish the goals of professional training. She advocates for the synthesis of 'being and becoming' in the development of the student learner and underscores the role of the supervisor in this process. She highlights the need to be able to develop a framework of assessing student performance and proposes a matrix for adaptive facilitation of student learning.

In the Conclusion chapter titled 'Issues for the future of field instruction in social work education', the editors consolidate all the significant themes emerging across the chapters on various aspects of field instruction and categorise what have emerged as significant issues and challenges. The challenges range from issues pertaining to the self of the social worker, the systems and cultural contexts in which the site of practice is located, and the solutions that stem from their actions. The self is the instrument that is used in social work, and that refers to the person – namely the student social worker and the supervisor. The system refers to the multiple intersectionalities that the profession deals with, namely, the sociocultural system, the organisation/agency, the school of social work and the larger context of education. The actions that result from leveraging the system are the results that student social workers and agency staff produce in the field. Undoubtedly the contours of social work are changing and expanding; however, there are some aspects of the profession that have stood the test of time. They include the values underpinning the profession, the challenges that the context or structure poses and the imperative need for solutions that make the profession relevant.

This book thus provides a very comprehensive and detailed description and analysis of the different components of fieldwork instruction/supervision, learner-supervisor-agency-curriculum related factors influencing supervision, challenges and suggested solutions. It is a reader or guide for social work faculty, students, agency supervisors and college/university administrators.

Note

1 To denote students, the terms students, student social worker, student trainee, social work student and supervisee are used.

References

Bhatt, S., & Phukon, D. (2015). *Social work education in India: A resource book*. Delhi: Alter Notes Press.

Global definition of social work. (2014). Retrieved April 14, 2019, from www.iassw-aiets.org/global-definition-of-social-work-review-of-the-global-definition/

Nadkarni, V., Balakrishnan, G., & Yesudhas, R. (2016). Education for social development: The case of India. In *Routledge international handbook of social work education* (Chapter 10), UK: Routledge.

Wayne, J., Riskin, M., & Bogo, M. (2010). Field education as the signature pedagogy of social work education. *Journal of Social Work Education, 46*(3), 327–339.

1
FACILITATING LEARNING OF SOCIAL WORK VALUES THROUGH STUDENT SUPERVISION

Lata Narayan

Introduction

Social work education is based on an interrelated system of values, theory and practice. Fieldwork is an integral part of social work education, and the goal of the fieldwork placement is to provide students the space and opportunities to integrate theory, learn practice skills, and experience the expression of values in social realities. Fieldwork instructors are considered social work educators in the field and the quality of field supervision is a major influence in the learning process of the student and his/her motivation to sustain in the profession. The components of fieldwork vary across Institutions of Social Work (ISWE) in the country. In this chapter, fieldwork refers to concurrent fieldwork of 15 hours per week or 3 weeks or more of block fieldwork in one setting or working with one population. Though the focus of this chapter is on experiencing values in fieldwork, it is to be understood that students understand social work values in the ISWE as taught in the curriculum, practiced in the culture of the institution and further experienced when facing social realities during fieldwork. It is therefore to be noted that field instruction is the joint responsibility of the faculty advisor of the ISWE and the fieldwork supervisor at the fieldwork agency.

This chapter emphasises the *teaching-learning process* in supervision, with a focus on the fieldwork supervisor who is in the agency/or at the ISWE and is in regular contact with the student during fieldwork. Some of the experiences that the supervisor could provide to the student during fieldwork, (opportunities and challenges) are discussed when helping the student apply and internalise the values and principles of social work in a context of a changing ecology which suggests ambivalence and unpredictability. The chapter is based on the experiences of the author as a fieldwork supervisor and a social work educator. Discussions were also held with fieldwork supervisors to obtain their perceptions and suggestions related to inculcation of values through field instruction. The chapter begins with identifying the social work values and then reflects on the context in which social work operates today. It further highlights the role of field supervision and roles of the fieldwork supervisor. Lastly, the author discusses key values which need to be reinforced in today's context and processes by which these could be experienced by students during fieldwork.

Social work values

Values are ideal norms which are largely accepted in society, e.g. speaking the truth. These are chosen qualities of life that are represented by on-going patterns of behaviour. Values are about living in a chosen and meaningful way (Luoma, Hayes, & Walser, 2007). These may be operationalised differently depending on the culture and the context. Ethics of a profession are the manner in which we choose when there is a clash between two values, e.g. woman's right to choose abortion and the right to life of the unborn child. Ethics involves 'doing' and provides a rational reasoning for the choice made.

In India, since there is no accreditation/licensing process for social workers, there are no regulatory mechanisms for screening ethical/unethical practices. There is no document on social work values which is accepted nationally for the social work profession in the country. However, there are key documents which state the values and principles to be practiced by the social workers in India. These are the values stated in the Bombay Association of Trained Social Workers (BATSW, 2002), Mumbai and the principles stated in the International Federation of Social Workers (IFSW) and International Association of Schools of Social Work (IASSW) which are quoted here.

The core values of social work profession all over the world are to uphold human dignity of every person and every person's right to self-determination, equality, freedom and justice. The overarching principles of social work are respect for the inherent worth and dignity of human beings, doing no harm, respect for diversity and upholding human rights and social justice (IFSW & IASSW, 2004).

> Besides these core values, within India the profession is naturally influenced by the values considered important in the Indian society. In Indian society, families and communities are important contexts for relationships, leading to more emphasis on duties than on rights. . . . Further, the Indian culture tends to be more holistic than analytical and wisdom-oriented more than science oriented. Additionally, the humanism of the *Bhakti* (devotion) movement, *Swarajya* (self-rule) and *Lokniti* (people's policy) of the Sarvodaya (well-being of all) movement and socialism, secularism and democracy promoted by the Constitution of India are among the ideologies that have shaped social work values in India.
> *(BATSW, 2002, cited in Joseph & Fernandes, 2006, p. 116).*

The International Human Rights documents emphasise the right to be human and the interconnectedness of all humankind. All rights and entitlements are considered as interrelated and interdependent components of one central, generative principle: human dignity (Reardon, 1997, p. 21). The documents reaffirm the 'human right to development'. Development is based on the principles of democracy, sustainability, and people-centred participation (Dias, 1997). Social justice refers to the ways by which society envisions a just society by addressing issues of injustice, inequity and promoting diversity, within the framework of human rights.

Based on their experiences and perspectives as social workers and their interactions with the social and ecological fields, the author and her colleague formulated the *Samagratā*[1] perspective and framework for social work practice and education in 2017 (Narayan & Pandit, 2017). This perspective is based on the realisation that for a holistic and harmonious relationship between all life and 'non-life' on the planet, it is essential to design our lives and work to explore the possible integration of the three major dimensions in which human life exists and participates. First is the way we experience ourselves (at the levels of body, mind and soul) and its connection with the whole, which falls in the domain of *spirituality and consciousness*. The second is the social dimension, which includes our interpersonal relations as well as our political, social, economic and cultural institutions (*society and social dynamics*). The third dimension, which includes our physical bodies, other sentient beings and the natural environment (earth, soil), is the domain of *ecology* (Narayan & Pandit, 2017, p. 535).

This perspective emphasises three core values which are depicted in Figure 1.1 – (a) compassion, which relates to the domain of spirituality and consciousness (b) social justice, which relates to the social dimension of human existence and (c) respect for life, which relates to the domain of ecology. Some of the key principles for

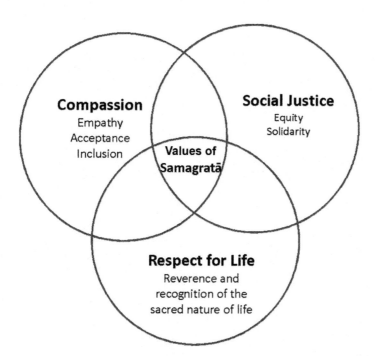

FIGURE 1.1 Core values of the *Samagratā* framework

Source: Author

the practice of compassion are empathy, acceptance and inclusion; social justice is articulated in terms of equity and solidarity and respect for life refers to reverence and recognition of the sacred nature of all that exists. This chapter focuses on the values highlighted in the *Samagratā* framework. Dignity is manifested when there is compassion for self and the other. In a similar vein, freedom is related to respect for life, where the freedom of self and the other is respected. As Figure 1.1 shows, the three values are interrelated and cannot be viewed in isolation.

The context of social work practice

The world has experienced more than a decade of globalisation which was the process by which all people and communities came to experience an increasingly common economic, social and cultural environment. By definition, the process affected everybody throughout the world (IFSW, 2012). Social workers, by the nature of their work, tend to meet those who were more likely to have suffered the damaging consequences of some aspects of globalisation (IFSW, 2012).

In the present times, one experiences a growing trend of extremism, intolerance and polarisation at the national and international levels, and one sees a sharp increase in inequities and oppressive forces. The increased infiltration of culture, religion, technology and media in every person's life has had both constructive and damaging effects on lives. A culture of instant gratification, impatience and violence seems to have permeated into the daily lives of people. At the same time, there is a gradual increase in sensitive responses to social ills and a gradual increase in consciousness towards building a humane and sustainable society (Narayan & Pandit, 2017, p. 534). Emerging perspectives which are gaining recognition in social work are anti-oppressive practice (Dominelli, 2002), feminist perspectives and practice (Menon, 2012), strengths perspective (Saleebey, 2002) and green social work (Dominelli, 2012). As stated earlier, the need to view the earth as an organic whole, 'humanity' as the common thread that connects us all and life as a unified field of experience is increasingly being acknowledged as essential. The People's Earth Declaration formulated during the United Nations Conference on Environment and Development (UNCED) at Brazil in 1992 also emphasised this need, which is seen as an awakening in the global society (Korten, 2010).

The energies unleashed by this awakening are coalescing around a people-centered citizen's vision of just, inclusive and sustainable human societies dedicated to enhancing the social, intellectual and spiritual growth of all people, celebrating the unity and diversity of life and maintaining a sustainable balance between the human uses of natural wealth and the regenerative limits of Earth's living ecosystem (Korten, 2010, p. 3).

It is in this context that students and fieldwork supervisors have to define social work, define their roles and be aware of the values required to bring about social change, as they are challenged to meet the demands of the changing external environment.

Stakeholders in field supervision

The three major players in supervision are the learner (student), fieldwork supervisor,[2] and faculty advisor from the ISWE (if the supervisor is in the fieldwork agency).

The learner (student of social work) arrives in the field with his/her own personal values and motivation for social work. Fieldwork is the learning arena, which often reveals the true motivation of the student towards social work itself and shapes it more decisively.

> The student of today is usually more independent, has often been more exposed to several opportunities, and, hence, has different expectations than the students of earlier years.
>
> *(Senior Fieldwork Supervisor with more than a decade of experience in health, TISS, 2017)*

The fieldwork supervisor's motivation, enthusiasm, skills and knowledge about social work and the congruence in approach and perspective and values of the ISWE with the fieldwork agency, are a major influence in inculcating values in the student. The faculty advisor represents the ISWE and enables the students and the fieldwork supervisor to integrate the theory to practice and also provides certain opportunities at the ISWE to the student, in order to further strengthen his/her learning in the field.

Supervisory roles

As stated earlier, in the teaching-learning process, the supervisor plays a crucial role in facilitating the student's learning and assimilation of values and ethics in field practice. The major roles of the supervisor are as follows:

Role Model: The most important role expected of a supervisor is that he/she acts as a role model for the professed competence and values expected through her/his behaviour in the field. He/she can be an inspiration for the student and motivate him/her towards effective practice. He/she also is expected to set high standards of practice in his/her work.

Educational Role: The supervisor facilitates the students' learning of social work skills and practice through the fieldwork tasks provided. Time is ensured for individual and group conferences which are the structured learning spaces planned for students. The tasks which promote the students' learning are planned and opportunities for the same are provided.

Facilitator and Mentor: Fieldwork is an emotional space and often throws up feelings of doubt, anxiety, guilt and other negative emotions in the student. The supervisor is expected to play a supportive and mentoring role by providing a safe space for the student so that he/she is able to express his/her thoughts and feelings openly.

Facilitating the student's learning of values is an underlying expectation of supervision in all the roles mentioned earlier. The next section details the core values and some practices which may be used to enhance the inculcating of these values.

Operationalisation of values through fieldwork

Before discussing the key values, it is important to consider the overall outcome expected of social work for individuals, groups and communities. The term *empowerment* is an encompassing term used across social work practice and has been defined as an *outcome* of social work interventions and *as a process* of achieving this outcome. All social work aims to empower the person/people and works towards enhancing agency of individuals in order for them to act towards a goal or a solution to the problems they face. The Field Action Projects (FAPs) of the TISS articulated empowerment as "The empowerment of the marginalised populations by building inner capacities and humanising the external environments." Narayan & Pandit, 2017, p. 491

The terms used to denote empowerment by the FAPs were: experiencing a sense of well-being; recognising and valuing one's identity and the power to make choices. This would also imply building self-esteem, confidence, resilience, autonomy and experiencing personal space. (Narayan & Pandit, 2017, p. 491). It is essential that every step in the fieldwork supervision process is an empowering process for the students' growth, if they are expected to enable the empowering process for their clients and populations. The core values discussed later are integral to the process of empowerment for all persons.

Spiritual dimension of the self

All values are sourced from the spiritual dimension of the self, as these are experienced qualitatively at a personal level. Spirituality is often confused with religion, and social work has been skeptical about including this dimension in social work practice. In the *Samagratā* perspective, spirituality is viewed with the following attributes: (i) Being spiritual is to be related to the visible, invisible and the infinite aspects of life simultaneously; (ii) When we are committed to the totality of life, we belong to the whole global family and are not bound by any human made divisions in the name of nationality, denominations, creed and dogmas and (iii) spiritual inquiry is not withdrawing from life and living but bringing a qualitatively new approach to the act of living (Thakar, 1985, cited in Narayan & Pandit, 2017, p. 536).

Hart (1999) addresses the spiritual foundation of Aboriginal social work approaches, where he focuses on an interrelationship within a framework that recognises the interconnection within and between all beings (pp. 93–94). He uses the medicine wheel common to many Aboriginal approaches, which reflects five key and interrelated elements to helping: "wholeness, balance, connectedness or relationships, harmony, growth and healing" (p. 92).

The spiritual dimension is now recognised as an important resource, rather than as a problem, in social and therapeutic work (Beevar, 1997). It has also been a source of motivation and hope and ethics for social workers (Hodge, 2005). The core values associated with the spiritual dimension are compassion and love. (Narayan & Pandit, 2017)

Compassion and love

Compassion is used commonly in social work terminology, and it is expected that this value and feeling is experienced by all. Compassion is core to all the other values and needs to be emphasised, as all life promoting values spring from compassion and love. It is an important source of empowerment and challenges and resists domination. Compassion is associated with empathy, sympathy and feeling for the other. Empathy is clearly defined as the ability to understand and resonate with the feeling of the other person. Compassion, in contrast, is defined as an emotional response when perceiving suffering and involves an authentic desire to help alleviate that suffering (Seppala, 2013). This actually gives us energy and a sense of purpose and direction. When we act upon this motivation, both we and those around us benefit still more (Dalai Lama, 2015, p. 55; Seppala, 2013).

Freire, in his Pedagogy of the Oppressed (1972), stresses that true liberation is an act of love. "The naming of the world, which is an act of creation and re-creation, is not possible if it is not infused with love. Love is an act of courage, not of fear, love is commitment to other . . . the cause of liberation. . . . Love must generate other acts of freedom; otherwise, it is not love" (p. 22).

Practices for enhancing compassion

Students can be encouraged to experience and learn compassionate training practices such as mindfulness and use of silence, meditation and practice of self-compassion which facilitate the process of greater awareness of our thoughts, feelings, body sensations and the surrounding environment in a caring, non-judgmental manner (Brown, 2011).

Neuroscience has shown that mindfulness gives people more control over their lives. Such practices reduce our ego-centric bias or the tendency to interpret things for self-benefit and gratification. It also facilitates the noticing of the suffering of others and builds the capacity to be compassionate. A study by Dr Davidson (2009), who studied the meditative states of Buddhist monks, found that through training of the mind, the brain can be transformed and generate compassion. Siegel, founder (1999, 2007) of the emerging field of interpersonal neurobiology, has found evidence that meditative exercises and mindfulness promote the growth of integrative fibers in the brain, and integration is the fundamental mechanism of self-regulation. Through his studies of the brain and the 'mind' he shows how we can experience a sense of deep wellbeing and compassion for ourselves and others, and we are an interconnected whole (Siegel, 2007).

A study in School of Management, IIT Bombay showed that in a compulsory course on self-awareness in the first year of the management course, the students who were taught and encouraged to practice mindfulness meditation surpassed the control group and scored higher on all parameters of traits of mindfulness, egocentric bias, compassion and moral reasoning (Pandey, 2017).

Practices of gratitude and forgiveness

A daily practice of gratitude and forgiveness in spite of all the challenges of life is another way of nurturing the compassionate self. There are several exercises to cultivate gratitude, such as maintaining a gratitude journal, gratitude practices for daily experiences and so on. The supervisor could facilitate this process for the students, in relation to the experiences in the field, e.g. appreciating strengths of staff, students and others is another practice which could be role-modeled by the supervisor. Students could be encouraged to practice gratitude in their own lives.

Practicing forgiveness is often more difficult, yet it is essential for the 'forgiving' student's peace of mind, rather than the person being forgiven. There are practices such as circle work, which facilitate the process of forgiveness. At the agency, learning to apologise for mistakes and clarification of misunderstandings in communication could be processes which enable forgiveness.

Earth as a living organism

Historically, communities lived with an understanding and reverence for the earth as a living organism. Social issues and concerns, including Urbanisation and urban issues have arisen due to understanding space and the earth as a commodity to be used for human survival (Narayan & Pandit, 2017). This is not just an issue for those in rural/tribal locations but life in all habitats.

Impact of urbanisation on ecology

For example, mangroves, forest areas, and open spaces are fast disappearing in cities as these are being destroyed for development programmes such as housing and transport for urban cities. Displacement of rural/tribal populations for development projects such as big dams results in disconnection from their natural habitat, loss of culture and traditional livelihoods and loss of sense of 'community'. Increased migration to cities results in unemployment for the migrants and, hence, influences their state of living, identity and increased vulnerability to being exploited in the city. This can no longer be ignored and it seems imperative that social workers reconnect with the earth and understand the planet and ecology as part of their social analysis and interventions. "The native wisdom of treating the earth as a living organism would enable a transition to a more connected, ecological and sustainable way of being and heal the damage done to the earth, build resilience of communities, and work towards the well-being of all" (Narayan & Pandit, 2017, p. 537). Students could be helped to reflect on their lifestyles and the values indoctrinated by the paradigm of consumerism and its effects on all aspects of human life, such as the health of the citizens.

Ecological degradation and impact on health

Unfortunately, efforts to mitigate the harmful effects of ecological degradation are made only when the situation becomes a crisis. e.g. the effects of air pollution on the health of citizens was evident in New Delhi, and the government had to impose strategies by legal measures such as odd and even days for using vehicles, keeping schools closed on certain days when the air pollution limits showed high toxicity, banned construction and stricter laws for burning of leaves and garbage (Singh, 2016).

Apart from being sensitised through knowledge about the urgent need to integrate the ecological perspective in all development analysis, being with nature in any form is increasingly occupying centre stage in promoting our wellbeing. Ayurveda, the ancient tradition of healing in India, recommends spending time with nature every day. Nature allows us to shift our attention beyond the domain of our ego and to recognise that we are inextricably connected to the universe (Brieske, 2018).

Suttie (2016) shows through studies that being with nature helps reduce anxiety and stress, increases attention capacity and creativity, increases ability to connect with people, enhances physical health (lowers heart rate, boosts immunity, deeper sleep) and helps one see the larger picture (Bratman, Daily, Levy, & Gross, 2015; Lee et al., 2014; Zjang, Piff, Iyer, Koleva, & Keltner, 2014). According to environmental psychology, spending time with nature has three positive effects which are, reduced stress, improved mood and improved cognitive performance (Positive Psychology Program, 2014).

Practices for connecting with nature

Apart from including the ecological analysis when understanding society, *reconnecting* with nature is essential for students and this can be facilitated in several ways. Experiencing working with clay, sand, painting with hands using natural colours and being with nature strengthen the awareness and relationship of our physical bodies and our larger ecological body, the earth. The supervisor can encourage the use of outdoor spaces for meetings and conferences, rather than being confined to the four walls of the agency. Students may be encouraged to use art forms such as clay work, sand and painting with hands with their clients and groups. Growing plants and taking responsibility for the environment of the agency are other ways of connecting with nature. Such activities make them more compassionate to the larger issues of global ecology.

> **EXAMPLE OF PRACTICE OF CONNECTING WITH NATURE**
>
> Given here are comments of students who had an exercise of communicating with a tree, as part of a course conducted by the author. Feedback from a course taken by the author in 2016, where the focus was on the personal and interpersonal development of the self:
>
> > "First I thought it was a stupid exercise, and found it very difficult to open up, but after a while, I realised that I could talk to it without inhibitions, and experienced unconditional love, and a friend I can rely on."
> >
> > "A humble tree taught me more than a human could – live to our potential, flow, blossom, and give out the unique fragrance of our positivity, kindness and genuineness."
> >
> > "Give when you can – my tree taught me that."

Social justice

Social justice involves addressing injustice, power imbalances and exploitative and oppressive processes, and interventions to address these concerns. Equity and solidarity are inherent in the value of social justice. Today, it is very difficult to establish clear and simplistic cause-effect relationships between the victim and victimiser, and, hence, it is important to recall the Freirian pedagogy (1970) where the oppressed and oppressor are participants in the liberation process, and, in the long term, co-own the change process and outcome. Gandhi too spearheaded the resistance to colonial rule with non-violence, consistently choosing not to breed ill feelings towards the British.

After several years of participating in politics and practice and having witnessed activist organisations break down due to judgmental views, self-righteousness and despair, Butot (2005) writes,

> I have come to question whether radical societal and individual transformation can be realized if it is not grounded in a loving stance toward others, especially those considered "other" from ourselves. I wonder if deep and sustainable change towards social justice and individual well-being can arise, or even be fully conceived, if the context for the change process does not include recognition of unity and diversity as coexistent.
>
> *(Butot, 2005, p. 2)*

Values linked to democratic participation (respect for all) for meeting the needs of the marginalised can no longer be based on collaboration and acceptance of the decisions of dominant groups (which may include the social work agency). It would need to be done through collective visioning of all those affected and "*co-creation of new systems for the well-being of the whole*" (Narayan & Pandit, p. 538).

> **AN EXAMPLE OF THIS IS DEPICTED HERE**
>
> In 2017, reputed women's groups in Maharashtra and interested men and women, under the auspices of the Mrinal Gore Interactive Centre for Peace and Social Justice in South Asia, were engaged in Dialoguing Masculinity and co-creating a "Manual Towards Comprehending Masculinist Politics of South Asia". This dialogue aims to go beyond the binaries of man/woman, male and female differentials constructed by societies and culture. The group has conducted workshops with academia, activists and survivors of violence in Pune, Jaipur and Guwahati, Nagpur and Dhule and have collectively evolved this perspective, which is not just going beyond binaries but locating violence embedded in the structures of South Asian societies and heightened in the intersectionalities of patriarchy, caste, religion and ethnicity. The workshops have involved youth but more importantly women, legal activists, community leaders, media representatives, writers and others across from rural Maharashtra and the States of Gujarat, Rajasthan, as well as some of the North Eastern States. This process was launched at a South Asia Conference held in Mumbai in collaboration with the Tata Institute of Social Sciences in December 2014.

Open community settings (urban workers' colonies,[3] street people, rural or tribal communities) are more likely to provide a direct experience of social justice, as community work necessitates confronting the inequalities and oppression faced by the people. When the setting is within a larger system, e.g. school, hospital, the issues of injustice are not always taken at the systemic level, and the client system is rarely mobilised to take action in order to obtain better services.

Practices for values of social justice

Creating awareness about the concerns faced by the population which the fieldwork agency works with is the first step towards sensitising the student to issues of injustice in the field. This process enables the student to reflect on his/her personal position on injustice and the experience of personal 'privilege' in his/her own life.

The students can be made to engage with the issues faced by the client system in different ways. Students can be helped to create awareness in the larger community about the social injustices faced by the client system. Use of street plays, posters, exhibitions and so on can be methods used for such purposes, e.g. issues of disability, cleanliness and sanitation in slums. In such situations, the agency's support is essential, so that follow up tasks may be undertaken by the agency staff. Students can be also encouraged to get associated with an issue related to the agency's goals, through a network or another organisation which works on advocacy issues, e.g. safe spaces for women. Case studies or articles may be discussed and reflected upon in individual/group conferences. These activities need to be linked consciously to the values of social justice. The boundaries of engagement of the agency on an issue could be a realistic challenge, and students need to be given the space for such deliberations and simultaneously be exposed to opportunities for engagement outside the system. It is also crucial that all students be placed in an open community for at least one year of their fieldwork, in order to really understand and experience people's overall state of marginalisation.

Peace and non-violence

Discussions of social justice are usually accompanied by confronting issues related to conflict and violence and the student is often required to deal with this at the personal and professional level. According to Reardon (1997, p. 23) the forms of violence are physical violence, structural violence, political violence and cultural violence. The current paradigm of development itself is a significant cause of human rights violations. Gandhi knew that the desire to amass wealth, when resources were limited, would inevitably lead to violence both at the individual and societal levels. Hence, he pleaded for a life of simplicity and self-control (Narayan, 2000). Freire (1979) also said that, personally, he does not advocate violence as a strategy for social transformation though he accepted that the existential reality of many developing countries was itself violent and unjust.

The UN Human Development Report (1994) states that "without peace, there may not be development, and without development, peace is threatened". It further states that peace and security will not be achieved except in the context of sustainable development that leads to "human security" (United Nations, 1994, cited from Andreopoulos & Claude, 1997, p. 91).

Working towards peace and harmony on the planet is inherent in the values related to compassion, human dignity, and respect for all life. Hence, though students need to be aware of issues and take stands against issues of social injustice, it is also important that students learn practices which lead to peace and non-violence.

Practices for peace and non-violence

Peace is the absence of conflict or a state of being which one aspires to have. One major goal of peace education is to teach how people can be in conflict while maintaining their dignity and the dignity of the other. Today, there are several mechanisms by which peace-building, healing and reconciliation of communities and populations are attempted successfully. Students may be exposed to some of these activities and, if possible, learn some of the techniques of peace building.

Education for sustainable development, such as education for conflict resolution, healing and reconciliation of communities, multicultural education, developmental education, human rights education and non-violent communication are all termed as peace education.

Circle work which is an ancient practice is being revived for building communities and is being used for conflict resolution, building trust and problem solving. It provides a safe, non-judgmental space for sharing and deep listening. "Circle refers to a process of facilitating dialogue wherein, (i) a talking piece is the primary mode of regulating the conversation, so that each person has an equal opportunity to speak; (ii) participants engage in an intentional conversation about values and a set of guidelines for how they want to be together; (iii) the process opens and closes with some form of ceremony; and (iv) building relationships precedes and is treated as equally important as tackling difficult issues" (Narayan & Pandit, 2017, p. 543).

The Peacemaking Circle process is one of the several practices now being used as an alternative to traditional sentencing and other criminal justice mechanisms for responding to violence and harm (Boyes-Watson, 2008). Some of these processes may be included when learning group work practice in the field.

Students can also be encouraged to understand, be sensitive and non-judgmental about the local culture in situations where they come from a different context or region. Opportunities for interactions with populations/people during their indigenous cultural practices and learning about their lifestyle would enable students to respect and accept diversity in varied communities.

Core skills for practice of values

Specific skills and processes for developing key values have been mentioned in the earlier paragraphs. Two core skills which are essential in all the skills and processes mentioned earlier for the expression of values are the skills in communications and, therefore, skills in nurturing relationships.

Communication

All students of social work learn about and practice communication skills such as verbal, non-verbal, asking questions listening, clarity of words, tone of voice and so on. All the skills of communication contribute to the process of interaction between 'us' and 'the other', whether in working with individuals, groups or communities. For this process, *dialogue* is a well-recognised practice in social work.

Dialogue goes beyond a two way communication and is a tool for change in a peaceful manner. It requires operating in a non-judgmental space, accepting differences or opposing views, and empathetic deep listening. Dialogue does not necessarily come up with solutions but genuine questioning and interaction for problem solving. It provides the space for an open and inclusive process based on mutual respect, and those involved learn democratic processes. These would include practicing of listening, providing space for authentic and free expression for each person, learning to give and accept feedback and allowing for different opinions. (Holloway, 2004).

According to Freire, a dialogue needs to be such that it has profound love for the world and people and humility and intense faith in the listeners (Narayan, 2000). These are skills which students can imbibe through the observation of the fieldwork supervisor at work and also the manner in which the learning spaces, such as the individual and group conferences, are used to practice dialogue.

Non-violent communication (NVC) is form of communication which is value-based, a process developed by Rosenberg (2003), which aims at a particular form of consensus, where needs of both parties are met. NVC focuses on words as conscious responses, based on an awareness of our observation, feelings, needs and request. NVC suggests two key elements essential to creating change even within systems of domination. One is a re-examination of our deepest assumptions about human needs and motivation; the other is an understanding of power and our ways of using it. It is an approach that can be used at all levels of communication and in diverse situations (Killian & Lasley, 2008). NVC is a relatively new process which students could be exposed to at the fieldwork agency or the ISWE, as it directly relates to the practice of social work values.

Use of language

Words are always value-laden and this is evident in the changes in social work vocabulary over the years. The social work profession has been making efforts to modify words to convey sensitivity and humaneness and also to be non-judgmental. Thus, women engaged in prostitution are known as sex workers, and the disabled are now persons with disability. In India, with a large number of local languages and students hailing from various locations in the country, it is likely that the student may not know the language of the people. These students tend to get overwhelmed or reluctant when they have to work with people whose language is not familiar to them. Though language is an essential tool to communicate with people and it is important that students learn the language of the people, the lack of it need not imply that no communication is possible. Sometimes the use of sensitive non-verbal communication can convey caring, compassion and empathy more than words.

> Many students do not know the state language, (e.g., Marathi, in the state of Maharashtra, India), when they begin fieldwork, but they soon learn to communicate with a smattering of Hindi (the national language of India), or through learning the key words. Language is not an impossible barrier as it is sometimes made to be.
> *(Senior Fieldwork Supervisor with experience in Health, TISS, 2017)*

Lack of knowledge of the local language can also be a factor which can help in equalising power between the student and the client, especially when the student is an eager learner and willing to learn the language from them.

Nurturing the inner self

Inculcating and assimilating the values mentioned in the earlier sections is part of the internal personal journey of an individual which is a lifelong process. Hence, it is crucial that time and space are provided in the supervisory process, to enable students to identify, reflect and make choices, as they transition from personal values gained as part of their life socialisation processes and attempt to assimilate values expected of a trained social worker.

> Students come with their own perceptions about populations they engage with the field, views about poverty. They need to unlearn many of these perceptions, especially in the first phase of fieldwork. They need the space and freedom to learn from their own life journeys, and JUST BE! Facilitating their learning to build connections with those around is a major role of the supervisor.
> *(Senior Fieldwork Supervisor with experience in the field of health, TISS, 2017)*

Some of the attributes of self which need to be nurtured in the process of field supervision include the following: self-awareness and self-esteem are essential for the process of empowerment which enables one to identify one's stand vis-a-vis a social issue, to communicate these stands authentically and to commit to them through action. Engaging in the process of change affects the self and often surfaces emotions such as fear, guilt, anxiety, despair and dilemmas related to acceptance of diversity, self-acceptance and negotiating and aligning personal needs and professional expectations, accepting and dealing with complexity and uncertainty. These are often the causes of angst, cynicism, a sense of victimisation and alienation and burnout among social workers. Thus, there is a need to create spaces within fieldwork and supervision that allow for verbal expression and exploration; stress release; holistic growth of the social worker through physical, emotional, intellectual and spiritual processes and reflection on application of values in personal lives or collective spaces. Creating a culture of self-care, self-healing and collective healing processes enables social workers to be more authentic and caring as well as operate from a sense of well-being.

Wong (2013) includes mindfulness exercises, Circle sharing and silent retreats in social work classes with students and faculty, where the participants reflect on their experiences and its implications on their personal and professional lives. Feedback from the students showed that these practices deepened their awareness through the five senses and were able to connect to all parts of themselves. They were able to embody critical reflective practice in a way that is not achieved through conventional teaching and learning of practice only with the mind.

Supervision and facilitating learning of values

Having discussed the key values and some practices for the same, this section relooks at the supervisory roles and the ways in which the supervisor could facilitate the student's learning of values. Values of the profession help practitioners to negotiate spaces for practice, provide the foundation and background to foster critical thinking and analytical competencies, assist in decision making towards interventions and act in an ethical manner that is beneficial to all parties concerned. It becomes the responsibility of the supervisor to provide opportunities to foster such learning. The practice of values has to be woven into everything that the supervisor does during the time when the student is at the agency, or in the supervision process.

The supervisor primarily demonstrates social work values through her/his very being and role-models what is expected of a social worker, e.g. how is respect for a person demonstrated in the agency? It could be as basic as the welcoming ambience in the agency, such as offering water, the seating arrangements which denote equality, where the workers, students and group members are seated at the same level or demonstrating respectful behaviour through their communication to everyone in the agency and in the field. Engaging students in decision making processes and other activities can teach them principles of participation and skills of dialogue.

The organisational culture is a strong determinant for the way in which students imbibe values of social work. The students appreciate those who are friendly, informal, democratic and make time to listen to them. In certain agencies, the office is seen as a space to drop in, and this creates a sense of 'ownership' about the agency. "*We are involved in the mental journey of the youth. This can be quite strenuous, but is required*" Youth worker at the NGO, Samvada, Bangalore, 1994. When the students experience a sense of ownership of the organisation, they are willing to learn and change much faster.

For her/his role as an educator, the individual and group conferences and recordings of the students are the structured tools in social work education. The time for the conferences should be considered sacred and 'protected time' for the student. Supervision 'on the run' does not provide adequate time to fulfil the supervisor's role as an educator. The dedicated time of the conferences provide the safe, non-judgmental space, where students can be facilitated to learn the skills and values related to practice. Reflections on work done, dilemmas faced and challenges faced may be discussed. Some of the practices mentioned in the earlier sections related to mindfulness; silence can also be introduced and practiced during the conferences. Group conferences offer tremendous opportunities for discussions, dialogues and group learning. If there is only one student in the agency, a group for learning may be formed which may include volunteers, staff and so on. Fieldwork recordings of the students form the basis for the discussions held during the conferences, and guidelines for writing recordings should contain reflections on the practice of/ challenges faced when practicing values in the field. Recordings are also a major tool for students to learn the value of accountability to the client system.

> I am very particular about students submitting recordings regularly and on time, as this is the basis on which they plan their work for the next week. The message has to be clear and loud, that fieldwork is not ad hoc . . . you do not just go and decide the tasks on the day itself. They are accountable

and responsible for the decisions they make for the people. The value of time management is taught through the time diary, and this is also related to their responsibility to the people and respect for their time.

(Senior Fieldwork Supervisor with experience in the field of Health, TISS, 2017)

Providing the students opportunities to shadow and observe the fieldwork supervisor and other staff enables the student to observe the skills and the expressions of values through behaviour.

From day one of fieldwork, students are part of all the activities of the tribal Sangatna (collective). They accompany the contact persons in the field (tribal areas), and observe them, their language, their communication and behaviour. They are also part of the process, and are given roles to play in meetings, and other interactions.

(Senior Fieldwork Supervisor with experience in Rural Communities, TISS, 2017)

Fieldwork challenges the student to confront the ethical realities of the field setting (for example, the student may face conflicts at being exposed to different cultures, over his/her role in influencing other people's lives and maintaining balance between personal and professional values). This is where the mentoring role of the supervisor comes into play. The supervisor would need to guide the student in the transition from the values followed as layperson to those of a professional worker.

Conclusion

Contextualising and operationalising values and ethics is a challenging task today. To address ambiguities, paradoxes and seeming contradictions, there is a need to be rooted in social work values to steer social work practice. In this chapter, the core values of social work are identified within the *Samagratā* framework, namely, human dignity and respect for all life, compassion and social justice. Fieldwork is an important arena in which to practice and emulate the values of the profession. Fieldwork supervisors and the faculty of the ISWE have the major responsibility of helping students to understand and imbibe these values.

It is to be acknowledged that some of the practices mentioned in the chapter are relatively new in social work in India. The practices mentioned are not exhaustive, and the author has included only those which she is aware of. Attending to the inner self and adopting practices for personal well-being and effectiveness as well as developing collective competencies as social workers and practicing professional values and experiencing the interconnectedness between all life forms are essential for every social worker. Facilitating students to learn techniques of mindfulness, meditation and others would be the responsibility of the ISWE, as it would not practical to expect fieldwork supervisors to know the practices. Hence, the ISWE also has the responsibility of providing opportunities to the fieldwork supervisors to learn these practices.

Authenticity cannot be taught but can be enhanced by on-going self-reflection. This is the core of supervision whereby students and the supervisor co-learn and jointly experience a 'professional conscience' in social work practice. It is essential that students learn and experience humane ways of interacting with people and communities.

Personal transformation is necessary to achieve social transformation.

Notes

1 *Samagratā* translates into inclusiveness or wholeness (Collins Dictionary, 2014).
2 The supervisor could be a social worker in the agency, or a faculty member of the ISWE.
3 More commonly known as slum communities.

References

Andreopoulos, G. J., & Claude, R. P. (1997). *Human rights education for the twenty-first century*. Philadelphia, PA: University of Pennsylvania Press.
Beevar, D. S. (Ed.). (1997). Soul healing and the family. In D. S. Beevar (Ed.), *The family, spirituality and social work* (pp. 1–11). New York, NY: The Haworth Press. Co-published simultaneously as *Journal of Family Social Work*, 2(4).
Bombay Association of Trained Social Workers (BATSW). (2002). Declaration of professional social workers 2002. In J. Joseph & G. Fernandes (Eds.), *An enquiry into ethical dilemmas in social work 2006* (p. 116, Appendix IIIb). Mumbai: Research Unit, College of Social Work, Nirmala Niketan.
Boyes-Watson, C. (2008). *Peacemaking circles and urban youth: Bringing justice home*. Minnesota, MN: Living Justice Press.
Bratman, G. N., Daily, G. C., Levy, B. J., & Gross, J. J. (2015, June). The benefits of nature experience: Improved affect and cognition. *Landscape and Urban Planning*, *138*, 41–50.
Brieske, T. (2018). *Healing through nature*. The Chopra Center. Retrieved February 6, 2018, from https://chopra.com/articles/healing-through-nature
Brown, M. (2011). *The presence process: A journey into present moment awareness*. Mumbai: Jaico Publishing House.
Butot, M. (2005). Reframing spirituality, reconceptualizing change: Possibilities for critical social work. *Critical Social Work*, *6*. Retrieved January 27, 2018, from http:///criticalsocialwork/reframing-spirituality-reconceptualizing-change-possibilities-for-critical-social-work
Dalai Lama. (2015). *Beyond religion: Ethics for a whole world*, p. 55. Noida: Harper Element.
Davidson, R. (2009). Transform your mind, change your brain. *Google Personal Growth Series*. Retrieved January 20, 2018, from http://www.youtube.com/watch?v=7tRdDq XgsJ0&NR=1
Dias, C. (1997). Human rights education as a strategy for development. In G. J. Andreopoulos & R. P. Claude (Eds.), *Human rights education for the twenty-first century* (pp. 51–63). Philadelphia, PA: University of Pennsylvania Press.
Dominelli, L. (2002). *Anti-oppressive social work theory and practice*. New York, NY: Palgrave Macmillan.
Dominelli, L. (2012). *Green social work: From environmental crisis to environmental justice*. Cambridge: Polity Press.
Freire, P. (1972). *Pedagogy of the oppressed*. London: Penguin Books.

Freire, P. (1979). To know and to be: A dialogue with Paulo Freire, *Youth Affairs*, New Delhi, June.
Hart, M. (1999). Seeking Mino-pimatasiwin (the good life): An aboriginal approach to social work practice. *Native Social Work Journal*, 2(1), 91–112.
Hodge, D. R. (2005). Perceptions of compliance with the profession's ethical standards that address religion: A national study. *Journal of Social Work Education*, 41(2), 279–295.
Holloway, D. (2004). *A practical guide to dialogue*. The Community Dialogue Critical Issues Series: Vol. 2, Belfast: Community Dialogue.
International Federation of Social Workers (IFSW). (2012, February 23). *Globalisation and the environment*. Retrieved September 22, 2017, from http://ifsw.org/policies/globalisation-and-the-environment
International Federation of Social Workers (IFSW) and International Association of Schools of Social Work (IASSW). (2004). Ethics in social work, statement of principles. Retrieved February 27, 2018, from www.iassw-aiets.org/wp-content/uploads/2015/10/Ethics-in-Social-Work-Statement-IFSW-IASSW-2004.pdf
Joseph, J., & Fernandes, G. (2006). *An enquiry into ethical dilemmas in social work*. Mumbai: Research Unit, College of Social Work, Nirmala Niketan.
Killian, D., & Lasley, M. (2008). Using NVC to create social change (introduction): A telecourse recording. Retrieved January 15, 2018, from http://nonviolentcommunication.net/index.php?option=com_ixxocart&Itemid=250&p=product&id=28&parent=12&vendorid=2
Korten, D. C. (2010). *Economy, ecology and spirituality: A theory and practice of sustainability*. Asian NGO Coalition, NGOC, IRED Asia and the PCD Forum, Living Economics Forum. Retrieved February 10, 2018, from https://davidkorten.org/economy-ecology-spirituality/
Lee, J., Yuko, T., Takayama, N., Park, B. J., Li, Q., Song, C., . . . Miyazaki, Y. (2014). Influence of forest therapy on cardiovascular relaxation in young adults. *Evidence-based complementary and alternative medicine*. Article ID 834360. Retrieved December 10, 2018, from www.hindawi.com/journals/ecam/ 2014/834360
Luoma, J. B., Hayes, S. C., & Walser, R. D. (2007). *Learning ACT: An acceptance and commitment therapy skills-Training manual for therapists*. Oakland, CA: New Harbinger Publications.
Menon, N. (2012). *Seeing like a feminist*. London: Penguin Books.
Narayan, L. (2000, April). Freire and Gandhi: Their relevance for social work education. *International Social Work*, 43(2), 193–204.
Narayan, L., & Pandit, M. (2017). 'Samagratā' framework for social work. *Indian Journal of Social Work*, 78(3), 533–560.
Pandey, A. (2017, November 24). Moral reasoning, compassion and mindfulness. *Speaking Tree, Times of India*, Mumbai, p. 16.
Positive Psychology Program. (2014). *The positive effects of nature on well-being: Evolutionary biophilia*. Retrieved March 1, 2018, from https://positivepsychologyprogram.com/why-nature-positively-affects-your-well-being-and-how-to-apply-it/
Reardon, B. A. (1997). Human rights as education for peace. In G. J. Andreopoulos & R. P. Claude (Eds.), *Human rights education for the twenty-first century* (pp. 21–34). Philadelphia, PA: University of Pennsylvania Press.
Rosenberg, M. (2003). *Non-violent communication, a language of life: Life changing tools for healthy relationships*. Encinitas, CA: Puddle Dancer Press.
Saleebey, D. (2002). *The strengths perspective in social work practice*. Boston, MA: Allyn and Bacon.
Seppala, E. (2013, July 24). Compassionate mind, healthy body. *Greater Good Magazine*, published by Greater Good Science Center at UC Berkeley. Retrieved January 5, 2018, from https://greatergood.berkeley.edu/article/item/compassionate_mind_healthy_body
Siegel, D. J. (1999). *The developing mind*. New York: Guilford Press.

Siegel, D. J. (2007). *The mindful brain – Reflection and attunement in the cultivation of well-being.* New York: W.W. Norton.

Singh, K. D. (2016). What Delhi government says it is doing to combat air pollution. *The Wall Street Journal.* Retrieved February 1, 2018, from https://blogs.wsj.com/indiarealtime/2016/11/07/what-delhi-government-says-it-is-doing-to-combat-air-pollution/

Suttie, J. (2016, March 2). How nature can make you kinder, happier, and more creative. *Greater Good Magazine.* Retrieved December 10, 2017, from https://greatergood.berkeley.edu/article/item/how_nature_makes_you_kinder_happier_more_creative

Thakar, V. (1985). *Spirituality and social action: A holistic approach.* Berkeley, CA: Vimala Programs.

United Nations. (1994). *Human development report.* New York, NY: United Nations Publications.

Wong, Y. R. (2013). Returning to silence, connecting to wholeness: Contemplative pedagogy for critical social work education. *Journal of Religion and Spirituality in Social Work: Social Thought, 32*(3), 269–285. Retrieved December 28, 2017, from www.tandfonline.com/doi/abs/10.1080/15426432.2013.801748

Zjang, W., Piff, P. K., Iyer, R., Koleva, S., & Keltner, D. (2014, March). An occasion for unselfing: Beautiful nature leads to prosociality. *Journal of Environmental Psychology, 37,* 61–72. Retrieved February 25, 2018, from www.sciencedirect.com/science/article/pii/S0272494413000893

2

FIELDWORK AND CONTEMPORARY REALITIES[1]

Convergence and complexities

Nagmani Rao

Professional journeys laid bare – useful lessons for supervision

Let me begin by sharing a few experiences drawn out from the pages of my learning and professional life.

Flashback to the days of my bachelor's in social work (BSW) training during the mid-70's – we were assigned to campaign for 'educating' families in the urban settlement adopted for intervention by our school, about the 'evils of child marriage'. Putting on our caps of 'social awareness raising', we walked into households, introduced ourselves as trainee social workers (TSWs), and began a monologue about the undesirability of child marriage and the law to prevent these. A woman in one of the hutments after listening to us quietly said, 'So, are you going to send me to jail because I have got my daughter married young? Are you going to bring her back from her husband and say the marriage is illegal? Then what will she do with her life? Do you know how important it is for our kind of people to get our daughters married when they are young enough to get a reasonably good match?' Her statements brought forth an important lesson – to find solutions to problems we must first reach their root causes and that there is a chasm between 'their' thinking and 'ours', which needs to be bridged with sensitive understanding.

As a young professional and an enthusiastic volunteer counsellor in a church set-up, I was dealing with a client who was dependent on alcohol. My job was to motivate him to give it up by appealing to his sense of rationality, convincing him to value his life as 'God's gift'. This man, in his early 30s, would faithfully report for his weekly sessions, politely listen to my 'counsel' and promise to make efforts. This continued over four to five sessions without an iota of progress. Unable to fathom his lack of motivation I finally used the technique of 'confrontation' learnt in case work. For the first time he seemed to show a spark – anger and pain in his eyes ... he animatedly opened up and exposed my outlook coming from a privileged perspective without understanding the struggles that had pushed him into this desperation. His story ...

> 'He came to Delhi as a landless migrant worker, just about managing to eke out an existence through his sparse daily wages, which were irregular, seasonal. After some years he gave in to family pressure to marry, despite knowing that he could ill afford family responsibilities. After two years, again under family pressure, he brought his wife to Delhi. Once his wife got pregnant his struggle worsened as he could not even manage sufficient food – required nutrition was a far cry. He watched helplessly as his wife's condition weakened. The baby daughter brought a fleeting period of joy into their lives, but due to health complications, extreme poverty and lack of access to welfare she died when she was barely six months old. His wife blamed him, went into deep depression and within a few months, also passed away. With deep desolation and a sense of guilt he turned to alcoholism to forget his 'failures'. His hard-hitting final words left me dumbfounded – "You talk of loving my God-given life. . . . Tell me, is there something I still need to live for? I pray that this alcohol kills me soon . . . so that I can join my wife and child, whom I could not keep happy in this world"'.

This interaction shook certain assumptions about professional roles, paving the road towards the first critical (albeit naive) engagement with the theory and practice of social work. Over the years these questions assumed concrete shape. How does one counsel and enable clients to 'develop coping mechanisms', when the real issue is not personal inadequacy but rooted in structural factors, extreme poverty and the vulnerability to exploitation in an unequal society? How does one adhere to the principle of 'controlled emotional involvement' when the client confronts you with systems that perpetuate injustice in society and deal with the sense of helpless anger that this evokes? Do social workers truly touch the root of problems through interventions? Can ameliorative measures sustain change when structural factors are overwhelmingly obstructive? How truly transformative is the profession?

The previously mentioned scenario gives an inkling of the numerous challenges spanning an almost 40-year journey, first as a dreaming young professional in the field and later as an activist, researcher and an academic – handling child rapes where patriarchal power and a society blind to this were the core issues; when *adivasi* women were cheated with job promises and forced into sex work to bail out their families' mortgaged lands but faced the prospect of social ostracism for breaking the 'moral norms' of tribal tradition; when women from drought-affected regions suffering abuse from alcoholic husbands or facing social pressures as 'deserted' women collectively participated in an uphill search for alternatives to realise their human rights for a dignified, humane existence, giving insights about 'feminist assertion' from the perspective of rural toiling women; when students, particularly those from subordinated, excluded and underprivileged societal sections, confronted and challenged idealism as a luxury that came from a privileged standpoint; compelling a consciousness about the 'crusader's arrogance of political self-righteousness'. These values were perceived as imposing and created discomfort in students about their pragmatism and aspirations, thus sensitising the academic practitioner to the changing perspectives of youth born in the competitive post globalisation era.

Engagement with the feminist movement since the late 70's opened the doors to an endless mosaic of questions and struggles to deal with the inadequacies of a profession that has yet to strengthen its roots to make sustained transformative impacts and the humility to understand that each 'success' is but a drop in a huge ocean of possibilities towards the vision of an alternate better world. Drawing from such experiences resulted in an empathetic approach towards supervision.

The major part of this chapter hereafter draws from the experiences as an educator, fieldwork supervisor, coordinator of the fieldwork programme, a member in the teams for curriculum development, policy making for various aspects of practicum and as a team member of the skill laboratory – a supportive component of training.

The discussion covers the following aspects:

- Importance of fieldwork and supervision in social work training
- The unique aspects of training in Karve Institute of Social Service[2]
- Challenges in training and supervision
- Learning the art and skill of supervision from students.

In supervision literature, while the term supervisor is used consistently, the learner is referred to by many terms – student social worker (SSW), intern, trainee social worker (TSW) and supervisee used interchangeably to mean one who develops personally and professionally through guided 'learning by doing and reflecting' in the human laboratory of social intervention.

Importance of supervision in social work training

The definition of social work has evolved through different perspectives and has been part of a contested terrain. Various definitions of social work indicate the professional nature of the discipline, which grooms TSWs through an integration of theory and practice, aiming for a convergence of theoretical knowledge with skills, values and attitudes that bring about social transformation. Intellectual and emotional stimulation and confidence building help achieve positive learning. Exposures are obtained through working with client groups, placement agencies and their teams, the welfare system and through insights about policies and programmes. These activate knowledge, skills and perspective building. (Singh, 1985; Lalwani, 2002; Roy, 2012).

IASSW General Assembly and IFSW General Meeting, July 2014 has expanded on previous definitions:

> 'Social work is a practice-based profession and an academic discipline that promotes social change and development, social cohesion, and the empowerment

and liberation of people. Principles of social justice, human rights, collective responsibility and respect for diversities are central to social work. Underpinned by theories of social work, social sciences, humanities and indigenous knowledge, social work engages people and structures to address life challenges and enhance well-being'.

(www.iassw-aiets.org/global-definition-of-social-work-review-of-the-global-definition/)

Fieldwork is seen by Hamilton and Else (1983) as 'a consciously planned set of experiences occurring in a practice setting designed to move students from their initial level of understanding, skills and attitudes to levels associated with autonomous social work practice' (Dhemba, 2012, p. 2). Fieldwork engages the student in supervised social work practice and provides opportunities to integrate theory and practice (Dhemba, 2012). Various schools and regions refer to fieldwork by different nomenclature – field instruction, field education, field placement, practicum, internship, etc. (Lalwani, 2002). Considered as the soul of social work education and training, it provides experiential learning under the guidance of expert supervisors to develop the personality and hone practitioner capacities for future professional roles. In the field, TSWs get opportunities to test out their classroom theoretical learning, evaluate its effectiveness in application during intervention and bring back the practice-based wisdom to classroom discussions. They also learn to critique and modify theory. Through fieldwork, TSWs understand, analyse and contend with socio-economic, cultural and political realities that would give them an orientation to the challenges they would face as future agents of social change and builds their credibility and identity with the profession. The learning components encompass factual (knowledge) content, problem solving and intervention (skills) content and critical self-understanding, and awareness (perspectives and attitudes) content. (Adapted from Trevithick, 2013).

Key elements of effective learning through fieldwork are TSWs and their expectations, goals and efforts; the agency; the curriculum and design; and last but not the least, the supervisor. While each component is important for a wholesome experience, this chapter will limit its focus on the TSW and on the supervisor as the key actors in the learning cycle against the background of the Institute's programme, where the author gained her experiences.

Supervision is a complex process that involves:

(a) Work planning and management
(b) Facilitating reflection and learning through the practice experience
(c) Giving intellectual and emotional support to TSWs
(d) Carrying out mediation roles – between TSW and client group, between TSW and agency personnel and amongst members of peer group in-group supervision in order to create a positive learning environment.
(e) Laying the foundation for TSWs' professional development.

(Marc, Makai-Dimeny, & Osvat, 2014)

The supervisor-TSW relationship is important to achieve work and learning related goals. Effective supervision is complex wherein the supervisor plays multiple roles – monitoring, facilitation, consultation and support. (Nunev, 2014). The skilled supervisor can balance these roles, both in relation to the agency as well as the TSW. As one who guides TSWs' growth and assesses their performance the supervisor must have the ability to give objective feedback and encouragement; s/he must also have the openness to receive and constructively respond to TSWs' feedback. As an active listener and facilitator s/he helps TSWs articulate their experiences, problem creating blocks and anxieties that negatively impact their work. The very nature of consultation with the experienced supervisor implies a hierarchical relationship and the supervisor should be conscious of this power relation so that guidance is not experienced as judgment and imposition but as one that supports growth. The supervisor hence needs to be a 'practitioner', 'field trainer' and expert in multiple pedagogical methodologies, a researcher, a role model, an innovator (Andrews, in Bhatt & Pathare, 2015).

The acceptance of supervision by TSWs is equally important. Here the onus to build a non-threatening environment and create conditions for open interactions lies with the more experienced and mature supervisor. The experience and aura of confidence of the supervisor can create a sense of awe amongst TSWs whereby they put the supervisor on a pedestal. Here again the supervisor has a role in correcting perceptions that lead to unhealthy deification. Selective disclosure has been used as an effective strategy by this author to show that supervisors are also continuously learning from their experiences and that TSWs are not clays to be moulded in the image of their teachers; TSWs have their own strengths that stimulate supervisors' enrichment.

Perceptions of TSWs about supervisory experiences have been highlighted by Moorhouse (2013). Even though located in New Zealand, the study points to the universality of experiences. A few key issues highlighted are mismatch or gaps in understanding between TSW and supervisor about the supervisor-supervisee relationship and expected task and learning outcomes. TSWs reported positive experiences when they perceived the supervisor as skilled, experienced, one who showed flexibility and with whom there was compatibility of viewpoints that created a mutual sense of comfort. The images about supervisors transmitted from previous batches are strong influences in shaping perceptions (Moorhouse, 2013).

Part of the role modeling responsibility is to uphold the ethical aspects of supervision (Hamse, 2000; University of Pretoria). To achieve this, the following need to be meticulously adhered to:

- Scrupulously avoid taking advantage of the power relation between supervisor and TSW
- Ethical and humane behaviour towards TSWs: congruence in embodying universal values – fairness, justice, courage and humility; as a supervisor, teacher and as a human being
- Addressing the legitimate needs of the TSWs
- Objectivity, transparency and fairness in evaluation

- Conscientious, honest and responsible role fulfilment
- Assigning task responsibilities to TSWs keeping in mind his/her abilities (addressing the potential risks of the human laboratory approach). For this, moving from simple, ability-testing task assignments before moving to challenges that are more complex and regular monitoring and feedback
- Practicing that which is preached – TSWs cannot be expected to adhere to professional norms and integrity if supervisors compromise on these.

The supervisor-TSW relationship, agency and field-based supervisory visits, regular individual and group conferences and meticulous perusal and discussion of recording are the essential tools for effective supervision.

Fieldwork at Karve Institute of Social Service: unique aspects

The entrants at the Institute come from diverse disciplinary and regional backgrounds and varying levels of exposure. While most entrants are fresh graduates in their early 20s, each year a few come into MSW after post-graduation in other disciplines or have resumed education after a break or a career span in other fields. While making the first-year placements consideration of these diversities is important.

The programme at the Institute follows a graded modular learning approach that is similar to many other schools, though there may be variation in the design and exposures.

- 1st semester: Induction through orientation programme and agency visits
- 1st and 2nd semesters: Generic, cross specialisation concurrent placements
- 2nd semester: Rural camp and specialisation-based Advanced Orientation visits
- 3rd and 4th semesters: Specialisation concurrent placements
- 3rd semester: Field assignments
- 4th semester: Specialisation study tour
- End of 4th semester: Block placement.

Fieldwork thus gives a wide array of exposures and experiences to the TSWs. The following paragraphs briefly describe three aspects related to fieldwork unique to the Institute – skill training, remedial fieldwork[3] and field assignments.

Skill training

Skill training is a supportive component to fieldwork. Three foundational workshops towards the end of the Orientation Programme and before the first semester concurrent placement begins are related to Self Awareness, Sensitivity Training, and Communication. Through the use of reflective exercises and other participatory methodologies, TSWs develop skills in introspection about their attitudes and values, reflected in their responses to and analyses of social situations. This begins the process of reflexive learning and developing sensitivity towards social issues, client group situations and learning basic communication skills that they would use in their professional interactions during field placements. Over the first two semesters regular skill laboratory sessions are conducted related to the three practice methods (case work, group work and community work), working with specific groups (for example, children, disabilities) and use of media (poster making, street play, slogans etc.), simulation games and some exercises for conducting group sessions in the field (Datar, Bawikar, Rao, Rao, & Masdekar, 2010).

Remedial (supportive) fieldwork

Although fieldwork is expected to give hands-on training resulting in personal and professional growth, it is also an aspect that can cause stress to many TSWs and affect learning and performance. Some of the stressors are:

- Conflict between roles and values (profession appropriate values that are taught and values that they may have imbibed through family and peer socialisation which they are compelled to question)
- Personal problems that impede concentration on fieldwork (relationships, illness, problems in adaptation to language, culture, course demands etc.)
- Self-esteem issues and competition and performance expectations
- Family problems (financial, family conflicts, family crises and feelings of guilt at 'not being there')
- Blocks in supervisor TSW relationship
- Fear of failure.

It is important that these problems which obstruct learning and growth are understood and tackled through the supervisor-TSW relationship. However, despite this, at times, TSWs do under-perform and may risk losing a year. Here is where supportive mechanisms become important. At the Institute these include:

(a) Extending the time period to help complete the assigned tasks and acquire the minimum competencies in this time to enable movement to the next level
(b) Having mid-term reviews for corrections and giving additional time and inputs
(c) A continuous period of fieldwork during part of the vacations, with change of agency and/or supervisor (in such situations written notes that spell out where the problems have been and how they should be addressed are recorded)
(d) Encouraging TSWs who have taken a drop, due to failure, to return and, with specific supportive inputs, helping them to complete the course
(e) Referral for therapeutic counselling and if required, involving a near family member/guardian (with the TSW's consent) to help overcome the stressors and move ahead.

These issues are either discussed collectively or through appointed sub-committees, considering the best interest of the TSWs, on a case to case basis. The results have largely been positive. However, where there are indications that a TSW may not benefit through supportive efforts (the stressors may be too overwhelming or the TSW is not ready, unwilling or unable to cope and make renewed efforts) s/he is advised to drop out and explore other courses or Institutes.

The important aspects to be considered in supportive supervision are:

- Facilitating removal of the factors that induce stress and affect performance, where these are within the ambit of supervisory inputs
- Counselling to deal with stressor conditions that need to be addressed and helping the TSW to build the capacities to confront and handle these
- Breaking up the learning process into sub-components that can be handled comfortably, such that the TSW takes small steps and builds up confidence and abilities through continuous encouragement and non-threatening, on-going feedback
- Looking realistically at the positive elements of the TSW's personality and potentials and weaving in tasks where s/he can utilise these, thereby rebuilding confidence.

Field assignments

Field assignments as a component of fieldwork were introduced at the 3rd semester level to cover additional credits given to fieldwork after the shift to new choice-based curriculum some years ago. These have proved to be very useful learning experiences for TSWs and as outputs for the collaborating organisations in their larger work canvas. This innovation gives autonomy to specialisations to carry out activities, often beyond the set curriculum. They enhance the knowledge and capacities and develop perspectives of TSWs and the opportunity for expanding the theory base through field application. The limitation however is that there has been no follow up to assess the sustainability of outcomes after the initial impacts. The chart gives a selective overview illustrating some interesting assignments during the past few years.

Challenges in professional training through fieldwork

(a) Finding the 'ideal' placement

Finding the perfect set of experiences and the 'ideal' placement for TSWs (from their standpoint) is quite a challenge. The following paragraphs discuss some of the issues faced drawn from the experiences of the author and her colleagues.

In case of the 1st year the coordinator and in the 2nd year, specialisation faculty, collectively decide concurrent placements. In the Community Development specialisation, TSWs are asked to submit their sector and intervention focus group choices at the end of the second semester in order to look for

TABLE 2.1 Specialisation-based field assignments

Specialisation	Nature of Assignment (Collaborators)	Methodology used	Content output	Learning for TSWs	Outputs for collaborators
Family & Child Welfare	Safeti-pin Campaign (SAMYAK Communication & Resource Centre)*	5 days of evening visits covered 200 locations spread across Pune city; dialogue with commuters, general public. The student doing audit entered the data at the location which got registered with the organization doing safety audit.	Sharing the data with the key stake-holders such as police, public transport service, NGOs or residents' association in the areas concerned. Once the Safeti-pin App is downloaded, commuters would be able to assess safety of the areas.	Being part of a wider international campaign for safe cities; understanding the use of GPS & mobile applications for public outreach; developing perspectives about safety issues for women	Feeding into their database and contribution to campaign outreach and impacts through partnership with governance systems and civil society organisations
	Child Labour Free Society (Network: Action for the Rights of the Child)	Students participated in a city level campaign 'Child Labour Free Society'. They contacted office bearers of 135 housing complexes, sensitised them about the situation of child labour and appealed to them to prevent child labour in any form.	Some societies passed resolutions for not employing child labour and were facilitated by the Institute at a special programme.	Being part of a network campaign, responding to queries and addressing resistances	Spreading awareness about social issues concerning child labour and building support from middle class for efforts to eradicate child labour

(Continued)

TABLE 2.1 Continued

Specialisation	Nature of Assignment (Collaborators)	Methodology used	Content output	Learning for TSWs	Outputs for collaborators
Human Resource Management	Awareness about water wastage & conservation (Hotels & Restaurants in Karvenagar & Warje areas)	Students visited the hotels and observed the use and wastage of water by owners, waiters and other staff and customers and discussed the importance of water conservation with the hotel proprietors.	The appeal for water conservation was accepted by the hotel owners.	Exposure to critical environment issues and public outreach skills	Hotel owners gave a commitment to put up posters/notices about water conservation.
	Internal Complaints Committee for Sexual Harassment (Deputy Collector and Companies in and around Pune)	A survey in 75 medium- and small-scale companies about existence of committees to deal with sexual harassment cases	The majority of the companies did not have such cells. Awareness generation about establishing such cells	Exposure to the reality in industries with respect to mandatory provisions about sexual harassment at work place	At least 10 companies came forward to make inquiries about establishing sexual harassment internal complaint committees.
Medical and Psychiatric Social Work	Organ Donation: Awareness Generation (S.P College, Pune and Tribal Girls Hostel, Hadapsar)	Awareness generation through poster and street play	Organ donation and legal aspects associated with this	Helped students understand an emerging area of social work intervention and the role of social workers in this	Helped generate interest and motivation in the younger generation about the value of organ donation
	Awareness about & prevention of child sexual abuse	5th to 7th standard children were shown a film followed by discussions.	Sensitization and opening young minds to discuss a sensitive topic	Skills in opening up young children to address issues of sexual	Teachers found the sessions very useful and wanted to

	(Collaborating Schools)		organise these with parents also
Urban & Rural Community Development	Slum rehabilitation and competing interests for urban spaces (MASHAL – SRA scheme, Community-based Organisations)	After orientation about SRA scheme and issues related to urban development, students were divided into three groups to interview 3 key stakeholders of this project – Govt. Officials, builders, and beneficiaries supportive of SRA and community groups opposing the scheme.	A comprehensive analytical report of the various perspectives and issues in slum rehabilitation presented in a seminar	abuse and child and family vulnerability; developing sensitive perspectives Students got insights about the complex and conflicting interests in the use of urban spaces and the political economy of urban expansion.	Identification of problems and areas for negotiations
	Groundwater situation and mitigating water crises (ACWADAM, Partnering NGOs/ CSR initiatives in the selected villages)	Two batches of students have carried out studies through measurements, observation and discussions with villagers on groundwater use and the imminent crises in select tribal villages in Pune district.	Prepared consolidated document, presented in seminar	Acquiring technical knowledge about emergent groundwater crises which can also be used in their community	Data used for future intervention on water use planning and management in the villages

Source: Institute's Annual Reports (2012–2016); NAAC Reaccreditation Assessment Report, Karve Institute of Social Service, 2015; and discussions with specialisation faculty colleagues, 2018

placements in line with their interests. However, there can be no assurance that agencies would always be available to cater to these agencies' policy and personnel constraints may not match the Institute's concurrent training framework. In such situations, these agencies are 'reserved' for the final block placement, which is far more flexible. Nevertheless, there is a specific responsibility to try to match TSW interests and capacity with expectations from agencies for achieving both agency expected task outputs and TSWs' learning outcome goals. As mentioned earlier, the diversity of background and exposure makes it difficult to ensure the perfect achievement of appropriate agency placements; the 'luck' factor does operate to some extent. (Moorhouse, Hay, & O'Donoghue, 2014). Though wary of expressing it openly, TSWs sometimes indicate that their learning 'would have been better if we had got better placements'. Agencies often express that 'useful' TSWs should have attitudes and capacities whereby they give desired outputs. There seems to be an inherent expectation that trainees would come as 'readymade pliable packages' to the placement, something unrealistic, as a host of factors influences the efforts and growth of TSWs. Some agencies overlook the fact that capacities and interests develop through enabling guidance. Occasionally, when agencies are hesitant, the rapport of the supervisor and the coordinator may be useful to negotiate placements and motivate TSWs to make efforts to measure up to expectations.

Contemporary issues cover the possibilities of macro, meso and micro levels of work. Not many agencies use a multi-pronged comprehensive approach, working at all levels and on multiple issues faced by their client groups. This places challenges in identifying placements that give a reasonably holistic hands-on exposure to work at different levels. Role models in the agencies are, at times, discouraging personalities and the faculty supervisor plays the delicate role of allowing TSWs to ventilate their disappointments and frustrations but is usually not in a position to make a direct intervention to rectify such situations, unless legal or ethical issues are involved. In such scenarios, at best, either the faculty supervisor or the coordinator would discuss the issues with a senior person (such as the head of the social work unit or the administrative head) to see possible ways of dealing with such barriers.

(b) Matching agency priorities and the learning framework

While the defined learning framework is communicated to agencies through regular interactions between faculty and agency supervisors as well as the annual supervisory meets at the Institute, flexible adaptations are also needed to fulfill agency expectations. To achieve this, faculty supervisors have to play interventionist roles to match the task output orientation with the process orientation. Agencies' supervisors, trained to carry out the work of the agency, do not necessarily have the experience and skills for supervision. Other factors include their workload and insufficient time and therefore the inability to fulfil, entirely, the TSWs' guidance needs. Here the faculty supervisor plays an important bridging role so that the TSW does not feel neglected and his/her motivation remains sustained.

Many agencies do not use a holistic and participatory approach model while addressing stakeholders' felt needs, while classroom theory advocates such an approach as being more useful for social transformation. Social action, which is taught and promoted as a method, is not a practice in many agencies, particularly those that operate within conventional welfare frameworks or reconstructive, development oriented approaches. When sensitive TSWs are given field intervention situations where macro level structural barriers are more overwhelming than micro and meso level personal and other factors, reaching towards problem resolution within the limited field placement timeframe is not possible and leads to emotional turmoil in the TSW. Encouraging the TSWs to work within the limited framework of the agency as well as to maximise learning despite the limitations is by no means easy for a supervisor.

Since the fieldwork days are interspersed with breaks, it presents time limitations for experiencing the continuity of process, thereby affecting in-depth learning of practice methods. There is a constant tussle between task orientation (which is more tangible) and process orientation, results of which may emerge much beyond the TSWs' term. Another issue is bridging the client orientation of agency supervisors and the TSW orientation of faculty supervision. This is particularly important when the human laboratory approach, which is inherent to social work training, compels addressing many ethical issues – how much leeway can be given to the trial and error learning of the TSW, that may be far more creative, and how structured and rigidly directed should the process be keeping in mind client interests?

(c) Standardising assessment

Another challenge is to bring about a standardisation in assessment mechanisms. Despite detailed parameters in the evaluation forms, subjectivity in assessment cannot entirely be plugged. Expectations of standards vary depending on the orientation and experience of supervisors; despite a defined range for numerical gradation from 'excellent' to 'not satisfactory', some supervisors are quite generous in assigning marks while others tend to underrate. The assessment parameters do not follow a standardised pattern across the specialisation groups. Faculty have often discussed these as a matter of concern and also felt the need to draw up more concrete guidelines for assessment against each parameter to minimise subjectivity and bring greater standardisation. A concrete step still needs to be taken in this direction.

(d) Preparedness for professional challenges

The development sector today sees the perforation by a range of non-social work trained professionals working with passion and commitment on social issues. A challenge of today and tomorrow is to train social workers to absorb a multiplicity of social and technical skills related to their specialisation areas of practice and stand up to the standards of working as an equal in multi-disciplinary teams rather than be seen as half-baked professionals who are, to borrow a cliché, 'jack of all trades but a master of none'. In the absence of a professional council or an effective platform of social work educators and practitioners to address and guide training institutes to adapt to the changing times, social work cannot aspire for a legitimate place in the sun as an important recognised profession that can have transformative impacts on social policy and society (Rao, cited in Sajid & Jain, 2018).

Need for convergence

Two aspects of convergence are discussed here – that of convergence between theory and practice, as well as of perspectives across the numerous subjects and that of agreement and convergence in styles, attitudes and approaches in supervision despite ideological differences within the faculty and between agency and faculty supervisors.

Students often say, '*Theory is meant for classroom learning and passing exams, fieldwork is for learning practice*!' Many of us may have held similar views when we were students. Our memories of fieldwork are far more vivid than what we learnt through classroom sessions. However, once we put on our educator boots and cap we are compelled to grapple with the challenge of demonstrating to the TSWs the linkages between theory and practice. It is important to engage in debates with students and colleagues about the value of theory and our approach at 'teaching theory'.

An issue with conventional approach to teaching is that educators tend to trap themselves in its jargon and abstract definitions rather than a lively dialogue with theory. There is a tendency to impart conceptual understanding rather than a cognitive, application-based and contextual understanding, thereby making theory 'information heavy' and dry. A student, Nazia, exemplifies this while capturing the difficulties she faced in working with street children and applying psychosocial theory of child socialisation which is taught within the framework of that which is the 'norm'. '*I felt the dimension of vulnerability of children is absent in theory that is taught to us, whereas for training I was placed with an organisation working for vulnerable children*' (Shodhganga, undated, p. 81).

Since many educators may also not have practice experience in all the field situations that TSWs deal with (or the experiences may be outdated, particularly if educators discontinue their engagement with the field after coming into academics), the teaching of theory may be perceived as 'bookish' by TSWs. A way to overcome this is to make theory come alive by using creative pedagogies where TSWs can bring in their experiences to the class and by simplifying abstract concepts with live examples. A colleague, who was considered a role model in creative teaching, brought in humour at appropriate points and raised questions that were applicable to the TSWs' lives while teaching psychology or conducting group work laboratory sessions. Yet another, who was a Dalit from a rural background and had made a place for himself through many struggles, taught Sociology and brought in his own experiences as well as those of other TSWs who had shared experiences with him. Students often said that they never realised that they were, in fact, absorbing theory and perspectives for societal analyses in the class, but these came alive while working in the field. The relevance of Paulo Freire's dialogic learning (1970, 1994) using problem posing pedagogy is important to facilitate student sharing and the educator also learning through these.

While talking about convergence of theory and practice Wrenn and Wrenn (2009) have impressed the importance of faculty engagement with practice. By relating field anecdotes, the faculty can relate it to the theoretical topic under discussion. For example, while teaching community organisation this author prepared case stories based on her practice and had students discuss these using guideline questions. While teaching ethics in professional practice, TSWs' experiences were made anonymous and presented for discussion on dilemmas in handling ethical issues. These stimulated active sharing of field experiences from other TSWs also. The use of extracts from TSW records with supervisory comments (Singh, 1985) is another way to engage in discussion amongst teaching faculty as well as with TSWs in small groups or though skill laboratory sessions.

Educators belong to different ideological and value orientations, as do the specialisations. A real challenge is to see how some basic common messages that are founded on the fundamental philosophical orientation of social work can be reinforced across the subjects – those related to human dignity, equality, respect and non-discrimination based on caste, class, gender, race, sexual orientation, disability etc. should be woven into all classroom teaching to build equality perspectives.

The last convergence highlighted here relates to styles and approaches towards supervision. There can be neither a permanently right or wrong approach nor absolute agreement of what is best for the TSWs. The styles vary from *laissez faire* to imposing and close monitoring and controlling approaches and each of these can be justified by the people who use them. Some supervisors are better listeners while others are better talkers. TSWs perceive some supervisors as being more motivating, non-threatening and approachable and others as dominating, rigid and pressurising. At times strongly positive or negative 'images' about supervisors, perpetuated by the subjective experiences of senior batches, trap TSWs as well as supervisors in a stereotype and create barriers in expectations and the supervisor-supervisee relationship; TSWs do not recognise that supervisors evolve through experience and feedback and do change positively as they go along. At the same time, considering TSWs' growth, it is important for supervisors to have continuous open debates and dialogues where they discuss their experiences and blocks as well as their views about styles of supervision and their impacts. If there is cohesiveness and a growth stimulating institutional environment it is possible for senior colleagues to take on positive mentoring roles. Where such an environment does not exist, it would be helpful to organise annual workshops with an external experienced expert to discuss these issues and define and test out paths to convergence. To prevent unhealthy comparisons, give common messages about professionalism in practice and develop ethical values through training, efforts for such convergences are imperative. Openness amongst faculty to discuss the diversity of learning and supervision needs according to the context of settings and client groups, discussing these with alumni and documenting these systematically can go a long way in developing different models of supervision.

The mirror that looked back at me – learning from students

The experience of supervision has been the most stimulating, exhausting and at the same time energising part of my experience as an educator. Discussing all these could form the subject matter of an entire book! A few illustrations would suffice here.

An important lesson that my TSWs taught me is that the socio-political environment of the 70's and 80's had almost died out by the late 90's and much of these histories were not even part of the lived experiences of the generation born in the post globalisation era. While the stories of struggle and achievement provoked their thoughts, the fragmented social movements that they saw also raised questions in their minds of how far we could achieve and sustain goals of social transformation through passionate interventions at the cost of personal life goals and status. The cynicism and pragmatism hit me hard enough to search for answers wherein I could engage such discerning TSWs in critical discussions about the value of commitment and struggle.

Often, as we become teachers, our own perceptions of teachers from our student days have faded. One of my students, who was quite irritated by my copious remarks on her recordings asked me during an individual conference, 'Do I never do anything right?' Puzzled by her question I pointed out to her various instances of the things that she had done 'right' and her relieved response – 'Thank god! I now know that I will pass' led to a healthy discussion about the importance of detailed reflective and analytical process recording. This resulted in a marked improvement in her records and work attitudes. I also learnt a valuable lesson of the importance of noting down encouraging remarks by the supervisor. The mutually strengthening experience of the supervisor TSW relationship stood reinforced.

A Dalit student from a village in a backward district discussed his aspirations of acquiring a middle level job in a well-paying NGO in a large city. I expressed my disappointment that he was not committing himself to work to bring about change in his native region. He said, '*You, with your privileged background could easily become 'mahaan' (noble) by choosing to work with toiling sections in rural areas. If I go back today to talk about social change in my village, forget about the established caste leadership, even my own community may ridicule me. I first need to establish myself and develop my confidence before I create a platform for change in my village*' (Rao, 2011, p. 72).

The significance of Babasaheb Ambedkar's slogan 'educate, organise and struggle'[4] acquired a new significance for me. I gratefully acknowledge how he brought home the fact that, unintentionally, I was projecting the superiority of my choices without recognising my privileged position to exercise these choices.

Rural camps are life-changing experiences for many TSWs – both rural and urban. Living with the TSWs in the same field conditions brings us in closer touch with them and helps diminish hierarchies. Many TSWs reveal facets of their personalities that we have missed in the formal set up of campus interactions. These insights, when shared with other faculty, help us to tap the potentials of shy ones to bring them to the fore through subsequent interactions in concurrent placements.

A challenge that I have constantly grappled with is to separate the supervisory role from the personal counselling role. (Hamse, 2000, pp. 19–20, which negates the therapeutic role of the supervisor) While there is logic in the position that supervisors should not become therapists to the TSW, the close engagement with them through the supervisory process develops a mentoring relationship that criss-crosses between the professional and the personal (the 'friend, philosopher, guide' axis), particularly when TSWs' personal problems affect their work. There have been numerous instances when individual conference sessions have compelled me to don the cap of a counsellor, when there seems likelihood of an emotional breakdown and the TSW expresses the need to talk to the supervisor. The positive outcome of these and the subsequent feedback that many students have given later in their professional life, confirms that it is not wrong to get into such interactions when one's student is going through a personal crisis. The skill in preventing conflict between the roles is to explain to the TSW that the role of personal counselling would not obstruct the supervisor from giving objective critical feedback when it is necessary and that the empathetic relationship as a personal guide would not come in the way of objective assessment of performance outcomes.

Conclusion

Effective learning through fieldwork is founded on a complex set of factors involving the TSW, supervisor, agency context, and learning opportunities. A weakness in any of these components can weaken outcomes. The discussions earlier have highlighted experimentation and experiences, with the aim that peer exchanges will bring in a process of shared learning. There can be no one universally applicable learning model. Some of the issues that bring challenges and possible measures to tackle them are highlighted briefly later. These can be tested and critically assessed as schools in each region evolve their own training modules.

Related to Agencies

Issue: Matching priorities of agencies, student learning goals and interests and training framework developed by the school

Measure: Involvement of the multiple stakeholders in evolving the fieldwork programme with periodic reviews according to changing contexts. This can be carried out through half- or one-day meets held annually and at the time of curriculum changes more extensive workshop discussions with senior practitioners and supervisors.

Related to the Student Learner

Issue: Diversity and changing contexts, which shape attitudes; fears and anxieties

Measure: Acknowledge rather than deny the power relations and their associated complexities and make conscious efforts to mitigate the negative effects of these.

Appreciation and spaces for diversities in a spirit of mutual learning; respect for feedback;

Flexibility in approaches to recording – structure, style, language of expression – to enhance reflexive learning;

The commitment to spaces for diversities could be developed as part of the institutional ethos. Where there are serious organisational dynamics this can be a challenge. Here an external experienced resource person or consultant advisor who understands academic challenges and is well grounded in the changing contours of practice may help through a facilitation role.

Related to Supervision

Issue: Convergences and agreement, transparency and accountability

Measure: This requires multi-pronged sets of measures that are interlinked:

Comprehensive mechanisms for transparency in supervision and assessment, clear concrete parameters for assessment;

Documented fieldwork policy and evaluation parameters shared and discussed with agency and TSWs in the initial days of fieldwork and reinforced through the interactive joint and group conferences;

Training and mentoring of new supervisors;

Moderation mechanisms built on collective trust and responsibility.

Related to the Curriculum

Issue: Inter-linkages, convergence and 'going beyond' as field demands change.

Measure: Developing opportunities and exposures to enhance multi-level skills, multi-disciplinary knowledge and perspectives beyond set curriculum;

Regular curriculum revisions;

Clearly defined fieldwork curriculum, communicated to TSWs and agencies.

Faculty engagement in the field as an in-built aspect of teaching responsibility is important to develop these measures. Through their involvement in field action and/or research, the faculty can bring new concepts into teaching, bring value addition during curriculum revisions and develop creative field exposures, interactions with practitioners engaged in innovative work and guide assignments that expand learning beyond the classroom curriculum.

If the profession is to emerge as one that is recognised as making impacts at all levels, from micro to macro, a serious evaluation is called for to develop a paradigm shift in social work training. This would involve a collective, sustained effort cutting across regions and schools with the participation of practitioners in designing fieldwork curriculum that gears social work trainees to learn to face the changing contexts of the contemporary period as well as develop an attitude to shape themselves to face challenges as future professionals.

Notes

1 No piece of writing is an entirely self-generated output. I would like to acknowledge the following for their support – Ruma Bawikar, Vimla V. Nadkarni and the editorial team of this book and K. J. Joy, for their critical comments on the first draft. Thanks are due to Ravi Dhadwad, Assistant Librarian, Karve Institute of Social Service, Pune, for fishing out the needed readings and Bharati Jagtap for mailing me the relevant documents. Candid sharing of experiences and specialisation related details by my colleagues at the Institute – Anuradha Patil, Dada Dadas, Devanand Shinde, Mahesh Thakur, Neha Sathe, Sharmila Ramteke, Ujwala Masdekar – helped me prepare a more comprehensive and inclusive chapter. Last but not the least, special thanks to the students of various batches who gave me the enrichment of the supervisory experience.
2 Karve Institute is a more than five decades old Institute located in Pune (Maharashtra). It is a Constituent Institute under Savitribai Phule Pune University. It offers post-graduate, M. Phil and PhD courses for professional training apart from involvement in field action, research and consultancy services.
3 While the term 'remedial' has a medical connotation, it is used at the Institute as a measure to help the TSW improve on work and learning outputs and is a supportive technique to prevent failure.
4 Babasaheb Bhimrao Ambedkar, Chairperson of the Drafting Committee of the Constitution of India and an iconic leader of the depressed castes (he coined the term 'Dalit' meaning 'the oppressed'). He believed that only if the Dalits moved out of the confines of the villages would they get opportunities for upward mobility through education and collective organising.

References

Andrews, J. T. (2015). Bridging gaps in professional social work in India. In S. Bhatt & S. Pathare (Eds.), *Social work education and practice engagement* (pp. 78–87). Delhi: Shipra Publications.

Datar, S., Bawikar, R., Rao, G., Rao, N., & Masdekar, U. (Eds.). (2010). *Skill training for social workers: A manual.* New Delhi: Sage Publications Ltd.

Dhemba, J. (2012). Field training in social work education: Issues and challenges in the case of Eastern and Southern Africa. *Social Work & Society (International Online Journal), 10*(1), 1–16.

Freire, P. (1970, Reprint 1994). *Pedagogy of the oppressed.* New York, NY: Continuum.

Hamse, A. D. (2000). *Social work supervision.* Pretoria: University of Pretoria. Retrieved October 14, 2017, from https://repository.up.ac.za/bitstream/handle/2263/26952/02/chapter2.pdf

IASSW. (2014). Global Definition of Social Work. Retrieved December 28, 2017, from www.iassw-aiets.org and www.ifsw.org

Karve Institute of Social Service. (2012–2016). *Annual reports.* Pune: Karve Institute of Social Service.

Karve Institute of Social Service. (2015). Reaccreditation Assessment Report (RAR) submitted to NAAC (National Accreditation and Assessment Council). Pune: Karve Institute of Social Service.

Lalwani, B. T. (2002). *Social work education and field instruction.* Pune: Centre for Social Research and Development.

Marc, C., Makai-Dimeny, J., & Osvat, C. (2014). The social work supervisor: Skills, roles, responsibilities. *Bulletin of the Transylvania University of Brasov, Series VII: Social Sciences, Law, 7*(1), 221–230.

Moorhouse, L. M. (2013). *How do social work students perceive the supervision experience?* MSW Thesis, Manabu, New Zealand: Massey University.

Moorhouse, L. M., Hay, K., & O'Donoghue, K. (2014). Listening to student experiences of supervision. *AOTEAROA, New Zealand Social Work, 26*(4), 37–52.

Nunev, S. (2014). Supervision practical training problems with social work students. *Trakia Journal of Sciences, 12*(1), 461–466. Retrieved October 14, 2017, from www.uni.sz.bg

Rao, N. (2011). Towards an alternate pedagogy. *Economic and Political Weekly, XLVI*(2), 71–72.

Rao, N. (2018). Making impacts: Contemporary challenges to social work professionals. In S. M. Sajid & R. Jain (Eds.), *Reflections on social work profession*. New Delhi: Bloomsbury.

Roy, S. (2012). *Fieldwork in social work*. Jaipur: Rawat Publications.

Shodhganga. (Undated) *Social work education: Practicum*. Retrieved February 21, 2018, from shodhganga.inflibnet.ac.in/bistream/10603/16128/10/10_chapter%203.pdf

Singh, R. R. (Ed.). (1985). *Fieldwork in social work education: A perspective for human service professions*. New Delhi: Concept Publishing Company.

Trevithick, P. (2013). *Social work skills and knowledge: A practice handbook*. New Delhi: Rawat Publications.

Wrenn, J., & Wrenn, B. (2009). Enhancing learning by integrating theory and practice. *International Journal of Teaching and Learning in Higher Education, 21*(2), 258–265.

3
COORDINATING FIELDWORK
Challenges and learning

Pamela Singla

Introduction

Coordination is an important aspect when heading an administrative position. It means organising people or groups together for a productive outcome or for the harmonious functioning of various constituents for effective results. Fieldwork in social work is an important component of the course which needs to be effectively coordinated for creating manpower which is skilled, capacitated and works towards better adjustment of groups and individuals in the society and challenges the existing social structures and practices which subordinate certain sections of the society.

Fieldwork requires effective coordination between three main stakeholders of the programme, namely the department supervisor; agency supervisor and the student (Figure 3.1) and hence is a serious responsibility for the person heading fieldwork unit.

As per the 2014 definition, social work promotes social change, problem solving in human relationships and empowerment and liberation of people to enhance wellbeing. Fieldwork in social work is a vital mechanism to meet these objectives wherein the students are trained to apply classroom learning into practice and vice versa enrich classes with experience sharing from the field, observe, and implement creative ideas. This fosters development of intellectual and emotional processes and attitudes. Hence, a supervised fieldwork curriculum is essential to develop the requisite skills for working with people and requires coordination between the three stakeholders mentioned earlier. Fieldwork curriculum in the various schools/ departments of social work is comprised of various components spread over two years of a Master's course.

The following sub-section provides an historical journey of fieldwork in one of the pioneer departments of social work in the country, followed by a section on components of fieldwork as practised in the various departments of social work in

FIGURE 3.1 Stakeholders in the fieldwork department
Source: Author

the country and also abroad. However, the discussion and narration are in backdrop of fieldwork as practised in the Department of Social Work, University of Delhi (DSW). The narration is powerful and examines each component in detail including the past practices.

Department of Social Work, University of Delhi (DSW): 1947 and hence

DSW, popularly known as the Delhi School of Social Work, is among the first institute in Asia to grant the Master's degree in social work. Not many know that the history of the department is intertwined with the history of the freedom struggle of the country. So, while the year of 1947 saw one of the world's biggest migrations across the border, it saw mass massacre, murder, rape, and violence of an unprecedented level. It was under such circumstances that the Young Women's Catholic Association, now DSW, shifted itself from Lucknow to Delhi and to the quarters of the Vice Chancellor Sir Maurice Gwyer. It was a tough time for the country and Delhi (Pathak, 2010). Under such circumstances fieldwork had started at the present DSW, with the city in flames and amongst riots. As Lucke (1965) writes, 'The fieldwork in those days had a different flavour and it was fieldwork in the true spirit. Students had to demand study at night after long hard days because they couldn't go on without thinking about the alternative plans and trying to figure out what more experienced social workers would have done'. Implying that fieldwork was humanitarian in nature and addressed the social situations as they existed, with '*shramdan*', apparently without worrying which method of social work practice would be more apt for the situation. It was more about responding to an immediate need and giving social work students an opportunity to be involved in the direct work of helping people. This is what the curriculum was eventually preparing students for.

Things have changed from 1947 to 2018. To get a M.A. Degree in Social Work in 1948 the student only had to have successfully completed the two years fieldwork signed and certified by the principal of the school implying that there were no marks for fieldwork but only internal grading. The importance of fieldwork in social work was such that each student was given a separate certificate with details of the fieldwork placement and the grade. While classes were held on six days from 8.30 a.m. to 12.30 p.m., fieldwork was done in the afternoons on five days in the rural placements in a village; a bus would transport the students to the village. Alongside was the public bus service for city-based placements which included LNJP Hospital (earlier Lady Irwin), Lady Hardinge Medical College, Beggar's Home, Remand Home for Children (Boys), and Nabi Karim Slum to name a few. There were no trained social workers then in any of the settings except for the Remand Home and later in 1951 at the Irwin Hospital and Lady Hardinge Hospital (Pathak, 2010). In 1956 for the first time marks for fieldwork performance were introduced into the educational curriculum. The requirement of the number of hours to be put in by a student were raised from 10 hours a week to 15 hours a week spread over 2 days of work in the field setting (Kumar, 1981). The person heading the fieldwork programme was designated as Head of the Field Work Department. This was subsequently replaced by Director of Field Work in the 1970s and in late 1990s (during the author's tenure in the department); the term 'Placements' was added thus designating the position as 'Director of Field Work and Placements', which continues to date.

Components of fieldwork

The following mentioned components of fieldwork are an integral part of practice learning in most of the schools of social work in India. Based on the experiential account of the author, this section describes each component with specific details and illustrations.

Orientation programme

The orientation programme is designed to provide the student with a bird's eye view of the course content. The programme is organised for students of both the first and third semesters in the month of July, as per the academic schedule of the University (the vocabulary during the annual mode was Previous and Final Year). While the programme for the first semester students is for ten days, for the third semester students it is for a week.

The ten-day orientation is the first exposure of students to social work education. The students are introduced to the course and fieldwork curricula and given field exposure through field visits. They learn about the course content, fieldwork programme, placement agencies, ethics, values, recording styles, supervision and evaluation, department staff (teaching and non-teaching), and departmental projects. The programme is conducted by the faculty members who add a lot of value with their rich experience. This is an important component of fieldwork because the students admitted to the course come from various disciplines, socio-economic backgrounds, and parts of the country. Hence, the objective of the programme is to bring the batch to a similar level of understanding about the theory papers and fieldwork training. So, while this is a general introduction to the course itself, it also introduces them to the component of fieldwork and helps form an important initial understanding about fieldwork.

One of the earlier practices at DSW was to conclude the ten-day orientation with an outing/picnic to an outdoor location, a practice which continued till early 2000. The purpose of the outing was multifold. While it facilitated better bonding between the faculty and the students, it also gave a platform for the faculty to check the suitability of the students for the proposed placement under their supervision, implying that it was the responsibility of the fieldwork unit to furnish the list of the concurrent placements on time to the faculty. Such was the seriousness of the task. One of the professors went to the extent of going through the autobiographical statement of each student in detail to understand the kind of supervision the student would require and also to avoid cases of dropout from the course due to any stress situation which could emerge due to the field setting and supervisor allocation. Gradually, the sanctity of the very well-established exercise got lost because of the relatively smaller number of teachers present during the outing/picnic and retirement of senior faculty. However, the relevance and importance of the practice cannot be undermined. The first semester orientation now ends with an indoor celebration which is more of a culmination of the ten-day orientation.

The third semester orientation spread over a week is organised to add to the existing knowledge and skills of the students who have undergone two semesters of training and a block placement. This is done through lectures and interactions with practitioners invited as resource persons. Teaching faculty from other departments with expertise in areas related to the social work discipline are also invited. The aim is to facilitate better understanding of the contemporary sites and challenges in social work practice, develop understanding of the emerging areas of social work practice, and enable the students to develop perspectives on the role of the social worker in such settings.

Concurrent fieldwork and setting

Concurrent fieldwork at the DSW, DU is understood as fieldwork alongside the classroom instruction. It is through this platform the students are expected to integrate theory and practice. Placement of students in the various agencies or communities/slums is the first step in concurrent fieldwork. The two days concurrent placement has been a practice at DSW since the 1980s (or even before) when I was a student in the department and continues to date in the semester mode. Every student is assigned a setting for the entire year. The students visit the field on Tuesdays and Thursdays, putting a minimum of six hours per visit under the guidance of a faculty and agency supervisor (in case of agency placement). Both, government agencies and NGOs, which offer scope for students' learning and growth in the social sector, are selected. Preference is given to organisations with the position of social worker primarily because of their understanding of the requirement of the course and nature of training to be imparted. However, due to an increased number of students over the years, finding organisations with a trained social worker is becoming difficult. Hence organisations which offer good work exposure to the social work students with experienced staff are considered for the placements. Practitioners who are newly inducted as supervisors need detailed orientation to fieldwork by the department supervisor and Director of Field Work by way of preparing the student, sharing the objectives of fieldwork both from the perspective of the social work course and requirements of the fieldwork agency, sharing the format for ongoing performance assessment and final evaluation, discussing the tasks based on the objectives as well as the line of communication in case of problems faced by the student, and setting timings for individual and group conferences and submission of student recordings. The student is also oriented to the team and other staff in the agency and most importantly the clients. These inputs are provided over time and not just in one sitting.

In the past the social work curriculum and concurrent placement were constantly trying to align with existing external field realities, thus re-defining the scope of the profession. For instance, in 1973–1974 the agency placements were replaced by the community placements in response to the curriculum focus on policy, development, and planning and constant discussions as to what contribution schools of social work could make to the process of development. For example, the national emergency in 1975 and demolition of unauthorised colonies uprooting many families evoked discussions among faculty with regard to the nature and content of field practice. The importance of these sites was felt not only for students' placement but also for identifying 'newer' demands around which the fieldwork practice could be reorganised (Kumar, 1981). Hence it is important that such practices continue to define the concurrent placements.

Individual conferences (ICs)

ICs are an integral part of the concurrent fieldwork wherein the student social worker and the supervisor collectively meet once a week for an allotted time of half an hour to discuss the progress of their work. Individual Conferences every week are to be held on the basis of fieldwork reports and hence it is imperative that the student social worker submits the reports within the time frame decided. The content of the reports should form the basis for discussion and supervisory inputs.

Group conferences (GCs)

The GC is an important component of fieldwork. It facilitates students to undergo a wide range of experiences in a structured and controlled setting. It trains the students into reflecting on their fieldwork, selecting a field situation for sharing at a wider forum extending beyond their respective supervisors, preparation of a formal paper, distribution of the paper on time, and performing the roles of presenter, chairperson and recorder on a fortnightly basis. GCs are held every alternate Friday afternoon for both the years and for one and a half hours with a group of approximately 15 students placed under 3 to 4 teachers who would be the resource persons. These conferences start around September, that is, after a month of visit to the field by the students. Under the GCs the students present their paper which has been finalised in consultation with their supervisor. The GCs are the only platform where all students are given an opportunity to present their field experiences and concerns within a theoretical framework. Since the presentation is in the presence of resource persons and classmates, it is also an exercise in the coherent articulation of arguments in public, which is an important skill in the social work profession. This is especially important for students who are not vocal in the classrooms and hesitate to put forward their views. A highly effective platform, it provides the students with exposure to different settings. This platform also provides a ground for the young faculty to learn from their senior faculty. The practice of GCs continued at the DSW, DU in the semester mode till the year 2011.

Supportive Field Instructions Programme (SFIP)

The SFIP, as the name suggests, was introduced to support fieldwork through compulsory field practice classes for both years (called semesters later) with the primary objective to enable the students to interact with practitioners and distinguished persons from the field on weekly basis. The method employed under this programme is interactive, with discussions, case presentations, workshops for skill enhancement, and sharing of information. The purpose is to add to the student's body of knowledge, their skills, and to keep them informed about the latest developments in the field. It also aims to bridge the gap between theory and practice. A faculty member is deputed to act as the programme coordinator. Holding the SFIP as part of the time table means compulsory attendance and the duration is one hour. Interested faculty can also attend.

In the annual mode the SFIP started in September and was held for one hour every Friday as part of the time table. Over the years there have been changes in the time table and the programme shifted to afternoons for two hours with variations in days. While the topics for the first year would cover areas such as how to enter and initiate work in the community, gender sensitisation, theatre as a means of communication, school social work, and use of communication skills in the field, the second year themes were more specific such as social work in industry, Right to Information, natural resource management, and employee social security to name a few. At times joint sessions of both years were organised considering the relevance for the students such as sessions on Participatory Rural Appraisal (PRA).

Rural camp

The rural camp was started to provide an exposure to students about rural life and the challenges faced by rural India. The students get an exposure to life in rural India, modes of governance, community-based organisations, status of women, class, caste, and power divides. The rural camp is one of the components mentioned in the UGC Model Curriculum Guidelines, (2001). In most of the social work institutes it is for a period of a week to ten days. An important task for the Director of Field Work, involves identifying and networking with a local NGO working in the rural area which can provide the requisite exposure to the students and arranging for boarding and logistics on a payment basis.

The camp, besides providing a rural or semi-rural exposure, aims to achieve good bonding among the students including building team spirit, undertaking leadership roles, and developing sensitivity to the needs of peer group and the field. It is a practice to have the camp in the month of December after the semester exams. In the annual format it was held after the mid-term evaluations in mid-December. Earlier, with a reasonable batch of around 55 students logistics were manageable but became difficult with an increased number of students.

Block fieldwork and winter placement

The block fieldwork includes training of the students in a particular setting of their choice for a continuous duration of 30–45 days within or outside Delhi and without faculty supervision. All expenses are borne by the students. The purpose is to broaden the students' experience before employment and guide them to take responsibility. This is a mandatory placement for the award of the degree. In the annual mode block fieldwork happened after the final year exams and was not evaluated.

In the semester system the block fieldwork happens after the end of the second semester. The shift was to facilitate students to join jobs immediately after their exam. Though it continues to be an unsupervised placement, it is evaluated out of 100 marks through a viva voce examination by an external examiner.

The winter placements are optional for the students. Those interested can take up around 15-day placements every year during the month of December to enhance their learning skills. The following two components, that is, study tour and group labs/skill labs, have not been a part of the DSW fieldwork, not for any specific reason, though their relevance for student's learning is immense.

Study tour

Study tour is a visit to a number of outstation institutions. The students use study tours to explore innovative special projects and initiatives in different parts of the country with an academic objective. The place and the organisation are collectively decided by the group of students in consultation with their faculty. The study tours are reported to give students a knowledgeable and worthy experience.

Group labs/skill labs

Group Labs are organised for the new entrants before sending them for field training. The students are oriented through several live experiences as the group labs engage students in real life activities to analyse social and structural issues from multiple facets. Group labs are a series of well-thought and tested games and exercises and are scheduled before starting concurrent fieldwork. Though some faculty have attended training courses on the same, it is not an integral part of the course structure unlike in some other universities like the social work department at Jamia Millia Islamia.

Job placements

The job placements are not considered a component of fieldwork practicum, but in DSW it forms a very important component of the fieldwork unit and is headed by the Director of Field Work. The job placements at DSW, DU started formally in the mid 1990s with a placement cell and have gradually expanded to ensure maximum placements of the students. An important contribution of the placement cell is the 'placement brochure' with the details of the students for the benefit of the placement agencies.

The various components listed earlier help us understand the structure and administration of fieldwork. There is a value and purpose for each of these. As times changed, the profile of the students, faculty, and agencies changed; there has been a need to alter and or improve some of these components to better administer the fieldwork experience for students. And yet documenting the past and the trajectory of the subsequent journey offers an important reference point to understand and reflect on the changing curriculum and the field and what adaptations they demanded.

This section presents the author's efforts towards an effective coordination between the different components of fieldwork, different stakeholders, and managing her roles and responsibilities to meet the set objectives as Director of Field Work and Placements from 2010–2013. The diversity of the experience is presented under the 'transitional period' which shares the discourses that happened while introducing the changes in the fieldwork curriculum. The second subsection enumerates the challenges faced and the learning in the due course.

Transitional period (2010–2013) and coordinating fieldwork

This period from 2010 to 2013 can be said to be transitional as the department saw a shift from the annual mode to the semester system. This was also the time when central universities everywhere had an increase in numbers of students.[1] At the department, a need was felt for revision of fieldwork curricula by faculty in the middle of the semester of 2011. The period saw new courses for faculty, to develop and teach, with the deadline to finish the course in four months, hence the need to simplify fieldwork. The suggested revision in fieldwork (mainly the evaluations and group conferences) suggested by one of the three stakeholders, the faculty, became challenging due to mid-session when rural camp and placements were around the corner and preparations for group conferences had begun by way of formation of groups. Changes were made as experiments to try out which various options would best fit the semester system. This section reflects on the discourse, highlighting what was retained and what got changed and can be a good lesson for other social work departments who are contemplating changes in their fieldwork curricula.

Concurrent fieldwork

One of the pertinent debates was to replace the two days fieldwork (within Delhi and National Capital Territory (NCT)) with one month consolidated fieldwork in the form of a block fieldwork (anywhere in the country). This meant placement for a month in one setting to meet the required number of days of 27–30 days. The proposal had its own merits and demerits. The merit was that the presence of the students in the field for a month would facilitate continuous exposure to the setting which gets missed in the twice a week format. However, the limitations in the system acted as a deterrent to its implementation. Firstly, it was not practical to supervise students beyond NCT due to financial constraints and getting the University to fund the travel was not within their existing rules. Secondly, the possibility of using technology/Skype for supervision was not considered practical due to poor network connectivity in many parts of the country, particularly in the rural areas, especially since students could opt for an organisation working in the interiors. Third, block placement was an existing component of fieldwork at the department wherein the students get an opportunity to intern for a month in the field after the second semester.

The positives of the twice a week fieldwork are that it ensures praxis of theory and practice on continuous basis. This format provides a holistic exposure to the students and orients them to activities happening during the year such as migration pattern, associated school drop outs, and mainstreaming of economically weaker children during specific months in the public schools, all of which may get missed in the block fieldwork. The two day format of fieldwork per week continues.

Students' choice for concurrent fieldwork

This practice which started in the year 2000 invited students to give their areas of interest for the concurrent placement. The practice was discontinued on various grounds such as difficulty to match the choice of the student with the agency due to the increased strength of students and hence the inability to have cent-per-cent choice-based placement. In the past also there were cases where the student's area of interest was not granted, thus resulting in dissatisfaction among the students. The matching of the student with the agency has to be done on more important parameters like distance between home and agency, not repeating the previous supervisor, area of work in the first two semesters, etc. Hence the practice of seeking the area of the student interest in placement was discontinued.

Students' evaluations

The fortnightly evaluation system was replaced by monthly evaluations (ME) in 2005. The proposal to replace the ME to 'end semester evaluation (ESE)' in the mentioned period was floated. The justification was that the semester system curriculum was heavily packed with many papers which made it difficult to continue with the fieldwork evaluation on a monthly basis. The change was also justified on the grounds that a month was too short a period to assess a student's performance, especially for those students who were either irregular or slow to understand the requirements of fieldwork. Plus, the provision of viva voce to assess the student's work was provided for under the semester system which negated the requirement for the monthly evaluations. The counter advices supported the benefits of regular evaluation (fortnightly/monthly) on the basis that a continuous evaluation never hurts the student learning. It could be an objective type evaluation with basic variables to monitor and evaluate the students working and enable their learning. The end result was the replacing of the ME with ESE to be done at the end of every semester i.e. after the end of four months. The evaluation proforma was changed to four different proformas for every semester. The comprehensive attendance sheet at the end of the proforma was replaced by basic data requirement on attendance.

Group conferences (GC) to Students' conferences (SC)

The group conference was changed to 'students' conference'. The new changed system was shifted to the second semester. It was designed to have presentation of the papers on two consecutive days by the students. The entire class was to be divided into two groups. It was decided that, based on pre-determined criteria, a few papers of the students would be selected for presentations. Though the idea was to promote healthy competition among students so that they strive for excellence, somewhere the essence of equal learning opportunity for every student seemed to get lost in the entire endeavour and would defeat the intended purpose of everyone striving for excellence. Thus, it was decided to have presentations from all the students dividing the class in two large groups.

The format given to the students for presentation under the new system includes review of literature, reflection on theoretical paradigms, and on the nature of engagement of the student. The students are free to consult any faculty for their paper which is a shift from the earlier pattern of preparing the paper under the guidance of the allocated supervisor. While the new format is seen to have its advantages in form of wider space to the students in planning their papers and nurtures reading habits, in the process the papers have become theoretical and fail to reflect on the learning in the field. They have become similar to a seminar paper and raise macro issues which are not connected with the student's fieldwork. Also, the continuous learning which was an integral part of the group conferences has evaporated making the new system symbolic and ritualistic. The training imparted in chairing a session, recording the minutes, and experimenting on alternate ways of presentation like skits or exhibiting through posters/material is lost due to the two day presentations. Some senior faculty still continue to guide their students towards reflections of the field in the paper.

Rural camp

The increased number of students posed a challenge in taking all the students to one organisation for the rural camp. One of the alternatives was to divide the students into groups of two or three and take them to different settings. This meant identifying suitable organisations and also faculty members to assist the students. Also, having the camp in December (after the evaluations) was problematic due to weather conditions not being conducive in most parts of the country and the students having different adaptations to weather. It was also difficult to find organizations to agree to host the rural camp for similar reasons of weather and the arrangements for boarding, logistics, and for other provisions like hot water and quilts for such a large number.

During her three years tenure the author took the entire batch together to one agency and split the batch into two groups for different project sites of the agency wherever possible. Though the task of identifying an organisation which would provide a good rural exposure and be willing to host a group as large as 80 students was not easy, it was worth the effort. Also, in order to facilitate the students' learning through the camp and to avoid becoming a liability on the host organisation, the camp was shifted to the month of October instead of December. This facilitated better camping due to friendly weather conditions and was managed well with the support of available faculty members. The students reported better bonding amongst themselves after the rural camp.

Supportive Field Instructions Programme (SFIP)

The practice of SFIP was discontinued on the pretext that since courses had to be finished in a limited time period there was requirement for more class hours. Hence allocating slot for SFIP was not feasible and was seen as justified due to lack of faculty's experience of teaching under the semester mode.

Job placements

Though not a part of the fieldwork practicum, job placements form a vital responsibility of the Director of Fieldwork. The job placements in the given three years were well planned and systematised and can be seen as one of the best phases for the DSW placements (The Hindu, 2013).

- The job placements were streamlined by completing the entire process of preparation of the Placement Brochure by the end of November or first week of December so that it was posted on time. To avoid any rush during the classes,

- a four-day placement fair was hosted for the first time in January 2011 to invite maximum organisations for recruitment within a given time period. The fair was a success and took care of on an average of 10–12 major organisations.
- Also, to avoid any kind of biases in selection, an equitarian approach was adopted with the objective to accommodate and secure job placement for most of the students. Hence a policy decision was taken that once a student is selected for two jobs he/she cannot sit for the third.
- Though only those organisations offering a remuneration of at least Rs. 15,000 per month were entertained by way of being invited for pre-placement talks (PPT), a minimum of Rs 20,000 per month was the quoted salary to the organisations. At the same time, students were kept apprised of the organisations which offered less salary so as to provide an opportunity for those who were interested to join in the offered amount. Spinal Cord Injuries is one such organisation which paid less but was good by way of the perks and health benefits. It was opted for by a student who worked there for many years.
- Presence of the Director of Fieldwork on all days of job placement to ensure smooth functioning.

The entirety of the placements was done by the four-member student committee along with the Director of Fieldwork.

Challenges and learning in coordinating fieldwork

This section delves into some of the working skills used for effective coordination at various levels and among partners to: ensure quality of supervision, explore new agencies for fieldwork placements, orientation of the new faculty, and interaction between academia and practitioners. Challenges that emerged and ways in which they were addressed form an important feature of this section.

Some of them are examined here.

Orientation Programme (OP)

The OP required coordination between resource persons-external and internal faculty, agencies, government departments, and the students at various levels. During the orientation programme, an effort was made to ensure that the coordination with the resource persons was clear and effective. This was for their timely arrival and addressing the theme as planned. There were occasions of last minute dropping out of resource persons and in one instance the resource person got delayed due to his poor time management. Such situations were taken care of by prior preparation of an internal faculty as a stand by, to fill in the slot at the last minute, if required.

OP also included field visits. The visit to the field required prior communication to the agencies. The agency linked to the Department of Women and Child Development was informed beforehand about the students visit through written communication to the Secretary, DWCD and for prior permission from the concerned authority. The field visits were planned to include one community, non-government organisation, government organisation and a charitable trust respectively. The entire programme was coordinated by dividing the class into two groups, allocating faculty to the groups, giving orientation one day before for timely arrival and other expectations.

Identification of placement agencies

Concurrent placement requires coordination with our very important partner – the agency, for the yearlong training of the student. This is challenging in terms of identifying new agencies competent enough to provide the required training to the student and continuing with the existing agencies approved by the faculty supervisors based on their past experience. For instance, one of the organisations refused to take the student due to the misbehaviour of the earlier placed student and put a condition that they would interview the student before consenting. In another situation, the new batch of students reported that due to non-communication by the previous student about the three-month long break, the community felt offended and were not welcoming to the new batch. Despite the orientation to the students on some of these pertinent practices, there are omissions which as Director were addressed with respective faculty supervisors.

Regarding identification of new agencies, an attempt was made to identify those with a professional social worker due to their familiarity with roles and responsibilities for the student, and at same time those without a professional social worker were also considered. Our past experiences and my visits to fieldwork agencies as Director of Field Work showed that a large number of agencies were without qualified social workers. Placement in a large number of them were still continued based on the positive feedback from the faculty. Simultaneously some of the agencies with social workers were seen to expose the students to a range of social issues such as homelessness, street and working children, school dropouts, poor health, inaccessible health services for the poor and lack of access to public spaces by women.

It is important to mention that as the Director certain important decisions were taken to streamline placements. These included:

- One agency per faculty to promote healthy supervision and ease the task of the agency who felt burdened with the visit of more than one faculty supervisor from the same department.
- Easing out the burden of large numbers of student placements in certain settings and under the supervision of four to five faculty.
- Maintaining objectivity in student placement to ensure that every faculty has mix of both sex students and also merit-wise to avoid any concentration of meritorious students in certain settings and with some supervisors.

Matching the field setting and student profile

This is a very serious exercise at coordination and from various angles. It means matching the profile of the student with the respective agency for the concurrent placement. The matching is required on various parameters (particularly in the third semester) such as previous supervisor, number of supervisors changed, previous field setting, nature of the present setting and area of work, residence of the student and metro service/bus service from residence to agency/community. Matching the student and the agency is a challenge when the number of students to be placed is large but vital for effective fieldwork and to avoid mid-session breakdowns. To avoid any kind of ignorance when approached by the students this exercise was done by the author herself by using Excel sheets.

Regular inputs and guidance to the ad hoc/guest faculty

One of the very important responsibilities of Director of Field Work is to orient and guide the ad hoc and guest faculty on the expectations from them as fieldwork supervisors. Meetings with the faculty and more meetings with the young faculty were organised to address their ongoing queries and update them with skills of supervision. This exercise was done frequently in the initial months of their joining along with giving them the flexibility of approaching the Director any time. Keeping in consideration the learning of the students, the matters addressed were: fixed and displayed individual conference (IC) schedule, IC interactions once a week which are formally announced to the student, avoiding change in the schedule unless very urgent, avoiding using social media for calling the student and any other meeting apart from the IC is unscheduled IC and should be accounted for. The Department has had a practice of inviting fieldwork files from the faculty any time during the semester, especially from the new faculty in the spirit of guidance and learning. Suggestions were given by the Director to respective faculty to enhance their learning. This practice ensured the timely upkeep of their records by the faculty. The practice was continued with the ad hoc, guest and the University Teaching Assistants (UTAs).

Points to remember

- Fixed weekly time for IC
- One photocopy of the report for the agency supervisor
- Fieldwork files not to be allowed outside department supervisor's room/library.
- Reports plus log sheets to be submitted together
- Fieldwork reports to be read before IC by supervisor
- Monthly meetings between the student and both supervisors

Example drawn from students' queries posed regarding fieldwork

'Should I enter the community alone or should all five of us enter together?' is the question posed by the student to her department supervisor for the first day of fieldwork, and receives the response that she can decide as per everyone's convenience. The student approaches the fieldwork Director of Field Work as the answer fails to satisfy her. The student is made to look into the advantages and disadvantages of both to facilitate decision making. For instance, entering in a group is bound to catch the community attention when the aim is to appear one among them for better interaction. Entering alone on the first day may be uncomfortable and intimidating, but her presence may not be conspicuous to the community. Care regarding dress and careful conversation is all reiterated and student made to ponder over. Hence the decision by the student is made with knowledge and creativity rather than convenience.

Change in supervisors and timely new allocation

Another challenge was to deal with the turnover of the guest teachers and other teachers going on leave. This requires timely re-allocation of the students to other supervisors or to newly appointed teachers so that fieldwork facilitation continues smoothly. This meant coordinating with available faculty to take additional students for supervision till the appointment of the new faculty. It also meant corresponding with the agencies regarding the change of supervisor, managing fieldwork files of the student before handing over to the new supervisor, display of the change on the notice board etc. For effective communication the notice would include the names of the student, earlier supervisor, new supervisor and the agency. The transfer involved taking a stock of the expertise and place of stay of the new teachers to optimise their inputs in the field similarly as it is done during the initial matching of students and supervisors. For instance, beginning 2012, 3 guest faculty did not join and the 15 students placed under them were transferred under 5 existing faculty supervisors. Care was taken not to disturb the linkage with the external partners and the student by continuing with the same placement. The University Teaching Assistants (UTAs) which was a new programme started by the University, had four persons as UTAs in the mentioned tenure who were given fieldwork supervision.

Agency supervisors meet in the department

A meeting was organised to ensure that interface between the department and agency supervisors was maintained and strengthened. This was also a platform where certain collective decisions were made and the roles of the department-agency supervisors spelled out. Issues like irregularity by student, no visits by the department supervisor or inadequate agency supervision came up and were addressed by spelling out department policies and following up with the department supervisors for their regularity.

Visit to the settings

As the Director, the author made it a habit to visit all the agencies at least once in a year which served many purposes. It helped to build and strengthen the contact between the Department and the field. It confirmed the agency's interest in supervising the students, ensured conducive surroundings for student's learning and allocation of work appropriate for the student by the agency. Names of new agencies for supervision were procured from faculty and those not considered suitable were dropped.

Coordination of block placement

The block placement, which is without any department supervision, puts a lot of onus on the Director with regard to coordination. The evaluation reports from the agency have to be received by the fieldwork unit in time so that they can be placed before the external examiner during viva voce. Due to unforeseen circumstances or casual approach of the student, cases where the reports did not reach the fieldwork unit had to be followed up on urgent basis, failing which the most vital stakeholder, i.e. the student, could get penalised.

Facilitating job placement

One of the major challenges faced was to send a draft copy to the university press as a mandatory requirement by the university, asking them to print it, only to get it back after two months, after regular follow ups and reminders with the note that it should be printed from outside through a private vendor.

Amidst all this the following deserve a special mention as experiences that were satisfying:

1   Visit to Bihar where the Department started the relief work after the Kosi mishap (when the Kosi river overflowed due to heavy rains and caused damage to settlements nearby). The team from the Department visited the site along with the team from the university to applaud the efforts of the people.
2   Coordinated the visits of social work students from other Indian universities during their visit to the department.
3   Informed fieldwork agencies two weeks prior to the student's placement to enable them to plan their schedule accordingly.
4   Started an annual calendar of fieldwork events.

A proposed pattern for fieldwork

Though there could be many options of fieldwork practice, the author suggests one such pattern of fieldwork practice:

Some of the lessons from Coordination are: first, there should be a designated individual or team to oversee the fieldwork programme. There should be orientation programmes for both students and faculty, especially new or visiting faculty so that expectations are clearly spelt out. The requirements of weekly ICs with students and bi-weekly GCs and end semester evaluations to be continued. There should be regular meetings with agency supervisors to strengthen fieldwork. This would give a platform to understand their problems in facilitating fieldwork and

TABLE 3.1 A proposed pattern for fieldwork

Fieldwork component	Present pattern	Remarks	Proposed pattern
Concurrent fieldwork*	– Twice a week Tuesday, Thursday – Two different settings in 4 semesters.	Field exposure is gained throughout academic year	Two options 1. The same format to continue, i.e. twice or thrice a week 2. Research-based fieldwork in the 3–4 semesters leading to empirical study
Block fieldwork	– After second semester, 30–45 days; June till mid-July – Without faculty supervision – Evaluated for 100 marks of viva voce	100 marks in hands of external examiner is not justified as objective assessment cannot happen in 5–10 min of viva voce	Options 1. With supervision: 100 marks to be equally distributed between external and internal examiner or even lesser marks with external examiner 2. Without supervision and no evaluation At end of second semester to continue
Rural camp	– Third semester – Sways between October and December	October is a preferred month as it is more weather friendly	1. Month of October. 2. Making a roster would facilitate faculty participation 3. Students go together for better learning, bonding and team work
Group conference	Students' Seminar	The students' seminar does not serve much purpose for students' learning	1. Alternative week for both semesters 2. 4–5 groups with 12–15 students 3. Faculty supervisors as resource persons. 4. Students share their field experiences through conference paper
Evaluation format	End Semester Evaluation	Just end semester evaluation is not very effective form of student evaluation	1. Fortnightly/monthly evaluations 2. Fortnightly/monthly proforma should be objective and brief 3. End Semester Evaluation continues with simple and straight questions to deal with diversity among students
Study tours	Does not exist	Expose students to successful to innovative efforts	Second semester in mid semester break for 4–5 days
Workshops-skill development	Does not exist	Will develop skills for better service delivery to address situations experienced during practice	4–6 full day workshops in entire 4 semesters

Source: Author

enable sharing of mutual information and inputs. Other components of rural camp, study tour and job placement should be placed in the semester schedule in such a way that all faculty members on rotation may be assigned responsibilities of nurturing each of these components. It has to be decided whether the final block placement has to be a supervised or unsupervised, graded or non-graded activity as each of these would have different repercussions in terms of both faculty input and student expectations. Since there has been a long history of various changes that the fieldwork programme has itself undergone for various reasons both internal and external, it would also help to develop a policy document or a manual that would be a good reference for fieldwork. This could be shared with the multiple stakeholders, mainly students, faculty and agencies.

Challenges and learning: a summary

Fieldwork has undergone substantial changes from the 1940s when it first began in India to now. The changes are also due to the changing national, social and political scenario of the country and due to the shift in the mode of examinations from annual to semester mode.

1. During the journey, the learning was on the skill of effective communication when dissent has to be given without getting emotional outbursts, meetings which get abruptly concluded and have to be reported factually correctly as 'inconclusive', fighting one's fears and anxieties.
2. The semester mode of examinations means increased workload for the students and faculty which has reduced the availability of time to reflect and ponder over work like 'fieldwork'. The students are under pressure to show results in four months which somewhat compromises the objective of fieldwork.
3. The environment for reflecting on one's work in the field and the learning involved seems blurred and fieldwork has somewhat taken a back seat though we still would like to believe that it's an integral part of social work practice.
4. The hurry to finish deadlines and attain results is contrary to the fieldwork practice which needs time to be with people, understand them, accept them and build rapport with them.
5. The fast and competitive mode of students somewhat is a hindrance to basic principles of social work practice which speaks of going at the pace of people, listening to their narratives, accepting them as they are and being non-judgmental.
6. The large student size is a challenge for fieldwork in terms of identifying appropriate agencies for fieldwork and doing justice by way of supervisory guidance.

Conclusion

Anyone who has worked as Director of Field Work would agree that managing routine fieldwork effectively is a lesson in itself, especially for academicians who otherwise do not have much scope for doing administrative work. There are inbuilt challenges in the designation which get addressed with experience and dedication towards the position. Importance of fieldwork in social work education should be reinforced with the ongoing debates and efforts to strengthen the programme as per the newer requirements and changing perspectives of the new and old faculty. The beauty lies in not letting the past go but restructuring the past with the new requirements. It is also crucial to hold as sacrosanct some components that are integral to facilitate this learning. For fieldwork to continue as an integral and indispensable feature of social work education it is important that the stakeholders are networked and linked to support each other and facilitate the students' learning with the feeling of humanity. Fieldwork often is a student's first venturing out to understand what the profession of social work itself is, thus making the programme and its coordination shoulder a higher responsibility of not only making the experience meaningful for young professionals in training but also hand holding them as they enter the world of professional social work practice. It is during this phase of learning that impressions are created about the profession and decisions made about their own career choices. Thus coordinating fieldwork is also about nurturing and coordinating the entry of a cadre of potential social work professionals.

Note

1 Implementation of the 27% OBC reservation in universities which was completed in 2011.

References

University Grants Commission. (2001). *UGC Model Curriculum: Social Work Education*. University Grants Commission, pp. 19.
(n.d.). Delhi School of Social Work (Department of Social Work), University of Delhi. Retrieved July 7, 2018, Sunday, from http://dssw.du.ac.in/about-us.html
The Hindu (New Delhi edition). (2013, June, Thursday). A rising graph. Delhi, India: The Hindu.
IFSW & IASSW. (2014). *Global definition of social work profession*. Retrieved June 2018, from http://ifsw.org/get-involved/global-definition-of-social-work
Kumar, K. (1981). Field instruction in social work education. Workshop on Field Work. Delhi: organised by Department of social work, University of Delhi, Unpublished.
Lucke, E. (1964, October-1965, January). Social worker's pledge: Gift to Gandhiji on his last birthday. *Social Work Forum*, *II*(4); *III*(1), 5–10.
Pathak, S. (2010). Short history of (Delhi School of Social Work), Department of Social Work. Unpublished, Bangalore. pp. 5, 9.

4

FIELDWORK SUPERVISION[1]

From vigilantism to nurturance

Neelam Sukhramani

As a social work educator in India, it is baffling that even while fieldwork has been considered as the principal tool for enabling the students to acquire the practice wisdom, there is limited debate and reflection in the contemporary time on the different components of fieldwork including fieldwork supervision. Barring a few schools of social work, there is no capacity building initiative for being a fieldwork supervisor. There is also limited discussion on how fieldwork supervision could respond to the altered context. The macro level policies appear to be impinging on the autonomy of core disciplinary requirements. Flooding of students, introduction of compulsory courses and altered qualifications for entry as an educator are an offshoot of these policies which are resulting in a compromise on the core disciplinary requirements. Fieldwork supervision appears to be competing with the other curricular components for time resulting in abridged and infrequent faculty-student contact. Within the limited time available, the supervisory process appears like a channel for facilitating task accomplishment without necessarily going deeper into the various dimensions of professional and personal development. The supervisor then stands a chance of getting reduced to a vigilante ensuring the accomplishment of different fieldwork components without necessarily being able to nurture the potential of the student. If the student has to imbibe the professional ethics along with the professional wisdom, fieldwork supervision has to move beyond vigilantism wherein the supervisor is primarily concerned with the completion of fieldwork requirements. The supervisor has to ascertain the specific requirements of each learner and accordingly nurture them since their performance as a professional is contingent upon their fieldwork experiences for which the fieldwork supervisor is the anchor. The current situation calls for a need to reiterate the purpose, ethos and functions of supervision as well as design and debate on mechanisms to deal with the altered contextual realities. This would not only be useful for social work educators but also for advocating at the macro level for the indispensable value that fieldwork supervision holds. The chapter, which is an attempt in this direction, would begin by spelling out the contextual specificities in terms of the learning environment, learner tools and learner characteristics. This is followed by a detailed discussion on the supervisory functions performed by the social work educator explicated with the help of examples from different settings. Finally, the challenges posed to the supervisory process and the possible means of reconciling the same are elaborated.

Before commencing this journey, the author would like to make two submissions. First, I would like to admit that even while one is acutely aware of the hierarchy implicit within the term supervisor, its embeddedness within the social work lexicon is resulting in its continued usage within this chapter as well. The discomfort cannot be discounted since the term opposes the ethos of social work profession. Social work profession continues to believe in a non-hierarchical positioning with any stakeholder and it is the spirit of togetherness which reflects the essence of social work. Whether a terminology can take that essence away is debatable, but for the time being we reconcile ourselves to the usage of the same. Second, while there are write ups mentioning the centrality of fieldwork in social work education, there are limited indigenous write ups detailing the supervisory roles/functions. This also results in over reliance being placed on the few available write ups which were written by some of the pioneers in social work education in India, during the initial few decades of social work education in India.

The context-field practicum, fieldwork supervision and the learner

This chapter locates itself in the context of concurrent fieldwork practice by virtue of it being the most widely adopted pattern in India as well as the comparatively greater opportunity that it offers for consistent supervisory inputs.

Concurrent fieldwork refers to weekly visits (usually twice or thrice a week) to the respective fieldwork agencies that are allotted to the students by the school of social work. By and large students continue in the same fieldwork agency for an entire academic year. The nature of settings in which students could be placed for fieldwork are institutional and community-based. Institutional settings are fairly varied in nature. These could be organisations working with various survivors of violence, offering mental health support, managing child care institutions, engaged in policy advocacy for varied groups, managing de-addiction centres, offering age care services, running inclusive or special education centres and working for rescue and rehabilitation of trafficking survivors, to name a few. The field agencies may not display exclusivity and have multiple interventions. They could be organisations that may be engaged in both direct interventions as well as in research and advocacy. They are managed by NGOs[2] (Non-Governmental Organisations) or by government departments. The community-based fieldwork placements may be either in urban or rural areas. In the urban context the students are placed in marginalised communities such as slums or resettlement colonies. These placements may be through NGOs working in these communities or they may be placed directly in what are referred to as open community placements. Field placements of students are dependent on the geographical location of the school of social work with urban areas having organisations working in a variety of fields which may not necessarily be the case in rural areas. The students are expected to devote a minimum of 15 hours per week to fieldwork. At the end of each week the student is expected to submit a report to the supervisor.

The students are assigned faculty supervisors and, wherever possible, agency supervisors as well. The onus of supervision, however, largely lies on the faculty supervisors in India. The agency supervisors even while allotted to the students may not have necessarily had the opportunity of being a part of a formal academic programme in social work. Thus, the responsibility of enabling the student to draw linkages between classroom and field-based experiences primarily lies on the faculty supervisor.

The agencies, which serve as the sites of learning for students have different perceptions about the value of providing training to the students. While some place the student's learning at the centre attempting to offer different learning opportunities to them, there are others who see the students as a helping hand enabling them to fulfil their tasks and thus the learning programme may not necessarily be designed as per the learner but based upon the organisation's requirements. These differential perceptions become a determinant of the role that they would assume in the student's learning.

The instrumentalities through which the practice of fieldwork supervision takes place are weekly reports of students followed by Individual Conferences (IC) and supervisory field visits. While Individual Conferences are usually scheduled once in a week and expected to be allotted at least one hour (UGC, 2001), the duration may vary depending upon the stage of fieldwork, the number of students allocated to the faculty supervisor and space available within the curriculum.[3] In some schools of social work, the Individual Conferences in the second semester of fieldwork have begun to be scheduled once in a fortnight, but this practice has been adopted in very few schools of social work. Further, the supervisory visits are expected to happen at least once in a month, but the frequency varies from one school to the other. The supervisory visits in the community-based settings are more flexible since they offer a faculty supervisor a possibility for going along with the student to different areas of the community, but in the case of institutional settings they usually entail a discussion on the nature of assignments that the student could possibly undertake, keeping in view the learning objectives as well as seeking feedback from the agency supervisor regarding the student's professional development.

The learners at the Master's level in social work enter into the course from diverse academic backgrounds such as social sciences, natural science, social work, commerce, law, media studies etc. (Desai, 2013). They come from different and distant parts of the country and even many parts of the world (Agnimitra, 2015). In the recent times, a few students are also entering social work after completing their professional education in disciplines such as engineering or architecture

(Agnimitra, 2015), which was earlier a rarity. At the Bachelor's level the students enter the programme with diverse understanding (Desai, 2013). Seldom are they aware about the nuances of the social work discipline. Its popularity as a professional course is sometimes the reason that is driving their entry into the profession. The absence of social work as a subject at the school level offers little opportunity for students to make an informed decision about entering social work education. There are instances where their siblings or other family members may have studied the course, which resulted in their desire to join it. At times, having confronted harsh social realities prompts students to take up a course in social work. Notwithstanding the differential factors that might have led to students joining an educational programme in social work, the understanding about the social work profession may be rather limited. The input available through the internet sources (if accessible to the students) does not provide them with a deeper insight about the profession, or more specifically, about the curricular requirements and thus certain students find it very difficult to cope with the requirements of the programme, which could be very different from the academic programmes that they have undertaken prior to that. The only exception to this would be the students entering into the Master's programme in social work after having completed their Bachelor's in social work, which are very few in number since a Bachelor's programme in social work is not a precondition for entry into the Master's programme, and the number of institutions offering a Master's programme are far more than those offering a Bachelor's programme in social work. To align the diverse backgrounds and motivations of this varied group of learners and to facilitate them in their professional journey is a compounding challenge for social work educators (Agnimitra, 2015, p. 30).

The previously mentioned contextual specificities thus place a demand on the faculty supervisors to pitch themselves at differential levels. An assessment of the understanding, motivation, background and prior experiences of the student on the one hand and that of the expectations from the fieldwork agencies on the other hand would be a determinant of the supervisory inputs. The supervision process has to combine the functions of knowledge and skill enhancement besides enabling the student to challenge their belief systems. Motivating them when the situation so demands and enabling the development of 'self' through a process of mentoring are also essential to foster personal and professional growth among the learners. The faculty supervisor has to be extremely reflexive since the supervisor-supervisee relationship can have a profound effect on the student.

Supervision as a channel for knowledge/perspective building

Knowledge and perspective building on issues that the student confronts in the field is an inalienable function of supervision. Banerjee (1975) also assigned significance to this role since in most cases the student is a beginner in the social work profession. Life experiences prior to joining social work may have prompted the development of a linear thinking which needs to be worked upon. Differential learning opportunities may have to be created for the student to develop these perspectives. Explaining the multidimensional perspectives from which an issue needs to be viewed and analysed is a part of the supervisory process. As an example, if members of the community are knowingly engaging in jobs which have several occupational hazards associated with them, the student would have to be helped to understand the varied factors that are compelling the people to put their own lives at risk. Providing readings to the students, engaging the student through reflective questioning and organising an interaction with another professional working on the area are some of the ways through which this could be facilitated. Asking a series of reflective questions brings home to the student the need to do so at their level when confronted with different situations in future. To cite another example, a student placed in a rural area finds the mother who goes to the field for the entire day leaving behind Rs 10 for the young child to purchase food articles (biscuits, chips etc.) from the local shop may perceive this as a lack of responsibility on the part of the mother or her unwillingness to cook before leaving which may be reported as such. The student has through this analysis drawn a linear cause effect relationship. The effect of consumerism may escape the student's attention or even, for that matter, looking at the issue from a gender perspective may have not struck the student. It is these lenses that we have to enable the student to wear through reflective questioning in the supervisory conferences.

The student also has to be helped to develop a legislative and policy perspective in relation to the issue being addressed by the fieldwork agency where they are placed. It is not just the reading of the legislation but also the implementation of the same, the challenges associated with the same as well as a critique which could form part of the supervisory process. There have also been instances where cross country analysis of policy has also been encouraged as part of the fieldwork process. The nature and depth of analysis would vary depending upon the nature of field placement, the stage at which the student is within the educational programme as well as the student's willingness and desire to engage in such an analysis. The cross country analysis is, however, useful for international students since they may eventually be going back to their native country.

Mathew (1975) responds critically to the oft repeated statement that the student is not able to integrate theory with practice. She says that the supervisor would have to lower their expectations for the student. She states that it is probably unrealistic to expect the classroom teaching to be so comprehensive and all embracing so as to provide answers to the situations that a student is confronted with in the field. The supervisor has to complement the classroom teaching. At times even in cases where specific aspects have been transacted in the classroom the student may find it difficult to connect their field experiences with that. The supervisor has to help the student to establish this connection to the extent possible. This movement from the intuitive to the conscious application of professional knowledge and skill could be fostered through the supervisory process (Mathew, 1975). This assumes greater relevance in the backdrop of the 'articulated approach' to field instruction which is followed by most schools of social work. Sheafor and Jenkins(1981) classify the approaches to field instruction as the 'apprenticeship model', the 'academic model' and the 'articulated approach'. The articulated approach refers to a pattern of instruction wherein the classroom learning (knowing) and the field instruction (doing) take place concurrently. Even while the articulated approach, which leads to a preference for concurrent fieldwork placements, demands a synthesis of the cognitive and experiential learning component, in reality this is a rarity which Sheafor and Jenkins (1981) also admit to since learning opportunities may unfold themselves at times even before the cognitive dimension related to that has been transacted in the classroom. As an example, one of the students who had shadowed a counselling session for the first time came to the individual conference stating that she was able to describe what she saw but was not able to move to a level of abstraction to state what the fieldwork supervisor was attempting to do. This is where the faculty supervisor had to step in to explain the purposes of counselling and the skills that the agency supervisor was using in the session that the student had witnessed. However, there are limits to which the faculty supervisor may be able to do this since expecting the faculty supervisor to be a know-all may be a pointer towards unrealistic expectations. Supervisory groups where discussions may take place on transactions within supervisory conferences while maintaining the confidentiality of the student could be a useful enabling tool.

As a supervisor stimulating the spirit of inquiry is critical to the student's growth. A student who was being constantly confronted with the issue of loss of livelihood by a community where the predominant occupation was waste picking was encouraged to read about the issue in greater depth. The readings on reasons behind the closure of landfills, the government's policy with respect to the people who are engaged in waste segregation and experiments related to management of waste resulted in the student understanding the issue multi-dimensionally. There are constraints to what they might be able to do as students, but an understanding of the issue is itself critical to the learning process. In fact, the student has also in the process understood the process of uncovering an issue that they may encounter in the field.

Recording, in some measure, mirrors the understanding of the student about an issue, their own attitudes with respect to the client system or prevalent practices and also demonstrates the skill set of the student to a certain extent. Careful segmentation of these elements from the reports and analysis of the same can facilitate a student's learning in the earlier defined dimensions. Mathew (1975) states that the situations encountered by the student in the process of fieldwork can be live opportunities for enabling the student to identify the knowledge, principles of practice and professional values and also to consider what cannot be explained on the basis of the existing knowledge available.

As a supervisor it is also important to explore possibilities of designing learning experiences based upon the learning needs or learning patterns of each student (Mathew, 1975). For students whose first language is not the same as the medium of instruction being followed, the pace has to be slowed down for ease of comprehension. Readings also have to be given to these students carefully in order for the student to not feel overwhelmed and those that the student would be able to grasp through comparative ease. A brief orientation about the reading may have to be given for them to be able to understand the context in which the reading is located. Students may also vary in terms of the ease with which they are able to comprehend inputs provided through the supervisory conferences. Eliciting their understanding allows for the supervisor to know if any additional inputs are required. The stage at which the students are in their curriculum is also a determinant of the inputs. As an example, greater inputs on the philosophical base of social work, functions of social work, are required for beginning level students.

Supervision and promoting self-awareness

Zeira and Schiff (2010, p. 428), while contrasting one to one supervision with group supervision, opined that the supervisor-student dyad parallels the process between the worker and the client in treatment. While this statement may not be accepted in totality, there are significant aspects which deserve ponderance. The statement needs to be understood from the standpoint of the potential that the supervisory process holds. Just as the worker envisages growth within the client, the supervisor does so with respect to the student and it is skills of intervention that are used while working with clients that stand the potential of being used with the student while maintaining the boundaries of a supervisor. The practice of social work as a profession requires the use of self, and the supervisory inputs could work towards promoting self-awareness. Banerjee (1975), while comparing social work to other professions, states that in social work the learner has to develop a greater degree of self-awareness as compared to other professions. She points towards the demands that the profession places on the practitioner in the areas of 'knowing', 'feeling', 'doing' and 'being'. The 'being' and the 'feeling' elements demand a greater degree of self-awareness. The skills of challenging on the part of the supervisor hold significant value in this regard. The supervisor could carefully and gradually bring about a recognition of the deeply embedded belief systems which the student may not have been able to recognise. A student in the first semester of her Master's course once wrote in her report the agony that she experienced while witnessing an adolescent girl carrying a gas cylinder (which weighs approx. 16 kg) on her shoulder over a flight of stairs. In her reflections she wrote that she wished there was a male to help her out. This observation was followed by a reflective discussion during the individual conference on the reasons which made the student feel the way she felt. She recognised that coming from an upper middle-class family she had never done something like that and therefore she felt that the girl would have also been discomforted by engaging in this action. The exploration helped the student in challenging her belief system. At a later stage, when the student was asked to reflect upon her experiences through supervision, the student, based on this discussion, wrote that the supervisory process allowed her to 'look at women as capable of being able to multitask and not being bound by 'feminine' roles expected of them'. Challenging this belief system is critical to be able to understand the complex interplay of factors which could be resulting in the reality that the student is witness to. Reiterating what has been stated earlier, challenging of belief systems has to be appropriately timed lest it backfire and become a roadblock for further interactions or prevent students from sharing their dilemmas. The purpose of challenging should be to allow the student to experience growth and not to point towards the anomalies in their patterns of thinking. The spirit has to be reflected both verbally and non-verbally in the supervisory interactions.

When students are unable to handle the dependence that the client may be developing towards them, they may become uncomfortable. Enabling the students to recognise the reasons that result in heightened expectations that the clients may have from them and the process through which independence could be instilled is necessary lest they start blaming the clients. A student placed in a marginalised community was working with a family to enable them to secure a wheelchair for a child who had an orthopaedic disability affecting his movement. The family was struggling to get their income certificate which was required for the purpose. The student was asked by the agency supervisor to facilitate the process since that would also ensure her own learning. While the student was working with the family in this direction, she would visit the residence of the child. During one of the interactions, the family shared with the student the financial hardships that they were facing. The family was engaged in home-based work which would result in extremely low wages besides the father of the boy also putting up a cart to sell items in the locality. While writing her reflections in her fieldwork report for the day, the student expressed her discomfort over the family beginning to load her with different problems that they were facing whereas social work as a profession is facilitative and does not intend to make the client system dependent on them. The supervisor was able to recognise that the student was feeling burdened by the narrative of the family and therefore chose to express these feelings. Reflecting and enabling the student to understand that even when we might not be able to address every situation of the client, it should not stop us from being empathetic towards them was important. Recognising that a sharing of financial challenges does not amount to them having developed a dependency towards the student social worker is important to allow them to feel for the vulnerabilities that the client experiences.

At times the belief systems that the students may hold about their co-worker in fieldwork training may also create feelings of mistrust, thereby affecting their functioning. In the Indian context, fieldwork is challenging for students from other countries or at times from other regions of the country because of the language and cultural differences. In some schools of social work, they are paired with local students[4] to facilitate their learning. This could turn out to be challenging since the local student has to take on the dual role of ensuring their own learning as well as facilitating the learning of the co-worker. An inability to understand the language may also create a feeling of mistrust. Any lapse from the local student may be construed adversely. The supervisor has to step in to help both the students reflect upon their individual insecurities that might have the potential of hindering their relationship.

Supervision and skill strengthening

Fieldwork training provides an opportunity to the students to acquire and strengthen skills critical to social work practice at the micro, mezzo and macro level. Faculty supervisors have to support the students in grasping the techniques of interviewing, recording, conducting home visits and other skills that are intrinsic to their domain of practice (Subhedar, 2001). Modelling of skills by supervisors is one of the mechanisms that facilitates students' learning (Ketner, VanCleave, & Cooper-Bolinskey, 2017). Supervisory visits to the field placements could be used for the purposes of supervisors undertaking a task and allowing the students to observe and learn (Singh, 1985). One of the fieldwork placements in most of the schools of social work is in marginalised communities. These geographical spaces could be baffling as well as intimidating for students. Students in the beginning do find it challenging to initiate conversations with people. The task of relationship building with the community which forms the foundation for future work seems like a roadblock to many. The demonstration of these skills by the supervisor can enable the student to clear/surmount the roadblock.

Supervisory visits can offer an opportunity in this direction. There are several examples, but for reasons of brevity I would like to cite one which demonstrates the role that supervisory visits could play in the development of relationship building and communication skills. A young child was playing with an object in an urban slum. Two male students had been placed in this community for fieldwork. The supervisor, as part of her visit, wanted to demonstrate the skills of communicating with a young child who was probably a little less than 10 years. Consistent with the developmental stage, the child would not stop and kept playing and moving next to the railway track that passed through the community. The supervisor also kept moving with him instead of expecting him to sit at one place and talk to her. The conversation started with the object that the child was playing with and thereafter moved on to the other activities that he liked to engage himself in. It then moved on to discussing about his peer group and then finally about his routine. The conversation went on for at least twenty minutes. The students were following the supervisor in close pursuit. The debriefing while walking out of the community entailed discussing about what they felt the supervisor was trying to do through the discussion, what skills were being used. Visits by supervisors as described in the earlier example not only aid the skill building of the student but also help the supervisor to understand the context of fieldwork practice as well as gain familiarity with the functioning or the interventions of the fieldwork agency. Reviewing literature on the challenges of social work field training, Tanga (2013) also points towards evidence that suggests that students feel discontented when supervisors from the university fail to visit them during their fieldwork placement or when the supervisors are not familiar with the fieldwork agency's work.

Individual conferences also hold significance in skill development. The practice of different methods of social work requires an array of skills which the student has to be helped to imbibe for strengthening their professional practice.

Skills of programme planning, budgeting, funding, monitoring and counselling, to name a few, have to be sequentially developed through the means of the supervisory conferences. Even while many of these skills may have formed a part of the other curricular components, the one to one conferences with the faculty supervisor help to provide individualised input and sharpen these skills further. The student may be helped to go through the different steps of designing a project proposal, as an example. Similarly, the student may be facilitated in designing group sessions with the client system that they may be working with in the field. Helping the student to understand different forms of recording is another area of skill development.

Skill enhancement is a progressive role wherein a delicate balance between support and independence has to be maintained. Mathew (1975, p. 328) opines that the supervisory role entails providing support wherever it is realistically needed and withholding it when the student should do it alone. This helps to foster growth and independence within the student.

Supervisor as a motivator

Students come into the social work profession with differing levels of motivation. The supervisor has to ascertain that and pitch themselves accordingly. Students may come into the profession holding glamorous ideas about transforming the world around them. When confronted with field realities which pose innumerable obstacles, they stand the chance of getting disillusioned. The belief of the supervisor in the profession and its abilities to deal with human situations is essential for them to be able to navigate such dilemmas. Mathew (1975) states that the students may begin to feel that with all their efforts as well they are not able to even 'scratch the surface of the problems'. These junctures could be very critical for the student as well as for the supervisor. Sustaining the motivation of the student or preventing the student's motivation from getting diminished is centric to the student's learning curve. The journey towards realism has to be steered by the supervisor lest the profession loses individuals with commitment. Support and reassurance from the supervisor are centric to sustaining the motivation of the students.

For some students coming in through other academic disciplines at the level of graduation, the social work curriculum could be very overwhelming. Requirements of fieldwork, where they are usually expected to devote at least 15 hours per week, the reports associated with it, simulation laboratories, classes and assignments could be anxiety provoking for some. This is particularly true where the student wants to give their best to each of the components but finds limited time for himself or herself. The silver lining is the availability of an individual mentor in the form of a supervisor. Recognising the emotional state of the student and getting them to verbalise their concerns and enabling them to design realistic goals for themselves can be therapeutic for the student. This may not necessarily be equated with therapy – it is the relationship which has the elements of empathy and positive regard which could enable the student to confide their worries.

The NGO sector where majority of the students are placed for fieldwork is also faced with its own set of unique realities. They are expected to deliver as per the funder defined agenda. They may have multiple funders having differing funding templates. Funding constraints are also tremendous and may result in a dis-satisfied work force. Students are not necessarily prepared to face these realities. They find themselves at crossroads where they are unable to visualise themselves in similar situations and begin to question the ethics of the profession. The supervisor cannot afford to be dismissive when these issues are brought in front of them. The supervisor's ability to understand the nuances of NGO management may enable them to address these questions, else they stand to lose the student's motivation. Recently a student of mine who is placed in an organization that works on alternative education came to me with the question of what made their organisation work on alternative education when the community was struggling with livelihood issues. As a supervisor, I considered it my responsibility to explain to the student the differential factors which operate on an NGO to determine its functioning. I also suggested that the student may choose to discuss this issue with those within the organisation who were there from its inception or had a longstanding experience within the organisation.

There are times when students experience tremendous self-doubt which impinges on their ability to function. One of my students used to constantly complain about not remembering things. She would read a lot, come prepared for every supervisory conference, but would always have a complaint about not remembering things that she had read. As a supervisor, I could sense her preoccupation with the thought which was definitely going to come in the way of her fieldwork. When a few weeks had passed by in supervision, without her knowing about the reason, I started flinging a battery of questions to her based upon the readings that I was aware that she had made in the past. When she was able to recollect all the answers, I posed her a question about the reason which had made me ask her so many questions. My intent as a supervisor was to work on her self-esteem as well as reassure her about her ability to remember material that she had read in the past. This might also be perceived as being dismissive of the student's belief, but somewhere as a supervisor I felt the student was inflicting a lot of pain on herself by continuously telling herself about her inability to remember, and I was also able to recognise that the student had to be helped to challenge her beliefs about herself.

Supervisor as a mentor

There are times when the student's life experiences may result in flashbacks when they might be engaging with clients experiencing similar issues. The student may experience discomfort which could be sensed by the supervisor. Depending upon the comfort level of the student, these issues may be discussed and relevant interventions made. As a supervisor, I have also come across instances where earlier life experiences may have affected the personality of the student. Students who have faced ridicule in childhood that has deeply affected them may be inclined to draw themselves into a shell lest any further hurt come upon them. With great caution and appropriate timing, these issues are touched upon in individual conferences. The critical element is not being dismissive about individualised concerns that may be affecting the growth of the student as a social work professional. However, caution has to be exercised in allowing the supervision process to remain focused on the impact of personal experiences on practice with clients (Shulman, 2009).

At times students feel overwhelmed by the traumatic experiences or challenges that a client may have been through. Providing for space within the supervisory conferences to discuss the same may help the student to feel more emotionally settled. One of my students was given the task of preparing a summary record of one of the clients that the organisation had been working with for about three years and who was also living in the organisation's shelter home. Till that time the student had not gone through the case file; she had been meeting with the client in the shelter home but was not aware about the life experiences of the client.[5] When she read the case file, the student was completely taken aback by the multiple forms of abuse that the client had been through which in a certain way made her feel very helpless as well as ignorant. The supervisory conference was used to discuss the student's feelings, the organisation's policy and the rationality behind the same which helped her to feel at greater ease.

We are unfortunately living in an era where the threat perception, particularly in the case of female students, is high. The daily reporting of incidents of offences being committed against women stands the chance of making the student as well as her guardian fearful of her going for fieldwork unaccompanied. This is further catapulted by the expression of similar feelings by the agency staff, to whom the student is attached for fieldwork. There are several instances where without an agency staff to accompany them, they would not permit the student to go into the community citing reasons of security and the student being their responsibility. Confronted with a situation such as this, the task of the faculty supervisor becomes extremely challenging. The faculty supervisor considers it their responsibility to build up the confidence of the student and facilitate her independent functioning. Understanding the way in which the student processes the information that she has been receiving from significant others in her environment, her own feelings associated with the same are relevant for the faculty supervisor. The supervisor does not want any harm to come upon the student, and yet she wants to build up the confidence of the student to work in the field without which her abilities as a social work professional would also be limited. As a supervisor being dismissive about the fears or apprehensions of the student does not serve the purpose. Instead, allowing them to talk about the same and discussing possibilities of protecting them from any harm may be a more desirable approach.

Mentoring also entails providing feedback to a student. However, when feedback is given only with the intent of evaluating a student's conformity with expected standards, it can be problematic. The faculty supervisors would need to take a more balanced approach wherein they should incorporate both the strengths and the potential areas of work on the part of the student. This is not only in consonance with the social work philosophy but also makes a student more receptive to feedback. Social work values and adult education principles could be the guiding thrust behind providing feedback (Bogo, Regehr, Power, & Regehr, 2007). The feedback by the faculty supervisor should also be ongoing and not come in at the end of the semester. This offers the student an opportunity to grow.

The supervisor-supervisee relationship is unique from other teacher-student relationships, which makes it possible for the student to discuss their career path as well. The understanding that the supervisor develops of the student through the course of fieldwork can help the student in making critical decisions regarding their professional path. This, of course, is contingent upon the student seeking such inputs.

Supervisor-supervisee relationship as a vehicle for self-development

To underscore the value of self in professional social work practice, Lynton (1960, p. 141) states that 'what he is sets the limits to what he does' (cited in Banerjee, 1975). Further Banerjee (1975, p. 312) elaborates that 'the efficiency of social work practice does not depend solely on what the social worker knows or poses to know but on what he is – not on what he 'can do' but on what he 'can be'. The UGC model curriculum, while highlighting the critical role of a supervisor, states that 'the learning of practice and professional role modelling is learnt by the instructors' being' (UGC, 2001, p. 117).

The supervisor can play a role in the student's emotional development (Shulman, 2009). If the supervisor models empathic skills in the supervisory relationship, the student learns through the process of observation. Shulman (2009) uses the phrase 'more is caught than taught' to explain this process. If the supervisor adopts an empathetic stance towards the student, there is a likelihood that the student would adopt the same towards the client. If a student who has been otherwise sincere with respect to his/her learning begins to fall ill frequently and the supervisor, instead of demonstrating empathy towards the student, asks the student to reconsider social work as an option given the challenging situations that are inherent in it, would find it difficult to empathise with clients.

The supervisor's belief in the supervisee's potential for growth amounts to modelling the desirable belief system that the student should have with respect to the client system. The respect accorded to the supervisee in the relationship also imbibes within the student the value of practicing the same with respect to the client system. The value of the supervisor being a role model for the student cannot be overemphasised in the development of the professional self. Banerjee (1975, p. 315) reiterates 'the supervisor's depth of knowledge, eagerness to acquire more knowledge, giving of own self to the clients and the supervisee ungrudgingly, poise, maturity, contribution to the field of social work and dedication to the profession would motivate the supervisee to identify with him and assimilate these qualities'. The philosophy of practice has the potential of being imbibed through the supervisor-supervisee relationship. The security of a student within a supervisory relationship also makes the student more receptive to feedback. In fact, a parameter for gauging the strength of a supervisor-supervisee relationship is when the student is able to talk about their shortcomings without a sense of fear.

The supervisor-supervisee relationship can also be a tool to demonstrate the relevance of feedback. If the supervisor encourages the student to provide feedback and demonstrates openness towards it as well as a willingness to work upon it, there is a greater likelihood of a higher degree of receptivity to feedback on the part of the student as well.

Historically tracing the journey of supervision in social work education, Pathak (1975) opines that the method of casework has a significant influence on the supervisor-supervisee relationship. It was believed that the knowledge and skills of casework practice could be utilised in developing and maintaining the supervisory relationship even while intense therapy may have to be excluded from its purview.

Supervisor as a learner

It might seem 'commonsensical' to talk about the need for the supervisor to continuously enhance their knowledge and skill base. However, it is the reality of the Indian context that makes an emphasis on the same a requirement. The faculty-student ratio deserves attention in this regard. What follows is the difference of settings, within which the large number of students allotted with a supervisor are placed. Each of the settings demands an understanding of the issue on which the fieldwork agency is working, the related legislative and policy framework as well as the distinctive approaches adopted in the field for working on the issue. Continuous upgradation is a sheer necessity. There is no harm in acknowledging oneself as a learner with the student. Differential modalities may have to be adopted for the process. Supervisory groups have been discussed in an earlier section as a possible modality for addressing this issue. This helps to maximise the learning opportunities for a student (Mathew, 1975). A critical self-reflection of the supervisory inputs also serves as a learning medium.

Mathew (1975) underscores the need for a supervisor to have dual abilities, i.e. skills of social work practice as well as the ability to teach. The reality may be contrary and even more so today where social work is equated with other professions and entry into social work teaching is not contingent upon the possession of practice experience albeit the presence of a doctoral degree. Consequently, today a number of social work educators in the Indian context may not have dabbled in the field before entering into teaching. Mathew (1975) thus suggested that social work educators should continue to be engaged in some practice that may not only aid towards keeping their skills alive but also strengthen their skills further. Mathew (1975, p. 330) laments that supervision without practice becomes lifeless and bookish, lacking in that freshness and dynamism which only practice can give. Nanavatty (1967, as cited in Desai, 2013) focused on the larger damage wherein the absence of field-based experiences not only prevent a social work educator from being able to apply theory into practice but also affects their own conviction in the ability of the social work profession to deliver. The limited field-based practice has resulted in pedagogy in social work becoming more macro-based wherein the students may be engaged in an analysis of a problem but its translation into practice is not learnt. The social work educators need to visit the field of the students more frequently so as to draw learning through partnership (Desai, 2013, pp. 49–50).

Challenges of the supervisory process

Several factors impinge upon the supervisor in performance of the multifarious roles that have been specified earlier. While some of these factors operate at a micro level, there are others which are macro in nature.

Supervisors do struggle to reconcile the conflicting messages that the students receive from the agency supervisors and faculty supervisors (Dash, 2017). The situation that was stated by Pathak in the year 1975 continues to date wherein it is challenging to have professionally trained social workers in the field agencies where the students are placed. At the same time, it is also true that in India very few schools of social work have their own field action projects even while the second review committee on social work education (UGC, 1980) had explicitly recommended the need to do so in the interest of social work education. Even if they have, they also possess a limited capacity to provide training to the students. The reality as it stands is that the primary sites for fieldwork learning are the agencies managed by Non-Governmental Organisations and in some cases by Governmental Departments. Bogo (2014), in her presentation at the 60th Annual Program Meeting on Advancing Social Work Education, while referring to the desirable pedagogy for field education emphasised the need for strong positive learning environments in organisations and teams where students receive their practice experiences. Teaching and learning should be viewed as being mutually beneficial. Faculty supervisors may also have to reflect on the nature of the role that they could play in this direction. Currently it is a one-way relationship where the schools of social work expect the fieldwork agencies to offer learning opportunities to the students. Social work educators could volunteer to take up the task of grooming the organisations which form the sites of learning for students. Since NGOs do not look at schools of social work as their competitors, the possibility of a positive growth-producing relationship are much higher (Sukhramani, 2002). Pawar (1999, p. 574) laments, 'Within the social work profession, there is no systematic link between social work educators and practitioners, which is so crucial to effective social work practice'.

Skill enhancement of students can be further strengthened if the supervisory inputs are based on observation of student's actual practice (Bogo, 2014). Such opportunities are limited in the Indian context where faculty supervisors take on the primary mantle for supervision. It is the reports as well as the limited opportunity of observation during supervisory visits that form the primary basis for providing supervisory inputs.

The reality that some students opt for social work even at the Master's level to safeguard their interests of professional engagement after completion of the two-year program also poses a challenge to supervision. As a supervisor one may be caught up between the dilemma of performing one's role adequately, which entails significant investment, while knowing that the student is there to only complete the course and has no intentions of taking it up as a career in the future. This concern has no easy answers, but allowing a student to acquire a degree without having imbibed the essences of it does not appear to be fair to the profession.

Working with students who may not display professionalism or the desirable work ethic can be challenging. Maintaining a non-judgmental attitude despite getting to know that the student may not be going regularly for fieldwork can be difficult for the supervisor. The rigor of social work training may not be compatible with the expectations from the previous educational engagements of the students, resulting in the student adopting a lackadaisical attitude. Even when supervisors may recognise their role as nurturing professional growth, in such situations, the supervisor may be compelled to lean towards being a vigilante particularly till the point of time that the student does not imbibe the professional spirit. The supervisors then find themselves contradicting social work values. They find themselves caught up in a dilemma where, with respect to the client system, they adopt a strengths-focused perspective, avoiding being judgmental or focusing on their deficits, but when it comes to the students they are compelled to take a differential viewpoint. The supervisors do not find themselves aligning with the social work philosophy which believes in the inherent potential of every person to experience growth (Bogo et al., 2007).

At the macro level, most universities equate social work teachers with those of other disciplines, without taking into cognizance other teaching responsibilities like field instruction and non-teaching work, which contribute to the total academic programme and field extension activities in the community. Hours devoted by the faculty to the field should be computed (UGC, 1980).

In the spirit of universalisation, the specificities of a course may stand to be sacrificed. As has been mentioned in the beginning, the Indian University System has unilaterally and universally applied the choice based credit system (CBCS). This has greatly compromised on the core curricular components. As the timings for classroom teaching have expanded, the timing for individual conferences is shrinking. While the spirit of CBCS is not to be challenged, it is not even fair to make compromises on supervision for the value that it holds, else supervision may just end up being a process of vigilantism with other elements essential for professional development taking a back seat. Group supervision has also been suggested as an alternative, but research has pointed towards group supervision not being a substitute for individual supervision.

It is a matter of concern that in the absence of a council and the significant increase in the colleges being run privately post globalisation, fieldwork requirements are being compromised on (Adaikalam, 2014). The axe appears to be falling on the individual conferences where faculty members have a large number of students to supervise besides performing other duties (Dash, 2017). Fieldwork instruction is neither structured nor systematised; hours of fieldwork being twisted to suit institutional needs and appointment of teaching staff without calculating fieldwork in the curriculum are some of the anomalies that have got into the system. There is a need for standardised guidelines and a mechanism for ensuring adherence to the same (Adaikalam, 2014) while undeniably making provisions for local specificities.

Conclusion

As has been evidenced through the course of discussion in the chapter, several contextual realities are a determinant of the supervisory process. The onus for making field instruction rewarding lies on all parties involved in the process (Schmidt & Rautenbach, 2016). This, however, does not take us away from our responsibility as social work educators, since the professionals that we are training would be working on issues concerning several human lives, which one would not want to be compromised on to any extent. Supervision is by no means an easy job; it demands a continuous reflection. It is a process which demands a high level of self-vigilance. Ensuring responsiveness on behalf of the field agency, enabling the student to fulfil the expectations of the agency and that of the curriculum and being equipped to provide inputs to the students in the diverse situations that they may encounter in the field is a continuous jugglery for the supervisor. The attempt is not just to make the students learn the knowledge and skills but also to groom them emotionally in order to be able to stand by the values that the social work profession upholds. It is to be able to mentor them to be responsive human beings who understand themselves and the people that they work with. The supervisor-supervisee relationship has to mirror the attributes that the student should be conscious of while working with the client system. It is equally important to understand the fears and apprehensions of the student as much as it to understand their strengths. Working towards the sustenance and enhancement of the motivation of the student despite the various odds that cross their path during the course of fieldwork is critical. Challenging deeply embedded belief systems which are not in conformity with the value framework of social work profession is also a delicate and yet critical task which requires skills and sensitivity on the part of the supervisor. Combining the various shades of nurturance in the process of supervision is demanding yet rewarding.

Notes

1 The author would like to acknowledge the contribution of her present and past supervisees (students) who have helped her to understand the various facets of supervision.
2 NGOs or Non-Governmental Organisations are run as societies, trusts or non-profit companies to engage with several societal concerns. They are voluntary in the manner that there is nothing in the statute which requires them to come into existence, they are not self-serving in aims and objectives and they are not for profit. Even while they are also referred to as independent in the way in which they can define their agenda, the reality

is a little contrary. There are funding constraints which also determine their direction of interventions even while the core area of their work may continue to be the one that made them feel the need to come into existence.
3 With the introduction of the Choice Based Credit System in the past two to three years within the Indian University System and it being made universally applicable to professional and other courses, the time available for Individual Conferences is gradually shrinking, which is definitely an area of concern.
4 The term local student is being used to refer to those students who are familiar with the language and culture of the region. They may not be from the same state where the school of social work is located but have familiarity with the language.
5 To prevent retraumatisation, the agency had a policy that there would be a single point of individualised interventions and the student trainee or any other staff member besides the one entrusted with the case would not engage the client in a conversation on the reason for their referral to the agency. They were, however, free to engage them in other conversations and also in other group activities that may have been planned.

References

Adaikalam, F.V. (2014). Contextualising social work education in India. *Alternativas: Cuadernos de trabajo social*, *21*, 215–232. doi:10.14198/ALTERN2014.21.11

Agnimitra, N. (2015). Field work in the contemporary context: Vision and engagement. *Journal of Social Work Education, Research and Action*, *1*(1), 28–49.

Banerjee, G. R. (1975). Professional self and supervision in social work. *Indian Journal of Social Work*, *35*(4), 309–316.

Bogo, M. (2014, October 23). *Developing the future framework for excellence in field education: Embracing the signature pedagogy of social work*. Tampa, FL: Council on Social Work Education. Retrieved from https://cswe.org/Centers-Initiatives/Initiatives/Summit-on-Field-Education-2014

Bogo, M., Regehr, C., Power, R., & Regehr, G. (2007). When values collide: Field instructors' experiences of providing feedback and evaluating competence. *The Clinical Supervisor*, *26*(1-2), 99–117. doi:10.1300/J001v26n01_08

Dash, B. M. (2017). Revisiting eight decades of social work education in India. *Asian Social Work and Policy Review*, *11*, 66–75. doi:10.1111/aswp.12114

Desai, K. T. (2013). *Paradigms of social work praxis: The case of street children*. Doctoral Thesis, School of Social Work, Tata Institute of Social Sciences, Mumbai. Retrieved from http://hdl.handle.net/10603/16128

Ketner, M., VanCleave, D., & Cooper-Bolinskey, D. (2017). The meaning and value of supervision in social work field education. *Field Scholar*, *7*(2), 1–18.

Mathew, G. (1975). Educational and helping aspects of field work supervision. *Indian Journal of Social Work*, *35*(4), 325–333.

Pathak, S. H. (1975). Supervision in social work: Historical development and current trends. *Indian Journal of Social Work*, *35*(4), 317–323.

Pawar, M. (1999). Professional social work in India: Some issues and strategies. *Indian Journal of Social Work*, *60*(4), 566–586.

Schmidt, K., & Rautenbach, J.V. (2016). Field instruction: Is the heart of social work education still beating in the Eastern Cape. *Social Work/Maatskaplike*, *52*(4), 589–610.

Sheafor, B. W., & Jenkins, L. E. (1981). Issues that affect the development of a field instruction curriculum. *Journal of Education for Social Work*, *17*(1), 12–20. doi:10.1080/00220612.1981.10778524

Shulman, L. S. (2009). *The skills of helping individuals, families, groups and communities* (6th ed.). Belmont, MA: Brooks; Cole Cengage Learning.

Singh, R. R. (1985). Proceedings of the workshop. In R. R. Singh (Ed.), *Field work in social work education: A perspective for human service professionals* (pp. 40–168). New Delhi: Concept Publishing Company.

Subhedar, I. S. (2001). *Field work training in social work*. Jaipur: Rawat Publications.

Sukhramani, N. (2002, October). NGO credibility and students' motivation: A challenge for social work educators. *Contemporary Social Work, 19*, 39–46.

Tanga, P.T. (2013). The challenges of social work field training in Lesotho. *Social Work Education, 32*(2), 157–178. doi:10.1080/02615479.2012.741578

UGC. (1980). *Review of social work education in India: Retrospect and prospect*. New Delhi: UGC.

UGC. (2001). *UGC model curriculum: Social work education*. New Delhi: UGC.

Zeira, A., & Schiff, M. (2010). Testing group supervision in field work training for social work students. *Research on Social Work Practice, 20*(4), 427–434. doi:10.1177/104973150933288

5

THE CONSCIOUS USE OF THEORY IN SOCIAL WORK PRACTICE

Illustrations from fieldwork

Sandra Joseph

The context and content of field instruction

The profession of social work has consistently been confronted with several challenges in India; first, in search for recognition as a profession in its vast areas of practice and second in gaining acceptance as a professional discipline in higher education. Ever since, much more has been emphasised on the urgency to indigenise the 'imported' profession to respond effectively to the plethora of local social issues that continue to stifle the nation (Nanavatty, 1993; Kulkarni, 1993). From its initial models of practice such as charity, relief and welfare to more current approaches emphasising participation, people's empowerment and human rights, social work is not duly recognised as a professional degree that offers specialised knowledge and skills, nor is it recognised for its scientific attempts at resolving challenges confronting humanity. While some countries are beginning to introduce more neo-liberal forms of social work and de-professionalising traditional social work owing to its rigid procedures and bureaucratic regulations (Dominelli, 1996; Lavalette, 2011), the profession still grapples in India with the issue of indigenising itself, gaining social acceptance and its rightful recognition as a profession, both in academia and the larger society (Nagpaul, 1993; Mohan, 1993; Drucker, 1993; Midgley, 1981; Rao, 1993; Roy, 2018).

There is a growing discontentment in the capacity of theory to capture the complexities of practice (Healy, 2000). It is imperative, therefore, that practitioners accept or reject theory in keeping with its adaptability or be able to generate indigenous theories that are compliant with the local context. While some think that the discipline can gain its identity only within its cultural context, there are others who believe that it can gain identity through a process of adaptation. Cutting across borders and cultures, theoretical perspectives are emerging as more acceptable to learning (Narayan, 2008). Features of a profession need to vary across time and space depending on socio-cultural values and beliefs (Desai, 1993). The interdependence of theory and practice wisdom crosses disciplinary boundaries (Kuhn, 1970) and is widely gaining recognition.

This chapter aims to articulate the application of two theoretical frameworks of social work, namely, 'eco-systems theory' and 'empowerment theory'. The conscious application of the two theories learnt in a classroom setting to a 'context-specific' empowerment programme for rural women forms the basis for field learning. It seeks to provide a model and arrive at an understanding of the applicability of theoretical knowledge through action, specifically explicating significance and importance of a methodological practice approach to empower women in a given eco-system. In the context of this writing, the ability of field instructors and student trainees to be able to link theory to practice is assumed, and the framework reiterates the profession's primary purpose of linking classroom learning with adequate field instruction. Concomitantly it seeks to enable the process of generating newer ideas and develop indigenous knowledge pertinent to social work practice in the Indian context. In working with women as the clientele, it further seeks to portend the significance of feminism and feminist practice ideologies in social work.

Relevance of social work in feminist practice

If social work is concerned with problems of deprivation then the most obvious client groups are the innumerable marginalised sections in society; among them those belonging to *Dalit* and tribal communities, backward classes and those affected by physical, social or political problems. Most of these sections will then necessarily include a large category of women. The status of women in India unfolds myriad ideologies which justify their subordination. The existence of such patriarchal notions reflected in the ideologies of biological determinism, sex roles, gender stratification and the inter-sectionalities of unequal relationships in caste, class, gender and region are some of the deep-rooted ideological constructs that govern women's status in the Indian society. In post-independence India, many women's groups sprang up challenging patriarchy and taking up a variety of issues such as violence against women, equal wages for equal work, greater share in political decision making etc. both at activist and academic levels. However, for most women in India, their status falls far short of the expected parameters of human development, dignity and equity. Voluntary social work to some extent addressed these issues in the form of welfare by responding to issues in health and nutrition, counselling, shelter homes, rehabilitation and other such supportive services. Taking a political stand has made small progress in its professional space. While there is no dispute on the need or relevance of such social services for women, emphasis on addressing issues from a rights-based viewpoint and understanding their origins from an academic or theoretical perspective has not gained ground in social work education and practice. The inter-sectionalities of caste, class, region and gender in the marginalisation of women certainly calls for more attention in the teaching and practice of professional social work.

With the growing importance of the developmental and empowerment approaches to practice in the Indian context, greater opportunities emerge for the profession to position itself by linking theoretical approaches to practice, particularly concerning women's issues. This is less difficult now than it was earlier when the practice of social work heavily depended on Western methods of social work, which were, basically, casework and group work. The approaches in these two methods focus on individuals and small groups that are attuned to the culture of the West and thus have been successful there. However, in India, community organisation as a method and its approaches have an edge over the other social work methods because of the 'community characteristic' prevalent in the nation. Little effort has been made at indigenisation or even at appropriate adaptations of Western knowledge to local characteristics. Academic support to encourage, develop and accept such efforts is correspondingly weak in the Indian milieu (Nanavatty, 1993). The profession of social work therefore has a moral obligation to broaden the understanding of applying appropriate theoretical foundations and inform social workers; set standards for formulating appropriate models, policies and research agendas and promote the feminist practice approach in social work. It is in this context that social work educators have the added responsibility to produce knowledge that addresses structural processes that hinder women's development irrespective of their social status or geographical location. In doing so, it will be in a position to validate gender-aware social work practice and convince policy planners, practitioners and the society at large.

Today there are more clear-cut and defined job opportunities to work for women's development in which social work profession can play a major contributory role. The profession, like feminism, is theoretically committed to improving the quality of life for all people (Van Den & Cooper, 1986). Social work shares almost all fundamental concerns of feminism. It emphasises that human capacity for adaptation and growth is present throughout the human life cycle. Human beings are capable of organising their lives and developing their potentialities if they have appropriate environmental supports (Maluccic, 1983).

These views link with the very purpose of social work as a way of releasing human and social power that promotes personal, interpersonal and structural competence that supports an 'empowerment' base for practice. Social work as a profession, however, lacks sufficient contribution to theory-building from practice orientations and vice versa. An effort to fill this gap is not a difficult task merely because social work as a discipline and as a field of enquiry equally refers also to a range of practice activities rather than only theoretical ideas (Healy, 2000). However, the reality is much more complex; practitioners need to integrate theoretical understanding and its applicability to practice in order to be competent. The following sections deliberate on two theories and their scientific application to a 'context-specific intervention' programme in the empowerment of rural women to enhance this understanding.

Mapping social work theory in a 'context-specific' intervention for women

There are several layers of understanding in social work knowledge, values and skills in practice (Devore, 1991). This layered understanding and the conscious integration of theory in the Indian context is not sufficiently written about and has left social workers far less equipped with the required levels of comprehension and skill in practice. The application of theoretical knowledge to practice in a context-specific intervention that seeks to empower rural women will provide clarity in the layered understanding and integration of theory to practice. It is therefore vital that field practice is accompanied by the application of proven knowledge, preferably locally generated and if not, locally adapted. Most importantly it needs to be culturally relevant to make meaningful connections within the local context. The inclination to directly apply theory with the belief that theory provides all answers in a direct or straightforward way is imprudent.

Eco-systems theory and social work

The 'systems approach' has gained wide acceptance in social work theory since the 1970s. An idea to unify the three social work methods such as case work, group work, and community organisation precipitated the search for a common framework for practice. The term 'systems theory' of social work was first introduced in 1930 (Hollis & Taylor, 1951). Even before the 'systems theory', social workers adopted a 'person-in-environment' perspective (Kemp, Whittaker, & Tracy, 1997). Systems theories provide an intellectual foundation for reintegrating the psychological and sociological discourses by recognising that a range of socio-economic and cultural systems impact people in myriad ways. The initial proponents of the systems theory highlighted its potential to provide scientific credibility to the profession and to develop an integrated theoretical foundation that would capture the central elements of social work practice in all its varied forms.

In the decades of the seventies and eighties, the systems approach in social work practice gained wide recognition and acceptance. The shift focused on a unifying perspective, one that was not bound by methods but shaped by situational or environmental parameters (Goldstein, 1973; Pincus & Minahan, 1973; Middleman & Goldberg, 1974; Siporin, 1980; Bronfenbrenner, 1979). To prepare social workers for practice, the social work curriculum needs to emphasise teaching practice perspectives that view the whole of social problems in a more broad-based understanding. An integrated practice framework for social work assumes that the root of problems originates in the larger environmental context and can be resolved by collective action.

Criticisms about the application of the systems theory to social work portray it as being weak in what should be its concern about oppressive forces: it does not consider the incompatibilities of capitalism and class and its hindrances to social integration. A major criticism has been in its limitations to define boundaries of systems and sub-systems in the realm of societal structures. Despite these ideological criticisms, systems thinking does enable a methodological and organisational rigor in practice (Milner & O'Byrne, 1998; Milner, Myers, & O'Byrne, 2015). The model is well suited to work in communities as it aids the practitioner in assessing the broader territory of intervention and to work in collaboration with other agencies. This experiment is an attempt to map the systems theory through a fieldwork project that provides a perspective to locate the practitioner and enhances an understanding of the complexities of social work practice.

In social work, the term 'system' means a set of dynamic general relationships that together process 'stimuli' (inputs) through a subsystem of closer relationships, thereby producing 'responses' (outputs). The process is one of changing inputs into outputs. In each case, the process takes place within boundaries. To place the eco-systems model in the context of a theoretical framework, an elucidation of several key concepts in the model, its goals and skills of practice is briefly discussed. The model is based on the eco-systems theory and opens-up a variety of opportunities for intervention and change. It subscribes to the philosophy of social work and to people's participation in development. The focus of social work practice is on the interactions between people and systems in their social environment. People are dependent on social systems for help in obtaining the materials, emotional or spiritual resources and the services and opportunities they would need to realise their aspirations that help to cope with their life tasks. The eco-systems theory views an individual as existing in a web of relationships (Evans & Kearney, 1996). While these theories do not necessarily address those factors that challenge the status quo, this chapter does not discuss oppressive systems that perpetuate unhealthy and inequitable structures but rather aims to explicate the importance of applying theoretical understanding to field practice.

There are six steps involved in the change process identified as the action system: engagement, assessment, planning, intervention, evaluation and termination. Engagement is when practitioners orient themselves to the problem and begin to establish communication and a relationship with the client system and others addressing the problem. Assessment is the investigation and determination of situations affecting an identified problem or issue as viewed from a micro, meso or macro perspective. It is gathering information about a problem so that decisions can be made about solutions. Planning specifies what should be done by whom and when. Intervention or implementation is the process whereby the client and the practitioner follow the plans to achieve the goals. Once goals are met and change takes place it is imperative to terminate the relationship. Evaluation is a process of determining whether a given change effort was worthwhile (Pincus & Minahan, 1973). Subsequently, follow-up is carried out to examine if the intervention is successful and moving in the right direction as envisaged in the planning stage.

Empowerment theory and social work

Development of the 'empowerment paradigm' and its application to different areas of social work concerns occurred alongside its early beginning. The Settlement

House Movement of the late nineteenth and twentieth centuries hailed the beginnings of the empowerment paradigm in social work in the sixties and seventies. While the 'treatment paradigm' foregrounded social work practice and education in the eighties, by the mid-nineties, the 'empowerment paradigm' was gaining its foothold. Following which theories and practices rooted in feminism, social action and community work or radical politics concerning empowerment of individuals, groups, organisations and communities gained firm ground. This involved the equation that effective practice was the product of practice 'with' rather than 'for' people. Subsequently, several practice models further influenced in establishing an 'empowerment paradigm' as a paradigm in social work.

Social work practice requires a coherent practice framework, resourceful ways to look at human and social systems functioning and dynamic processes for change (Miley, O'Melia, & DuBois, 2001). While Pincus and Minahan (1973) developed the social work practice framework based on the systems model, it was noted that the profession of social work suffered from the lack of a unifying framework that would bring diverse areas of expertise together within the profession (Ramsay, 2001). However, it may seem that a unifying framework does not embrace pluralistic and multiple intersecting perspectives. Exploring for such a framework is a necessity for the profession to design interventions that are relevant to the context.

Global Standards for Education and Training in Social work emphasises standards for development of core curriculum, with focus on capacity-building and empowerment of individuals, families, groups and communities through a human-centred developmental approach (IASSW & IFSW, 2004). Significantly, also, Standard No. 6 of the Standards for Cultural Competence in Social Work Practice refers to empowerment and advocacy in social work practice (NASW, 2015). It underlines the importance of social workers being aware of social systems, policies, practices and programmes and their impact on multicultural client populations and to advocate on their behalf (Carpenter, 2016). Empowerment also refers to the self-help movement, in which groups act on their own behalf, either in co-operation with or independently of the statutory services (Thomas & Pierson, 1995). Empowerment-based social work guides the practitioner to handle issues at all levels of practice – at the individual level it is garnered from within the individuals and at the societal level will benefit only individuals and groups in social, economic and institutional structures.

Several authors have termed it with distinctive features – such as a continuum, (O'Sullivan, 2003), as reflective practice (Schön, 1991), as a dialogic process (Freire, 1970) and as bringing together aspects of the work (Phillipson, 1992). The empowerment method focuses on the achievement of goals and change of systems by utilising available strengths, resiliencies and resources. By focusing on competence rather than deficits in individual or social functioning, the model supports resourcefulness and development of skills to remove social barriers for individuals and communities.

The empowerment framework describes foundations for an ecosystem approach in practice. It provides details of generic processes that frame generalist practice at all system levels. That includes the dialogue phase – forming partnerships, articulating challenges, defining directions; the discovery phase – identifying strengths, analysing resource capabilities, framing solutions, and the development phase – activating resources, creating alliances, expanding opportunities, recognising success and integrating gains. (DuBois & Miley, 1996. Using the empowerment-based social work model by O'Melia, Du Bois, and Miley (1993), an empowering process depicting the dialogue, discovery and development phases was identified. Having placed the two theories in perspective, the following discussions focus on explaining the intervention and its applicability in a 'context-specific' empowerment programme titled '*Mahalir Thittam*'. The Tamil term literally means 'Women's Plan'. This adaptation of theory should enable the social work educator or practitioner to comprehend the linking of theory to practice in a more explicit manner. The following is a discussion on policies of the government of India in empowering women and a brief description of the '*Mahalir Thittam*' programme that is implemented in Tamil Nadu.

The '*Mahalir Thittam*' programme

For empowerment of women in rural India, process-oriented empowerment interventions for women have been found to be successful mainly because of the contributory role that NGOs and committed individuals played in this regard. Professional interventions of social work methods or models have not been sufficiently expressed in rhetoric or research. Identifying such practices or approaches is very much the responsibility of social work educators whose contributory role is to link research findings and new theories with practice models. Several enabling frameworks have evolved in empowering women over a period of practice. Participatory approaches such as social mapping, resource mapping, gender equality matrix and vulnerability analyses are some of the frameworks that have had powerful impacts particularly in the empowerment processes of rural women, alternate visions, methods, and strategies formulated by governments, policies and laws have played a major role.

Beginning with the Constitutional and legal provisions for women and laws in entitlements, political participation, education, employment and laws to mitigate violence such as the Protection of Women from Domestic Violence Act (2005); Sexual Harassment of Women at Workplace Act (2013); and other initiatives like the National and State Commissions for Women; Ministry for Women and Child Development; the National Plan of Action for the Girl Child (1991–2000); National Policy for the Empowerment of Women – 2001 (Government of India, 2001); reservation for women in local self-government; Five Year Plans, gender budgeting etc., are some other policy frameworks that embrace the empowerment of women.

The Government of India's policy on women's development has taken on a variety of shifts in emphases. The most significant changes occurred in the mid-eighties with the Seventh Plan which initiated a move towards equality and empowerment of women. The Eighth Plan marked a further shift towards empowerment of women, emphasising women as equal partners in the development process. Ever since, women's empowerment was considered as an essential component in all subsequent Plans in India. One such initiative, the '*Mahalir Thittam*' programme, is a socio-economic empowerment programme for women implemented by the Tamil Nadu Corporation for Women in partnership with NGOs and community-based organisations, launched in 1996 and progressively introduced in all districts. It is based on the self-help group approach and implemented in partnership with NGOs.

The '*Mahalir Thittam*' project is one of the most popular efforts of the Government of Tamil Nadu in empowering women towards self-reliance through economic empowerment using self-help groups as a channel for operation. The prime objective of the project was to improve the social and economic position of women below the poverty line through the formation of women self-help groups (SHGs) formed with active support of NGOs.

The empowering processes envisaged in the '*Mahalir Thittam*' programme include several components within the three broad dimensions of empowering women – personal, social and economic. Assessments are made in keeping with the needs of the women across the three dimensions. The aspects of personal empowerment include women's understanding of their status, self-awareness, self-esteem, self-confidence, sense of achievement and belief in the capacity as some of the interventions are at the personal level. Social empowerment components include being able to voice opinions on their needs, breaking barriers of class, caste, and gender. Activities such as enabling women to engage in productive activity, access to work and wages, credit and savings and managerial skills are identified as expected outputs for economic empowerment outcomes.

Development programmes of this nature induce changes that alter the basic functioning of the system and its interaction with its environment. Thus, women's development is based on an understanding of how various systems relate and interact and how they are drawn in and are affected by planned change processes. This analysis captures the totality of systems processes through which development of rural women occurs and through which resources are mobilised towards their empowerment. The author maps both systems theory, a dynamic process which induces a change in the lives of rural women; and the empowerment theory, which powerfully seeks to build the inner strength of the women. Thus, integrating both theories in a context-specific reality, a model of intervention guided by the systems and empowerment theories is propounded.

Mapping the theories in a 'context-specific' programme

Titled 'Empowerment-based Eco-systems Model' by combining ideas from the two theories as discussed earlier, an attempt to identify and map the intervention processes guided by the theories in the '*Mahalir Thittam*' programme was developed. The mapping facilitates a deeper understanding for both the instructor and the practitioner. The intervention was carried out through a UGC funded Major Research Project in the Department of Social Work in 2012–2013 titled 'An Action

Research Project for Creating Sustainable Livelihoods for Rural Women' through the Stella Maris College Extension Project Centre located in Tiruvallur District, Tamil Nadu. The Postgraduate students of the Masters programme in Social Work specialising in Community Development were placed to fulfil the requirement of their concurrent fieldwork tasks on the stipulated fieldwork days (Friday, Saturday, and Sunday) for one semester (fourth semester). Among other requirements of the fieldwork practicum, students were specifically allotted to work with the women of self-help groups (SHGs) who were part of the '*Mahalir Thittam*' project of the State Government of Tamil Nadu.

Some of the tasks assigned to the students were as follows:

1 Identify women's livelihood and training needs
2 Motivate women to form and strengthen peer groups
3 Form and strengthen networks among women SHGs
4 Disseminate relevant information to women regarding the '*Mahalir Thittam*' project
5 Link government resources with the women SHGs
6 Identify competencies and strengthen leadership qualities among the women.

Students were enabled to identify the theoretical components and make their own analysis of the theoretical inputs. Subsequently, during supervisory conferences, students would share the strengths and challenges in comprehending the aspects of the theory. Further, they were guided to move at the pace of the women's convictions and decision-making abilities. The philosophical underpinnings of the profession such as its values, beliefs and principles were frequently examined and re-examined while on the field and during supervisory conferences.

Mapping the systems theory

Using the systems understanding of the concepts of input and output (Sadowski, 1999) the figure presented here will provide the reader with a pictorial view of the intervention. As a first step, the practitioner identifies the input as rural women, transformation takes place through the '*Mahalir Thittam*' programme and the resultant output is empowered women. Once the women are set to be part of the programme the various step-by-step components of intervention at the personal, social and economic levels lend themselves towards a progressive empowering process.

According to the systems theory, people basically look for support from three kinds of resource systems: informal or natural resource systems i.e. family, friends, neighbours, co-workers, and others who extend support; formal resource systems like organisations or associations such as trade unions or community councils, or self-help groups which promote the interests of their members; and societal resource systems such as schools, hospitals, government departments and funding agencies.

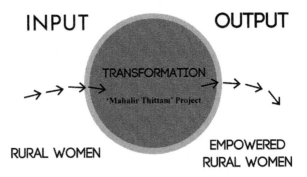

FIGURE 5.1 Input, transformation and output in the systems framework

Source: Adapted from Sadowski, P. (1999) *Systems theory as an approach to the study of literature, origins, and functions of literature* Lewiston, NY: E. Mellen Press

The four systems in the *'Mahalir Thittam'* project

The task to map the four systems in the project is a valuable learning outcome in the classroom where students are able to identify and map the systems within the project. This is a crucial point in the learning phase where the theoretical comprehension is experimented in the field. In the project, the client system, change agent system, target system and action system were identified as follows:

Client system: In the context of this study the client system comprises the women beneficiaries who belong to the larger network of self-help groups.

Change agent system: The concerned NGO, Tamil Nadu Women's Development Corporation, and the banks/credit institutions are identified as the change agent system. In this case, social work trainees will be identified with the Stella Maris College Extension Project Centre that works in collaboration with the Tamil Nadu Women's Development Corporation.

Target system: The target system refers to those people that the change agent needs to influence in order to accomplish the goals of the change effort. It could happen in some cases that the client system and the target system might be the same, as when a change agent accepts an individual client for help in solving a personal problem. Under the *'Mahalir Thittam'* project, the target system is comprised of women themselves, their families and the community at large. In other cases, the client system may be considered the target system in working towards some goals, but in respect to other goals, the target and client systems may differ and be apart.

Action system: A new system comes together with the expectation that the members of the system will be in direct interaction with each other. The action system in this context is the process of achieving the three main empowering tenets of the intervention process; social empowerment, economic empowerment and personal empowerment (capacity building) by

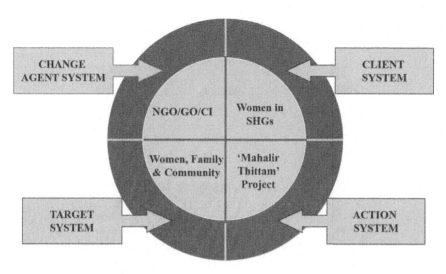

FIGURE 5.2 Mapping the four basic systems

Source: Author

setting into motion the other three systems: the change agent system (Government, NGOs, Banks, and the SHGs), the client system (the women) and the target system (the community members). It can be an existing system already in operation that may now take the shape of a new system that is put together by the change agent, or several people who may not at any one time be engaged in direct interaction with one another but whom the practitioner will coordinate and work with to change a target on behalf of the client system.

The key element of the model is a classification of the types of systems in relation to which the social worker carries out her/his roles. As a next step, the practitioner identifies and maps the four systems within the intervention as is explicated in Figure 5.2.

The four basic systems

Having comprehended the four major systems, the next step was to map the four systems in the larger eco-system in the community and identify its sub-systems. The diagrammatic presentation depicts the four systems within the larger systems and the sub-systems.

Systems approach in the *'Mahalir Thittam'* project

The four systems in the social work framework have been mapped within the systems of the 'Mahalir Thittam' programme through a process of defining the

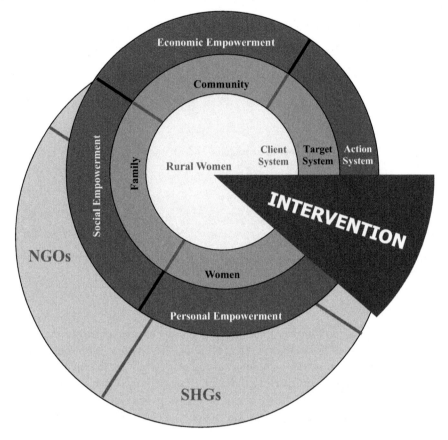

FIGURE 5.3 Mapping the four systems in the larger eco-system

Source: Author

determinants within the specific context in which the intervention is located as is explained in the diagram. Identifying the four systems in the larger eco-system, women beneficiaries of the programme are identified as the client system, the change agent system being the government, which is the main implementing agency, along with the NGOs, banks and self-help groups. Women, their families, communities and other women constitute the target system wherein the action system is set in motion. The action system makes up for the empowerment initiatives comprised of personal, social and economic aspects of the intervention programme that ultimately leads to the empowerment of women.

The four levels of analyses made in the study such as the individual, family/household, the enterprise and the community are further identified in a systems framework. The framework depicts the action processes from identifying women in poor living conditions to becoming empowered women. The proposed model is a presentation of the empowerment of rural women in the '*Mahalir Thittam*' project using a systems framework. The diagrammatic presentation is an attempt to identify and place in context the two theories of social work in the '*Mahalir Thittam*' project. The framework further depicts the action processes from identifying women in poor living conditions which eventually results in their becoming empowered women. Accordingly, the proposed model of the intervention using the systems framework and the empowerment framework is presented pictorially.

The eco-systems theory with its input, process and output on the one hand and the empowerment theory with dialogue, discovery and development on the other is mapped alongside the intervention process that is presented in the centre. The client system being the women living in poor conditions with specific needs and access to resources, change-agent system being the government, banks and NGOs, target system being women who require an action system that mobilises social, economic and personal resources to gain empowerment. While the systems approach talks about inputs, the empowerment model identifies dialogue as its first stage; a process of transformation in the systems approach is identified as the discovery stage in the empowerment model and the output of the systems model is aligned with the development stage in the empowerment model. The following diagrammatic presentation is an attempt to identify and place in context the two theories of social work in the '*Mahalir Thittam*' project.

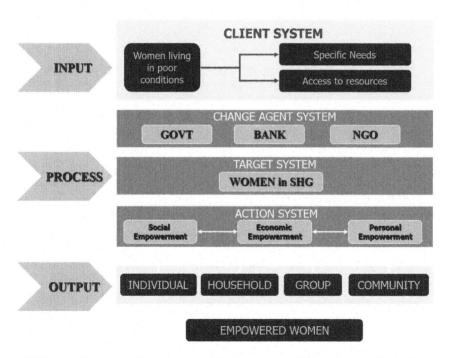

FIGURE 5.4 Integrating theory and practice mapping an 'Empowerment-Based Eco-Systems Model' in the '*Mahalir Thittam*' project

Source: Author

Women in SHGs become the action system and do not remain the client system or target system. The formation of the SHG itself is the evolution into an action system as the SHG's role is of empowered women who manage their own livelihood after learning all the skills of mobilisation and bookkeeping, liaison with the government and so on.

At this stage, the field instructor explains the 'systems approach' to the social work trainee to view the approach as a dynamic process, all of which induces a change in the lives of rural women. The rationale for using this approach is explained as follows: development programmes induce changes that alter the basic functioning of the system and its interaction with its environment. Thus, women's development is based on an understanding of how various systems relate and interact and how they are drawn in and affected by planned change processes. This analysis captures in totality the socio-economic processes through which development of rural women occurs and through which the sub-categories of personal, social and economic empowerment are identified and mobilised towards their empowerment.

Comprehending the praxis element through field instruction

In the field, the focus turns from the acquisition of knowledge to the application of knowledge. The mapping process of the two theories in a context-specific intervention allows the student trainee and the practitioner to apply knowledge by discovering the various components of theory in practice. In the first place, the field instructor needs to be acquainted with the theory and convinced about its applicability. Constant dialogues and discussions and openness to the rejection of the theory are important aspects of the instruction. This directs the student to consciously apply theories and build conviction about their applicability. It is at this juncture that higher levels of professional knowledge are proven and acknowledged and new ideas emerge. This, in turn, enables the student to demonstrate whether relevant theories are locally adaptable or can be locally generated. The fieldwork supervisor/educator and the social work trainee engage in a focused relationship that enables free dialogue. Furthermore, it enables the trainee to express her/his frustrations, difficulties experienced in the field such as lack of time, inability to complete time-bound activities and her/his inability in the application of theory, and comprehension of theoretical concepts.

Most important of all strategies would be to create innovative curricula where theoretical and practical learning experiments are woven together. Teaching and evaluation methodologies may be incorporated to enable students to demonstrate their learning experiences. Other strategies such as identifying appropriate projects and interventions that are viable for learning purposes, enabling students to see the linkages with theory and practice and exposing students to the applicability of the theory wherein the supervisor demonstrates field examples in the classroom by visually linking field reality to the theory (shown in the diagrams) would help in comprehending theory and practice. Drawing comparisons and assessments of similar projects and programmes will give the students wider knowledge and applicability of skills during practice. Most importantly, the supervisor will necessarily be acquainted with the theories and be ready to accept the relevance of application and the generation of newer and more relevant ideas from the students.

Outcomes of the intervention

Through the research project, the Department of Social Work has been able to establish concrete networks and tangible interventions for the women that enabled the establishment of an extension project centre namely Stella Maris College Extension Project Centre. Subsequently, the institution has also been able to establish direct intervention with the women. Some of the major achievements of the project are summarised:

At the classroom level:

- It provided an exceptional academic experience of integrating classroom and field-based learning through the application of theoretical understanding and exploration of methods and aspects in the discipline of social work education and practice.
- Students shared knowledge and skills, discussed, debated and reflected on learning experiences. Utilising their knowledge creatively, students made contributions from their own areas of knowledge.
- It provided an opportunity to reiterate the significance of institution-community partnerships.
- It was an opportunity for students emphasising in Community Development and faculty members to participate in the various initiatives of the government for rural women.
- This action research project created an opportunity for an interdisciplinary approach wherein students from the National Service Scheme and various departments such as Zoology, Chemistry and History were able to collaborate on the project.
- The project led to an exploration of further career opportunities for students as a result of the relationships built in the government departments.
- As part of the curriculum, rural camps (one-week duration) were organised to foster among the students the need for integral and reciprocal learning. Students were exposed to the realities of rural life and in turn the women were able to gain several skills that were mobilised through the faculty and students of the department.

At the field level:

- This project sought to bring about a transformation in the lives of women by creating an enabling environment for them. The livelihood needs of women were identified and resources and services in the location were made available.

- Financial independence opportunities were created for women through various livelihood training programmes and linkages with government and non-governmental bodies.
- Skills training was imparted to the women.
- A certificate course on jewelry making and tailoring was provided for the rural women for a duration of six months. The women were encouraged to set up small tailoring units within the village.
- Women were linked with the Gandhi Foundation for garments training with employment for the support of *Pudhu Vazhvu* (Tamil Nadu State Government poverty alleviation programme for the empowerment of women in SHGs).
- Life skills training on self-confidence, communication, assertiveness and leadership was organised to enable women to set up entrepreneurial initiatives/units. Local mechanisms for networking of women's groups and organisations were established. Specifically, rapport was established with the government and NGOs in order to link resources with the women.
- Women have gained greater awareness on how to avail government services. Both women and men were given awareness about the self-employment opportunities through the support of Micro, Small and Medium Enterprises, a central government initiative for entrepreneurship development. Self-confidence and a sense of oneness among the women was an outcome of this intervention. Through the network of Micro, Small and Medium enterprises of Tamil Nadu, women were motivated in self-employment opportunities and marketing practices.
- After several negotiations with concerned authorities such as members of the local governing body, Village Administrative Officer, *Sarva Shiksha Abhiyan* officials, District Education Officer, self-help groups and local schools, women have access to utilise common community resources such as the school premises, primary health centre, community hall, women welfare programmes and other government schemes.
- Increased awareness was generated among the women through programmes on women's rights with special reference to employment, health, education and other legal aspects using various intervention strategies: awareness building programmes such as exhibitions, street theatre by students and inputs by resource persons from the concerned fields.

Conclusion

Practice that is not guided by such knowledge fails to create consistent evidence and comprehensive information, which eventually falls short of informing the value in professional practice. The defining moment for the social work trainee occurs only when classroom learning relates to field experiences, where the idea of reflection (reflective practice) is influential in understanding theory in fieldwork. It is crucial to keep in mind that solving issues is not based on guesswork or habit but rather on reflecting and responding to client's needs based on an understanding of issues (Thompson & Thompson, 2008).

Academicians, researchers and practitioners contribute by way of generating knowledge and practice models. What is important and crucial now is the coming together of academicians and practitioners with a serious and committed effort towards the application of theoretical frameworks in practice. It is hoped that this field experience of applying theory to practice will contribute to filling in the wide gap between thought and action. Linking theoretical approaches to practice will, therefore, be the answer to gaining greater recognition and creating meaningful and scientific change.

References

Bronfenbrenner, U. (1979). *The ecology of human development experiments by nature and design*. Cambridge, MA: Harvard University Press.

Carpenter, L. (2016). The development of cultural competence in social work practice and education. Master of Social Work Clinical Research Papers, Paper 568. Retrieved November 21, 2017, from http://sophia.stkate.edu/msw_papers/568

Desai, M. (1993). Special issue: Social work profession in Asia: Editorial. *The Indian Journal of Social Work, 54*(4), 507.

Devore, S. (1991). *Ethnic-sensitive social work practice* (3rd ed.). New York, NY: Macmillan.

Dominelli, L. (1996). Deprofessionalizing social work: Anti-oppressive practice competencies and postmodernism. *The British Journal of Social Work, 26*(2), 153–175. Retrieved September 26, 2017, from https://doi.org/10.1093/oxfordjournals.bjsw.a011077

Drucker, D. (1993). The social work profession in Asia: Look homeward, 1968–1993. *Special Issue: Social Work Profession in Asia, The Indian Journal of Social Work, 54*(46), 513–536.

DuBois, B., & Miley, K. K. (1996). *Social work: An empowering profession* (2nd ed.). Boston: Allyn and Bacon.

Evans, D., & Kearney, J. (1996). *Working in social care a systemic approach*. Aldershot: Arena/Ashgate Publishing.

Freire, P. (1970). *Pedagogy of the oppressed*. Translated by M. B. Ramos. New York, NY: Seabury Press.

Goldstein, H. (1973). *Social work practice: A unitary approach*. Columbia, SC: University of South Carolina Press.

Government of India. (2001). *Policies and programmes for the advancement of women in India*. New Delhi: Department of Women and Child Development.

Healy, K. (2000). *Social work practices: Contemporary perspectives on change*, pp. 121–122. New Delhi: Sage Publications Ltd.

Hollis, E. V., & Taylor, A. L. (1951). *Social work education in the United States*. New York, NY: Columbia University Press.

International Association of Schools of Social Work (IASSW). (2004). Global standards for social work education and training. Retrieved from www.iassw-aiets.org/global-standards-for-social-work-education-and-training/

Kemp, S. P., Whittaker, J. K., & Tracy, E. M. (1997). *Person-in-environment practice: The social ecology of interpersonal helping*. New York, NY: Aldine De Gruyter.

Kuhn, T. (1970). *The structure of scientific revolutions* (2nd ed.). Chicago, IL: University of Chicago Press.

Kulkarni, P. D. (1993). The indigenous base of social work profession in India. *The Indian Journal of Social Work, 54*, 555–565.

Lavalette, M. (2011). *Radical social work today, social work at crossroads*, pp. 7–8. Bristol: Policy Press, University of Bristol.

Maluccic, A. N. (1983). Planned use of life experiences. In A. Rosenblatt & D. Waldfogel (Eds.), *Handbook of clinical social work*. San Francisco, CA: Jossey-Bass Publishers.

Middleman, R., & Goldberg, G. (1974). *Social service delivery: A structural approach to social work practice*. New York, NY: Columbia University Press.

Midgley, J. (1981). *Professional imperialism: Social work in the third world*. London: Heinemann.

Miley, K. K., O'Melia, M., & DuBois, B. (2001). *Generalist social work practice: An empowering approach*. Boston: Allyn and Bacon

Milner, J., Myers, S., & O'Byrne, P. (2015). *Assessment in social work*, pp. 77–99. London: Palgrave.

Milner, J., & O'Byrne, P. (1998). *Assessment in social work*, 90–92. London: Macmillan.

Mohan, D. (1993). Diversity and conflict: Towards a unified model of social work. *Indian Journal of Social Work*, 54, 597–608.

Nagpaul, H. (1993). Analysis of social work teaching materials in India: The need for indigenous foundations. *International Social Work*, 36, 207–220.

Nanavatty, M. C. (1993). Problems affecting the indigenization of social work profession in Asia. *Indian Journal of Social Work*, 54, 547–554.

Narayan, L. (2008). Contextualising social work practice in India: Some explorations. *The Indian Journal of Social Work*, 69(2), 107–110.

National Association of Social Workers (NASW). (2015). Global standards for social work education and training. Retrieved from www.socialworkers.org/LinkClick.aspx?fileticket=PonPTDEBrn4%3D&portalid=

O'Melia, M., Du Bois, B., & Miley, K. (1993). From problem solving to empowerment-based social work practice. In B. Du Bois & K. Miley (1996) (Eds.), *Social work: An empowering profession* (pp. 214) (2nd ed.). London: Allyn and Bacon.

O'Sullivan, T. (2003). Why don't social workers work in partnership with people. Unpublished Paper, University of Humberside, Hull. In Adams Robert, *Social work and empowerment: BASW: Practical social work* (3rd ed.). Series Editor: Jo Campling. London: Palgrave.

Phillipson, J. (1992). *Practicing equality: Women, men, and social work improving social work education and training*. London: No. 10, CCETSW.

Pincus, A., & Minahan, A. (1973). *Social work practice: Model and method*. Itasca, IL: Peacock.

Ramsay, R. F. (2001, February 8–10). Revisiting the working definition: The time is right to identify a common conceptual framework for social work. Paper presented at the Kentucky Conference on social work and education: *Reworking the working definition*, College of Social Work, University of Kentucky, February 8–10, 2001. Unpublished manuscript, University of Calgary. Retrieved from www.ucalgary.ca/sw/ramsay/papers2/Daly-03-practice-methods-comprehensive-framework-1.html

Rao, M. K. (1993). Social work education: Some questions on relevance, direction and emphasis. *Indian Journal of Social Work*, 54, 609–512.

Roy, S. (2018). *Social work in globalizing world: Practices and challenges*. Jaipur: Rawat Publications.

Sadowski, P. (1999). *Systems theory as an approach to the study of literature, origins, and functions of literature*, p. 19. Lewiston, NY: E. Mellen Press.

Schön, D. A. (1991). *The reflective practitioner: How professionals think in action*. Aldershot: Avebury.

Siporin, M. (1980). Ecological system theory in social work. *Journal of Sociology and Social Welfare*, 7, 507–532.

Thomas, M., & Pierson, J. (1995). *Dictionary of social work*. London: BASW/Macmillan.

Thompson, N., & Thompson, S. (2008). *The social work companion*. New York, NY: Palgrave Macmillan.

Van Den, B., & Cooper, L. (1986). *Feminist visions for social work*. Baltimore, MD: National Association of Social Workers, Silver Spring.

6
RECORDING AND DOCUMENTATION IN FIELDWORK

Mohua Nigudkar

Introduction

Fieldwork recording, a written or oral narrative of the learner's engagement at the fieldwork setting, is a significant component of fieldwork and social work curriculum. It is a holistic description of the fieldwork experience and reflects the fieldwork activities, tasks, learnings and insight. Fieldwork and fieldwork recording are closely interlinked with curriculum requirements and the larger goals of social work education. Through fieldwork recording, the social work student/learner is also enabled to analyse the extent to which classroom teaching, theoretical perspectives, social work methods and skills have been imbibed and applied to fieldwork. Further, the larger socio-political-ideological environment too influences social work and social change (Australian Learning and Teaching Council Ltd., 2010). In India and elsewhere, the nature of social work education too has been evolving based on changing social realities and our improved understanding of people and their situations. Bodhi (2012), comments:

> In India, efforts to insert liberatory and emancipatory elements into Indian social work education, are now visible and are being articulated in the public domain. New ideas, analysis and perspectives have now started to emerge with the convergence of perspectives between community social workers, development and rights social workers, political social workers, feminist social workers and pro-equality social workers.
>
> *(p. 2)*

All of these aspects have implications on fieldwork, thrust areas of organisation, nature of fieldwork settings and fieldwork recordings.

The two terms, *Fieldwork Recording* and *Documentation*, though often used interchangeably, are distinct in their meaning and scope. Documentation is the collection of all written material prepared or gathered by the learner during the course of fieldwork. Documents mostly include fieldwork recordings, activity reports, summary sheets, official noting, correspondence, *minutes* of meetings, programme report, project proposal and fieldwork evaluation formats that the learner/supervisor is required to complete as part of fieldwork curriculum. While fieldwork recording or report can be oral or verbal, documentation is invariably the written repository for future reference.

Over the years, while there has been Indian literature around different aspects of fieldwork (e.g. Andrews, 2014; Desai, 2013; Mallick, 2007; Devi Prasad & Vijayalakshmi, 1997; Gangrade, 1975; Mehta, 1975; Thangavelu, 1975; Maurya, 1962; Kapoor, 1961), there have been relatively fewer articles specifically on fieldwork recording and documentation. This chapter will primarily focus on fieldwork recording that social work students (henceforth interchangeably referred to as learners) have to undertake at their respective fieldwork organisations or settings. It includes an overview of fieldwork recording based on the author's own experience of over two decades of being a social work educator, fieldwork supervisor and coordinator. The author has had an opportunity to supervise a wide range of fieldwork learners across governmental, non-governmental and community-based organisations. The content in this chapter has primarily evolved out of the author's field experience within the Indian context; designing/conducting fieldwork recording related training sessions, review of some of the existing fieldwork manuals, as well as literature (especially academic papers published within *The Indian Journal of Social Work*), liaising with fieldwork organisations, and assessing individual student fieldwork recordings. The examples and illustrations, provided in this chapter, have been either adapted from student fieldwork recordings or based on discussion with students and social work colleagues. This chapter does not include research report writing or ethnography fieldwork writing.

The chapter is divided into three parts:

1   Understanding the Purpose and Significance of Fieldwork Recording
2   Examining the Writing Structure: Types of Fieldwork Recordings
3   Beyond the Written Words: Encouraging Excellence in Fieldwork Writing.

Understanding the purpose and significance of fieldwork recording

Fieldwork recording or writing is often perceived as a daunting task, a needless chore, especially for those who are diffident about writing or do not necessarily realise the significance of writing about their fieldwork. Moreover, many students prefer to engage with action-oriented social work but are not equally inclined to reflect and document about it. Writing has been recognised as an important tool for expressing thoughts, ideas, describing work, and communicating (e.g. Defazio, Jones, Tennant, & Hook, 2010; Hyland, 2008; Farell, n.d.). Defazio et al. (2010, p. 34) assert that "effective writing is a skill that is grounded in the cognitive domain. It involves learning, comprehension, application and synthesis of new knowledge . . . writing also encompasses creative inspiration, problem-solving, reflection and revision that results in a completed manuscript". Additionally, Defazio et al. observe, "from a student's perspective, writing may instead be a laborious and even dreaded exercise of attempting to place thoughts on paper while developing mastery over the rules of writing, such as spelling, citation format and grammar" (p. 34). Among the different advantages of writing, Hyland (2008, p. 10) emphasises that writing is about "discovering and formulating ideas as we create personal meanings". The "written report can present data and a level of analysis that would be difficult to convey in oral form" (Farell, n.d.). Within the context of social work education, the purpose of fieldwork recording is manifold. Fieldwork recording is useful for documentation and reference. It is also a medium through which the learner can express thoughts, emotions, questions, doubts and apprehensions, if any, about fieldwork. Fieldwork recording provides opportunity to the learner "to organise and present information, observations, reflections and actions in a systematic manner" (Desai, 2013, p. 332). Through the fieldwork recordings and writing, the learner attempts to articulate and verbalise the fieldwork experience. Besides, fieldwork recording does not exist in a vacuum and goes beyond mere narration of experiences and/or compiling a bunch of reports. It involves an analysis of the larger social context within which the organisation and the fieldwork is located. Through direct engagement with people, the learner also develops relevant skills at the grassroots level and a clear perspective on social work. The recordings facilitate knowledge building about diverse field realities and social work intervention/strategies on a micro-meso-macro continuum. Encouraging learners to understand the significance of writing about their fieldwork and utilising the fieldwork recordings as one of the tools for monitoring, feedback, and guidance are among the key responsibilities of the fieldwork supervisor (henceforth referred to as the supervisor).

The writing process improves both writing and analytical skills, which can be applied to other written work as well. Recalling, remembering and writing about work enables the learner to assess the activities or work undertaken and develops critical thinking skills. It enables the learner towards organising the thinking process and structuring the work plan methodically. For example, if the learner has attended a meeting with a government official regarding permission for a medical camp, the learner can systematically note the details about the meeting, analyse the outcome, and prepare a plan of action towards finalising the medical camp. Most importantly, recordings are a powerful medium of communicating about the learner's work and highlighting social issues. Specific reports create a forum for dialogue and debate. For example, a student social worker's short research report on existence of hidden child labour in a certain locality led to increased discussion for addressing child labour and initiating corrective action in that area.

Writing about the complexity of the field and lived experiences of people is insightful. Arora (2006, p. 140) reflects: "Fieldwork cannot be conceived of as an external encounter, as it involves an internal dialogue within the self". While this statement has been made in the context of ethnography, it is equally relevant for fieldwork within social work education. Fieldwork includes working with diverse individuals and groups. The learner may have certain impressions of people based on their own beliefs, values and socialization. Through fieldwork recordings, the learner can examine their own assumptions about people. Assumption, an unexamined belief or notion, may not always be accurate. It can lead to incorrect conclusions and/or erroneous inferences. Writing brings clarity about the learner's own thoughts and outlook on people, their life situation and social issues. The following examples of fieldwork recording (Illustrations 1 & 2) are instances of developing greater sensitivity and examining pre-conceived notions through the process of reflective writing.

ILLUSTRATION 1   REFLECTIVE RECORDING (EXAMINING PRECONCEIVED NOTIONS)

"A woman walked into my organisation and quietly stated that she needed help. Her neighbour had suggested that she could contact our organisation. She mentioned that she had no money and no food to feed her children. She added that her husband had expired. She had two young children and was unable to leave them alone and go for work. She had no other family members. She shared that she had already spoken with another social worker (who was my colleague) during her last visit. I observed that the woman was well dressed. Her hair was neatly combed. She was also wearing good footwear. She spoke calmly and even smiled occasionally. I started doubting whether she was really speaking the truth about having no money. I decided to enquire about her with my colleague who then told me that the woman was in a crisis situation over her husband's sudden death. She had borrowed her neighbour's clothes and footwear as she did not want to come to an organisation looking shabby and untidy. She also did not want to cry in front of strangers. She wanted support but not pity. That day I realised that I had my own preconceived notions of how a poor person should look and behave. We are very quick to judge based on our perceptions about people. Henceforth I will be more careful about forming impressions without having adequate information".

Source: An illustration of a reflective writing based on a discussion with a social worker working in an organisation which supports vulnerable children and families

ILLUSTRATION 2   (EXAMINING ASSUMPTION, BUILDING SKILLS AND PERSPECTIVE)

"Today was a fruitful ending to the work. I wanted to organise a meeting with the youth in the community, aged between 20–25 years, on livelihood options. This group of young men was generally whiling away their time and were perceived by

> *the community as 'bad company'. It was a community of lower socio-economic groups. With great difficulty I had got a group of six young adults together. Even though it was a small number, I thought of beginning with them. I wasn't very motivated at the beginning of the day as no one had arrived when I reached the meeting venue. Slowly they turned up. After meeting the youth and interacting with them, I was reminded of my purpose. I had to try my best to motivate the youth. I got re-energised and discussed with them the different vocational options. I encouraged them to think about it. Two of the boys agreed to come with me to the vocational guidance centres and find out more details. I appreciated their initiative. The other members too got excited that they may soon learn a skill and get a job. One of the members wanted to work during the day and re-join his night school.*
>
> *For me, it is always a moment of achievement when a concrete work gets done. Initially I was thinking that the meeting would not achieve much. But I realize that it is important to work without biases and assumptions about youth or any person that we work with. Further, the life span perspective informs us that during the life stage of youth and young adulthood, some of the priority areas are career opportunities, skill building, and a purposeful life. Seeing the renewed hope in the eyes of my group, I was able to relate with the life span perspective and the stage of being part of youth. I also realised that it was not merely about enrolling them in school or training courses. Everyone has a right to a life of dignity and purpose. Information and access to resources is an entitlement for all".*
>
> Source: An illustration of a reflective writing based on a discussion with a first year student social worker undertaking fieldwork in a community-based organisation

Determining Factors in Recording: Effective fieldwork recording necessitates an understanding of various contexts and factors to produce the desired outcome. As stated earlier, fieldwork or fieldwork recording does not happen in a vacuum. The learners' motivation, beliefs about people and understanding of social reality does impact fieldwork, especially during the beginning phase. At the same time, the organisation's work priority, their response to social issues, combined with curriculum requirements for fieldwork and quality of supervision determine the overall fieldwork experience of the learner, including fieldwork recording. Thus, the multiple contexts and factors that impinge upon fieldwork and thereby fieldwork recording (see Figure 6.1) are:

- The context of the learner (motivation, beliefs and approach towards fieldwork),
- the context of the organisation (areas of work, requirements from learner and extent of learning opportunities),
- the context of the supervisor (level of expectation from the learner, nature of supervision, perspective, supervisor skills),

110 Mohua Nigudkar

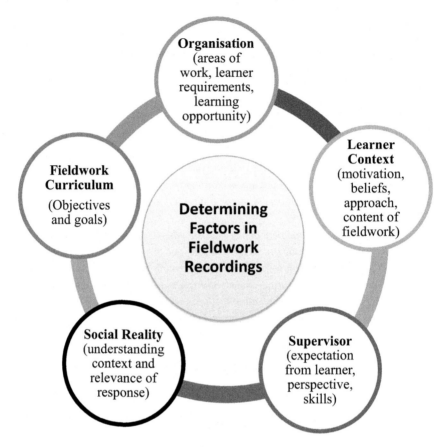

FIGURE 6.1 Multiple contexts and factors that impinge upon fieldwork
Source: Author

- the curriculum context (fieldwork objectives and overall curriculum goals), and
- the context of social realities (understanding the "field" and relevance of response).

In addition, minimal scope of fieldwork, inadequate planning and repetitive work, also limits the scope of recording and thereby skill building in writing. Diverse learning and/or work opportunities in fieldwork increases the scope of fieldwork recording. For example, if a learner is engaged with a range of responsibilities such as direct work with individuals, group sessions, awareness and advocacy programmes, or developing a needs assessment tool, the fieldwork recordings too have varied and substantive content. Moreover, an organisation may require different kinds of reports and documents. For example, if the organisation requires information about the community, the learner writes an information-based report about the community profile. If the organisation requires the learner to review one of their projects, the report is largely evaluative. For fundraising purposes the learner will need to prepare a project proposal, concept note and budget. In process oriented work such as opening bank accounts for the homeless youth to motivate them to save money, detailed process recordings and reports will be relevant for tracing the developments, monitoring progress and designing action steps.

Ethics and Writing: The core values of social work such as dignity, respect, accepting of diversity and self-determination are intrinsic in people-centered work. As the learners come from different socio-cultural backgrounds, it is important for them to adapt to the culture of the community (e.g. Nasreen & Singh, 2018). Especially in India, "reality could present itself in very complex ways especially when it comes to inter-sectionalities of caste, religion, ethnicity, language and gender" (Bodhi, 2012, p. 4). Fieldwork related writing is closely interlinked with values and ethics of social work. Practising these core values while working with people and writing about them gives an insight about internalising human values and engaging in the lives of people without bias and prejudice. Fieldwork recording is a tool to integrate knowledge, skills, and values of the profession not just intellectually but emotionally as well (Desai, 1975).

One of the key responsibilities of the supervisor is to guide the learner towards imbibing some of the basic principles in fieldwork recording, notably:

- Writing objectively without bias
- Using words and language which is non-labelling and non-discriminatory
- Endorsing human rights and dignity through language and communication
- Maintaining accountability to the organisation and the people
- Documenting accurate information and not falsifying details
- Maintaining confidentiality
- Believing in the significance of writing and documentation as a medium of advocacy and social change.

Incremental Learning Through Recording: Apart from learning opportunities and writing skills, the quality of recording also depends on the stage of fieldwork and the level of the learner. For any kind of effective writing, clarity on the purpose of writing is a must. There will be differential expectations from a graduate (Bachelor's) level learner of social work vis-à-vis a Master's level learner. As stated earlier, fieldwork recording is closely linked with the organisation and its nature of work. The learner begins with gathering information about the organisation, recording the same and preparing a report about the organisation. These details assist in preliminary planning of fieldwork. From simple narratives of work undertaken, a steady progression towards in-depth analysis and critical thinking skills ensues. During the initial days of fieldwork, the recordings are largely information-based with some observations. As the pace of work and learner involvement increases, the scope of recordings also widens. Towards the completion of fieldwork, overall consolidation of learning is documented. Through the process of fieldwork, the learner also learns to use specific terms such as "rights", "empowerment", and "justice", relevant to social work practice. The supervisor ensures that terms are used and written purposefully and not merely as jargons.

Fieldwork recording also depends on the quantum of work done. On certain days there may not be much to write. Every recording may not have the same amount of content. The scope and thrust of areas in fieldwork recording will depend on the priority areas and nature of work, curriculum requirements and expectations from the organisation. Finally, the quality of fieldwork recording is dependent on the learner's excellence at fieldwork, inclination to write and sincerity of efforts.

Transferring Knowledge into Practice: Skill building has to be in "the *real* world and not *imagined* world" (Bar-On, 2001, emphasis added). Applying classroom teaching in field practice, documenting the process and discussing new field learnings, is part of the critical reflective practice of fieldwork. For example, if the learner has been taught about "communication skills" in class and "listening" as a skill, the student applies the skill of "listening" while working with people during fieldwork, writes about the experience and reflects on the positives as well as areas of improvement. A learner may also gain insights at fieldwork about factors that hinder listening and share the field experience in the classroom discussion. Over a period of time the learner imbibes the skill of listening and is able to practice active listening effortlessly. Alongside skills, the learner also integrates theory with practice, another crucial element of fieldwork. Ross and Ncube (2018) conducted a study to explore the perceptions of third year undergraduate social worker students attending a South African university regarding their experiences of field practice supervision. A total of 93 out of 101 students participated in the study. While the study was primarily on supervision, it included student experience of writing fieldwork reports. Some of the student narratives were that report writing was "cumbersome" and they were further challenged by the "need for theory integration". One of the students shared that, "it was nice writing verbatim reports, but it was challenging to me when it comes to integrating theory" (p. 42). In another study conducted by Desai (2013) to examine the theory-practice relationship in field practicum, one of the student participants of the study observed that "when she initially read feminist theories, she felt that they were full of jargons and western-centric; but, through fieldwork placement in an urban slum she experienced how these theories transcend their spatial origin and play out in women's lives in India" (p. 334). To be able to do well at fieldwork and thereby record well, it is expected that students enter the field with a certain theoretical base which they can either observe in practice or use theory to design their programmes (Bar-On, 2001). Through fieldwork recording, writing about the theory-practice integration increases the understanding about the application of theory in social work practice. For example, the anti-oppressive perspective examines the disparity of power, linking personal and political and the inherently oppressive structures in society that get institutionalised through culture, practice and policy (e.g. Clifford, 1995, as cited in Burke & Harrison, n.d.). A learner working with a tribal group on forest rights can work within the anti-oppressive framework while advocating for equity and social justice.

Putting theory into practice requires thinking, reflective knowledge and willingness to write about confusions too (Bar-On, 2001). The learner can analyse whether a theory is enabling towards developing a critical perspective or elements of a theory can be applied in actual practice. For example, while working with destitute children in institutional care, theories that may be found useful are attachment theory, social learning and ecological perspective; for working on domestic violence against women, the feminist perspective may be considered relevant whereas in fieldwork with the elderly, the life course theory is often applied. No one single theory or perspective can explain/examine every aspect of the social phenomena or reality. Depending on the nature of fieldwork placement and the learner's own inclination towards a particular theory, adapting either a single theory or integrating an eclectic framework of theories is attempted by the learner. The following example (Illustration 3) demonstrates integration of theory with practice through the process of critical thinking and writing.

ILLUSTRATION 3 (CRITICAL REFLECTION AND THEORETICAL PERSPECTIVE)

"In a recent group session that I undertook with women, many women in the group shared about the vulnerabilities that they themselves faced due to the fact that they were "women" and that women in their communities did not have much "freedom". Some even narrated their experiences of living in poorer families and the double problems they faced of both economic suffering for the entire family alongside violence and discrimination in general against women of their community. There were no proper hospitals, schools or drainage system. There were fewer jobs. The women expressed anxiety that crime too was increasing in their locality. The conflict theory and the feminist perspective become significant in understanding the realities of the women. Different kinds of hierarchies, lack of resources and the conflict that arises leads to the entire community and especially the women being deprived of basic necessities and autonomy of choice".

Source: Adapted from a second year student social worker's recording. The student was placed for fieldwork with an organisation working on issues pertaining to marginalised women

---

Examining the writing structure: types of fieldwork recordings

While there need not be one single standard format for fieldwork recording, each curriculum and fieldwork programme typically has specific requirements or expectations from fieldwork recording. Process recording and report writing are two writing structures usually applied in fieldwork recording.

Process recording

Process recording is a narrative structure and requires sequentially writing about events and happenings as they unfold. Historically, process recording was introduced for noting details of *case work* with individual clients. For example, in case work with an elderly person on health concerns, the learner noted details about the nature and content of interactions, which included writing about the feelings, emotion, reaction, responses, self-reflection and use of skills and concrete future plans. Though case work as a method of social work and applying the problem centered on diagnostic approach continues to remain relevant, the scope of working with individuals has expanded in response to changing social realities. Not all learners are equally engaged in case work. Newer interventions have been formulated that focus on mobilising individuals/groups/communities, creating networks, coalitions, consciousness building processes, human rights advocacy and vocalising issues of oppression and structural inequalities. While process recording has been critiqued for being "time consuming" and not necessarily producing an accurate account of work (e.g. Mallick, 2007), nonetheless, process recording does have the scope to encapsulate the myriad forms of social work intervention especially within the context of fieldwork recording and learning. Process recording is relevant for a range of preventive, developmental, therapeutic and/or radical social work.

Although standardised parameters to define process recording may not be necessary, an effective process recording requires a systematic and sequential presentation. Process recording is an ongoing documentation of events or a one-time narration. It can be a verbatim recounting of interactions with individuals or an experiential portrayal of the daily experience of fieldwork: Work schedule, description of fieldwork activities, the planning process, implementation, reflection and insights. It can either be a detailed account of every aspect of fieldwork or select highlights of the work. For example, if the learner has organised a group session involving persons with disability, the process recording could either cover only certain aspects about the group session and its outcome or include details of the background work, planning and other information.

Process recording generally outlines work plan, schedule, description of activities/programme, observation, analysis, reflection and goal setting. The different tools/kinds of process recording mostly, but not only, used are:

1 **Daily log of activities**: Writing about schedule of work, analysis, reflection, goal setting
2 **Narrative recording**: Describing the details about an incident, event, individual or group work
3 **Case study recording**: Working with individuals and individual sessions
4 **Group work**: Documenting group sessions
5 **Summary recording**: Summary of work undertaken over a period of time
6 **Journal keeping**: Examining learning especially related to one's assumption, belief, values, biases, behaviour, insights into self-awareness, behaviour, and growth

7 **Audio/video recording**: Medium for documenting interactions and activities
8 **Ethnographic writing**: Immersion in the fieldwork through ethnographic study.

The following example (Illustration 4) is a sample of process recording.

ILLUSTRATION 4   PROCESS RECORDING (NARRATIVE, OBSERVATION, REFLECTION)

"I reached the residential care home for children around 10:00 am with the objective of meeting two newly admitted children who were staying in the home for the past three days. Their regular social worker was on leave. I was requested to speak with the children and gather the preliminary information. I was also informed that some parents of other children had assembled near the main gate of the home to meet the social worker. I was told to meet the parents too. I began by starting to read through the case files of the two new children. The house master had filled in the basic information. The two children were brothers from a small nearby town. I called for the two boys. Both boys rushed to me and said that they want to go back to their house and started asking about their mother. I told them that I will try my best to find their address and would like to ask them a few questions.

I engaged with the elder brother first and made the younger brother comfortable in one corner of the room by giving him crayons and colouring books. The case file stated that both children were missing children. I started asking the elder boy about his home. The elder boy, who was around nine years old, could only manage to give the name of a railway station. I asked him whether there was any accompanying adult with him when he had left home. He was unable to say anything much. In the meantime the younger brother had left the crayons and was standing close to his elder brother. The younger one, aged around six years, displayed signs of hesitation in having a conversation with me.

I read the case file again. The case file mentioned that they had been found alone and crying at a large railway station. Hence they were taken into safe custody by the police and admitted in the home. I started asking about their journey. The elder child then started mentioning that they had travelled with their neighbour for securing admission in a boarding school. However the neighbour allegedly left them in the train with the promise of returning but failed to turn up even after a significant period of time. The younger child also talked about the same neighbour but went to state that the neighbour was taking them to work in a nearby factory. The younger child also mentioned about the wages and other benefits, which the neighbour had agreed to pay their mother with the promise of escorting them back to their village after a period of one year. The neighbour allegedly left them on the platform of the station after the brothers started crying for food.

I started asking them about their parents. They stated that their father was very ill and unable to move from the bed. Their mother was working on a neighbour's land. They seemed to be staying in a village.

The children did not have any phone numbers that I could contact. However, they gave a description of their locality and the name of a local market place. When I asked them about names of any other person, the elder brother remembered the contact details of a shop keeper in the village who would often allow the use of his phone. I called him up and, much to my relief, he could identify the parents of the children. He went to say that the parents have had filed missing complaints with the police authorities in their village and even posted printed photographs of the children in prominent places across the village. I provided him the contact number of the home and requested him to convey the message to their parents. The shopkeeper spoke with the two children and assured them that their parents would soon contact them. The two brothers hugged me and rushed out of the room with large smiles on their tearful faces.

I was very happy that their family had been traced and the children were smiling. However, there are questions in my mind. Were the children missing or were they being sent for child labour? Who was the neighbour? Was the neighbour a genuine person or a prospective child trafficker? If the family themselves were sending children for work, will the best interest of the child get met by sending the children back to their family? What are the underlying factors that make families vulnerable? Reflecting on the process, I was happy that my patience with the children in asking questions made them comfortable to share details. The next step would be to meet the parents and get more details. Soon thereafter, I went to meet the other parents who were waiting near the gate of the home . . ."

Source: Adapted from the recording of a first year student social worker doing fieldwork in a residential children's home for children in need of care and protection

Report writing

Reports focus on a specific activity or event. While there need not be a mandated format, a report is ordinarily not as detailed as a process recording. It analyses and presents information about specific programmes or events without in-depth reflection and introspection on the background processes. *For example, if the learner has organised a fund raising charity event, a report about it gives specific details about the objectives of the event, summarises of the processes undertaken and analyses the outcome. Detailed description of self-learning and insights may not get included. As per the requirements of the curriculum/organisation, a learner may write one comprehensive report including reflection of the experience, or aspects of self-learning and introspection may get separately documented in a reflective process recording.*

Some of the different kinds of reports conventionally but not only written on fieldwork, are:

- **Information-based report**: Documenting facts, evidence and concrete details based on literature review, enquiry, survey or field visit
- **Reports of field visit**: Details of home visit, school, hospital, police station, office, government department and other visits as per need
- **Client/Case Study report**: A report on the sessions, progress and future plans
- **Activity-based report**: Report on special programme/event/project/campaign
- **Mid-term reports**: Interim or ongoing progress reports of a project or programme
- **Final fieldwork report**: Concluding report of fieldwork
- **Administrative related report**: Minutes or summary of meeting with fieldwork supervisor, group meetings, staff and team member
- **Project management report**: Project, rationale or purpose of project, objectives, requirements, tasks to be undertaken, next steps, progress, future plans

Through practice, the learner becomes aware about the broad distinction between a process recording and report and the structure for different kinds of recording. Where formats are not available or there is flexibility, the learner creates a structure to the recording with appropriate titles and sub titles. For example, in closed settings like a residential care institution for children, there may be a specific structure for case documentation. In such a situation the learner can prepare the case reports as per the established structure. In an open setting such as a civil society group, which is campaigning for areas such as low cost housing, mobilising public opinion and influencing policy change, the organisation may require a different kind of documentation of the processes involved. The learner may be required to prepare an impact or evaluation report of the campaign. In some organisations, the learner may be expected to conduct a short-term research or survey and prepare a report. A point to be noted is that research reports are different from fieldwork reports. For any research-based activity, all parameters of a research process need to be adhered to, including research ethics, protocols and established norms of writing a research report. If a learner engages with research at fieldwork, while the process recording may include a reflective account of conducting the research and learnings, the research report will need to be written as per the standard requirements of a research report.

Nuts and bolts of fieldwork writing: contextualisation, observation, analysis, reflection

Learning through fieldwork recording is enhanced with context-based understanding and writing observations, analysis and reflection of work.

Contextualisation: To undertake any social work intervention, understanding the context within which the work is located is imperative. Hamilton's "person-in-situation" concept being critical for social work (Mailick, 1977, as cited in Fook, 2012:4), awareness of social context and its importance in understanding individual experience and informing practice are considered as some of the principles in social work (Fook, 2012). At the same time, "changing people's consciousness is a pre-requisite to changing society" (Mullaly, 2007). Recognising the underlying oppressive structures in society that impact and influence people's lives and situations is equally necessary to bring about long term social change (Mullaly, 2007).

In fieldwork recording, writing about the context provides a backdrop or point of reference for work and deeper analysis. For example, if the learner plans to start a recreation programme and adult literacy classes for women in a community, it is important to understand the profile of the women, their socio-economic background, daily experiences of life, cultural practices, health and emotional wellbeing, resources available and level of interest. If traditionally the women have rarely considered recreation or literacy as an important need for them, the learner begins by motivating them to participate in a group meeting where the learner proposes the plan, discusses and encourages the participation of the women in designing the recreation/literacy programme. Gradually the learner also initiates a conversation with the women around the causes of lack of literacy among women and recreation as an important but often neglected need. Contextualised work and subsequent recording about the same generates critical thinking and meaningful intervention.

Fieldwork Observation: The tool of observation is valuable to understand the phenomenon as it exists or appears. Observation, if noted methodically and without bias, provides basic information and details about the situation. Observation can range from noticing particular features or characteristics, to patterns of behaviour and interactions. For example, in a home visit the learner can notice the physical characteristics of the home, the living conditions and amenities in the locality as well as the nature of interactions among family members, and dispute, if any. However, caution must be exercised that no conclusions are made solely on observation without examining supporting facts and other analysis. Observation can also enable the learner to make modifications to existing programmes or suggest newer initiatives. For example, while doing group sessions with adolescent girls on self and personality development, the learner finds that the girls are reluctant to participate. They do not seem interested to discuss about their individual "self". The learner also observes that the girls are eager to get information especially on job opportunities. Through reflective writing on the group work session, the learner analyses the reasons for non-participation of the girls. The learner infers that the girls do not seem to find the group work sessions relevant. The girls are more interested in discussing career goals and absorbing new information. The learner discusses with the adolescent girls and takes their opinion. The girls agree that they are worried about their future and want some inputs on career opportunities. The learner suggests appropriate modifications to the group work programme within the existing framework of personality development. By involving the girls, the learner also practises group participation and democratic decision making processes.

Analysis: Fieldwork recordings are inherently analytical. Analysis guides nuanced thought and action. For example, if the learner organises a campaign against domestic violence at a busy railway station, through the fieldwork recording or report, the learner examines in detail the planning process, extent of resources mobilised, implementation, outcome, feedback given by audience and reflection on skills. The learner prepares an overall assessment of the campaign and lessons for the next campaign.

Reflective Writing and Critical Thinking: Alongside analysis, through the process of introspection or reflecting on fieldwork, the learner delves into a deeper self-understanding about work, skills, abilities, perceptions and potential areas of growth. Fieldwork recording provides the learners an opportunity to reflect upon their role in interactions with people, administrators and research as social workers (Desai, 2013). Reflection is an exploration and an explanation of events and not merely a description of them. It includes description, interpretation and recording the outcome (Hampton, n.d.). Reflective writing also develops the skill to consistently review work and modify as and when required. Greater insights about self are obtained while writing. Critical reflection, an extension of critical thinking, is the "process of analysing and questioning our experience, practice and ideas and then challenging our own thinking" (Australian Learning and Teaching Council Ltd., 2010, p. 56).

The following example (Illustration 5) provides an indicative paragraph related to reflective writing.

ILLUSTRATION 5   REFLECTIVE RECORDING/ JOURNAL ENTRY (SELF-AWARENESS AND GROWTH)

"Over the last few days, I have found that it takes time and efforts to build a trusting relationship. When people are nice to me, I am satisfied. But sometimes, I am considered too young for the work and not taken seriously. I get upset then. Also, the authorities are quite resistant to any kind of change that I propose. At the same time they also give me freedom to plan my work. I need to persevere and not give up so easily. Actually I am keen that they listen to my idea. I am very much interested in social work and making a difference. My supervisor has given me feedback that I need to improve my communication skills. Maybe I need to plan my points better and present them systematically before the authorities. Maybe I need to be more positive about my efforts".

Source: Adapted from a discussion on recording with a first year student social worker

---

Fieldwork recording assists in developing critical thinking as the learner is required to carefully assess the situation based on facts and not merely on opinions or subjective views. Critical thinking also means the ability to question certain taken-for-granted practices. For example, child marriage in many parts of the world is culturally accepted and even justified as a traditional social practice. To develop a perspective on the issue, the learner will need to examine all aspects of child marriage: Collect facts and figures, interact with the children or other persons connected with child marriage, understand the negative impact of child marriage especially on the child brides, analyse factors for child marriage and form a well-informed position before advocating for elimination of child marriage. Similarly, for example, if a learner wants to convince parents to send their children to school instead of child labour, the learner will first need to study the issue of child labour, assess approach of parents towards education, analyse societal apathy towards child labour and review livelihood options for poorer families. The learner thereafter can intervene at different levels (micro-meso-macro level) to effectively address the issue of child labour and write accordingly.

Fieldwork, a combination of tangible and non-tangible outcomes, is a multi-sensory experience. Through language and words, fieldwork recording is an expression of the learner about knowledge, perspective, feelings, verbal and non-verbal behaviour, insights and application of skills. It facilitates newer ways of understanding, thinking and behaviour. The following example (Illustration 6) narrates insights obtained through the recording process.

ILLUSTRATION 6 PROCESS RECORDING (INSIGHT AND SENSITIVITY)

"A male resident, aged 70 years, in a home for the destitute elderly always appeared cheerful and ready to help. He was an informal leader of the group and was given additional responsibilities by the authorities. He would regularly go the market and buy things on behalf of the other residents. Whenever I went to the home to do my fieldwork, he would be the first person to greet me and enquire about my studies. I started thinking about his family background and reasons for his admission into a home for the elderly. Later I was informed by the staff that he had lost his entire family of 17 members in a train accident. His family, comprising his wife, three children, parents, siblings, and other relations had gone to attend a wedding in another city. He had stayed back due to work. On the day of their return, he went to the railway station to receive them. While he was waiting at the station, there was an announcement that due to collision of two trains many passengers were grievously injured. He rushed to the site of the accident and found that his entire family was no more. After this shocking incident, he did not want to live any more. He had no interest in his work and began drinking heavily. After one year, he sought therapeutic care. He sold all his possessions and got himself admitted into the home to stay among people. He now tries his best to bring cheer into the lives of other elderly. He is also undergoing counselling and medication. Hearing about his life situation brought tears to my eyes. My respect for this person increased. We had been taught in class about trauma, coping and resilience. I think I now understand these terms better. I also need to read more about needs of the elderly".

Source: Adapted from a recording of a second year student social worker doing fieldwork in a home for the elderly

Beyond the written words: encouraging excellence in fieldwork writing

In a study by Ross and Ncube (2018), the findings indicate that the students mentioned report writing as "time-consuming, challenging, and exhausting" but also endorsed that it was an important skill that needed to be learned. Some of the students shared that "the experience is time-consuming but writing reports helps to look at the client in an objective manner" or "it was difficult the first time but through guidance I think I am getting much better" (p. 42). Ross and Ncube recommend that since report writing is a "signatory feature of the social work profession" students need to be equipped with both time management skills to complete their reports as per schedule as well as techniques to integrate theory with practice.

Nasreen and Singh (2018), undertook an in-depth study of two international social work students who were undergoing their social work training in India. While the focus of the study was to understand competency development at fieldwork and challenges experienced by international learners in a cross cultural setting, the findings indicate that competency development (which includes documentation and report writing skills) can be increased if all concerned stakeholders (learner, co-worker, supervisor, organisation, community etc.) work in coordination with one another.

Fieldwork recordings are individual recordings of each learner since the experience of each learner is unique and contextual to the fieldwork setting. The supervisor has a central role in the learner's journey of social work and self-discovery. Irrespective of whether the learner has an aptitude for writing, there is a higher likelihood of effective documentation when the learner recognises the scope and relevance of writing about fieldwork. Through discussion, inputs, motivation and feedback, the supervisor emphasises the purpose of fieldwork recording (see Figure 6.2) and nudges the learner towards optimal fieldwork and writing.

In this context, fieldwork records, reports, and other documentation are valuable to both the supervisor and the learner as ready reference about fieldwork. Different kinds of writing require differential skills. As early as 1975, Desai had appropriately noted: "In field work instruction the student's recording is an essential tool for formulating educational diagnosis of his capacities and limitations. It helps the supervisor to set realistic and achievable goals at each stage of the student's learning process within the broad framework of social work education. Through it the student is helped to identify, understand and accept his strength, limitations, develop meaningful skills etc. and integrate basic concepts in professional social work with field practice. He needs help to reflect in the records his growing sensitivity to persons, situations, goals and the process of working with people." (p. 346).

In the more recent study and analysis by Ross and Ncube (2018), a majority of the students mentioned that through supervision they also learned the skills of goal setting and report writing. Monitoring and feedback improve the quality and efficiency of writing. The details in the narration are also a tool for self-learning and

FIGURE 6.2 Purpose of fieldwork recording

Source: Author

discussion with the supervisor. The following example (Illustration 7) elucidates the use of recording as a supervisory tool to generate discussion around fieldwork.

ILLUSTRATION 7 (EXPANDING FIELDWORK SCOPE THROUGH SUPERVISORY DISCUSSION)

"I went to the state tribal welfare department to meet an official. I wanted to get some information about the welfare schemes for a particular tribal community. I was asked to wait. After waiting for nearly 45 minutes, I was able to meet the concerned officer. He was very busy and asked me whether I had any letter from my organisation. I did not have any such letter. He then asked me about my knowledge of the local tribes. I told him that I did not have much information. He then asked me about the purpose of getting information on welfare schemes. I told him that my organisation wanted these schemes to be accessed by the tribal community. He commented that although there are a lot of resources allocated for the tribal community, it is not being utilised properly. I kept quiet. He asked

> *me my opinion about it. I did not know what to say. He gave me the information. I returned to the organisation.*
>
> *I met my supervisor with the earlier recording. Using the recording as a starting point for discussion, my supervisor first appreciated that I had waited patiently for 45 minutes to meet the official and had not returned without obtaining the information. Rather, I had completed the task that was given to me by the organisation. My supervisor then asked me to reflect or think about the meeting. We had a wide ranging discussion about issues concerning the tribal community, and the role of the tribal welfare department. I was given additional information about tribes. My supervisor also gave me a feedback that henceforth I need to plan better for a meeting and do some reading. This will enable me to present my thoughts in discussion with others and improve my analytical skills as well."*
>
> Source: Adapted from a discussion on recording with a second year student social worker doing fieldwork in a community-based organisation.

The grading and evaluation of fieldwork is a challenging process as it attempts to quantify the student's learning and experience (both tangible and intangible outcomes) into a specific score or grade (Nigudkar, 2017). The fieldwork recordings are one of the parameters for assessment and evaluation as the recordings reflect the content of work undertaken, the learner's ability to integrate experiences, develop perspective on social issues and skill building for intervention. Managing the administrative aspects and logistics of recording is equally important. The supervisor steers the learner towards preparing a schedule for writing, organizing thoughts and material, understanding important terms/concepts, developing formats, scheduling a time for submission (manual/online) and receiving feedback from supervisor. These seemingly obvious area, are often neglected, resulting in inadequate or delayed submission of recording.

Each learner has their own learning style and preference for writing. Learners who are analytical, interested, sincere and skilled in writing are largely enthused about fieldwork recording. Some learners are excellent at fieldwork but do not write promptly. Others have an anxiety about their writing ability. For example, if a learner does not submit fieldwork recordings as per schedule, it could also mean that the learner requires suggestions on time management. Sometimes learners do not realise that they need to plan for the writing as well. The supervisor can guide the learner accordingly and actively structure the learner's work and schedule till the learner is able to do so independently. For example, if the learner is reluctant to write, the supervisor could discuss with the learner the reasons for the same. If the learner is not confident of the language, then supervisor could suggest some additional reading on improving language or writing skills and give small writing tasks to the learner. If the supervisor finds that the learner is dynamic at the field but "bored" of writing, the supervisor could engage in a verbal discussion first with the learner about fieldwork and then instruct the learner to prepare a short report on the supervisor-learner discussion. In all such situations, it is preferred that the supervisor assigns manageable writing tasks and gradually increases the level of complexity.

The supervisor's discerning and yet facilitative approach will encourage learners to improve themselves or enhance their skills. Whereas some learners prefer a free flowing unstructured narration or a critical essay, others may write better through a structured format with titles, sections and paragraphs. The supervisor's acceptance of different writing structures encourages learners to write unhindered. The supervisor will need to set aside their own personal preferences for a writing style and objectively assess the writing style of each individual learner and guide accordingly. Fieldwork recordings often reflect the learners' interest and level of commitment with the field. There can be a few learners who may project minimal work as substantive efforts. For example, minimal recording could indicate a lack of interest and motivation at fieldwork. In some instances the learner may possess superior writing skills and amplify more work than the actual task done. In some other situations the work itself may be repetitive or limited. The time sheet of the learner or an account of the time being utilised at fieldwork could provide the supervisor a cue about the type of work being assigned, management of time and extent of learner engagement. In all of these scenarios the supervisor will then need to take the cue from the recordings and focus more on increasing the learner's enthusiasm for fieldwork itself, or expand the scope of work rather than discuss only the content of recording. In a few situations lack of engagement with fieldwork recording could also reveal other reasons. For example, a learner may be preoccupied with extraneous stressors (money, interpersonal relationship, health, familial crisis, cultural difference), which impact fieldwork performance and recording. The supervisor will need to discuss with the learner about addressing the stressors to the extent possible, seek help, if required as well as guide the learner towards concrete tasks and different ways to focus better. To strengthen the quality of fieldwork recording, the following points may be of relevance to the supervisor:

- Recognise that each learner comes with their individual context and there could be different factors that affect fieldwork recording and documentation
- Objective discussion with the learner about the challenges in writing, if any
- Understand the learning style of each learner
- Periodic individual and group discussion with learners about definition of key concepts and terms relevant to fieldwork recording (such as process recording, reflection, empathy, empowerment, analysis, goal setting)
- Inputs on sourcing information and building knowledge
- Tips for improving study habits and time management
- Sustained encouragement and motivation to every individual learner
- Timely feedback with constructive suggestions
- Clear and unambiguous supervisory comments especially if the feedback mechanism is through distance and online mode only.

Conclusion

Any activity pertaining to social work entails planning, goal setting, implementing, fund raising, monitoring and evaluation. All of these processes necessitate systematic writing, reports and documentation. At fieldwork, the learner has an opportunity to learn about different dimensions of social work, including the skill of recording and documentation. Fieldwork would be considered incomplete without recording and documentation. Recording skills is not just useful for fieldwork but for the social work profession too, as writing is a powerful medium for communicating about social work, creating awareness, dissemination of knowledge and advocating for change.

References

Andrews, T. (2014). Exploring ways of strengthening fieldwork training in social work. *The Indian Journal of Social Work, 75*(3), 365–374.

Arora, V. (2006). Continuing engagement of fieldwork and the writing machine. *The Indian Journal of Social Work, 67*(12), 135–148.

Australian Learning and Teaching Council Ltd. (2010). A guide to supervision in social work field education. Retrieved January 8, 2018, from http://socialworksupervision.csu.edu.au/resources/docs/CSU-guide-social-work-field-education.pdf

Bar-On, A. (2001). When assumptions on fieldwork education fail to hold: The experience of Botswana. *Social Work Education, 20*(1), 123–136. doi:10.1080/02615470020028427 Retrieved April 10, 2019, from www.tandfonline.com/doi/pdf/10.1080/02615470020028427

Bodhi, S. R. (2012). Reassembling content and pedagogical processes in fieldwork supervision: Reflections from a critical social work episteme. *The Indian Journal of Dalit and Tribal Social Work, 1*(1), 113. Retrieved January 8, 2018, from www.ticijournals.org/reassembling-content-and-pedagogical-processes-in-fieldwork-supervision-reflections-from-a-critical-social-work-episteme/

California State University, Los Angeles School of Social Work. Educationally based process recordings. Retrieved January 8, 2018, from www.calstatela.edu/.../School%20of%Social%20Work/.../msw_1st_year_pro

Clifford, D. J. (1995). Methods in oral history and social work. *Journal of the Oral History Society, 23*(2), as cited in Burke B., Harrison P. (1998) *Anti-oppressive practice*. In: Adams R., Dominelli L., Payne M., Campling J. (eds) *Social Work*. Palgrave, London

Defazio, J., Jones, J., Tennant, F., & Hook, S. A. (2010). Academic literacy: The importance and impact of writing across the curriculum: A case study. *Journal of the Scholarship of Teaching and Learning, 10*(2), 34–47. Retrieved April 29, 2018, from https://files.eric.ed.gov/fulltext/EJ890711.pdf

Desai, K. T. (2013). Field practicum in social work education: Some reflections on the theory-practice relationship. *The Indian Journal of Social Work, 74*(34), 323–340.

Desai, M. M. (1975). Student recording in field work supervision. *The Indian Journal of Social Work, 35*(4), 345–352.

Devi Prasad, B., & Vijayalakshmi, B. (1997). Field instruction in social work education in India: Some issues. *The Indian Journal of Social Work, 58*(1), 65–77.

Farell, W. J. 1992. The Power of Writing. *Plymouth State College Journal on Writing Across the Curriculum,* 3 (2), 1-3. Retrieved on October 03, 2019 from https://wac.colostate.edu/docs/journal/vol3/vol3.2.pdf

Gangrade, K. D. (1975). School of social work: Field work agency liaison. *The Indian Journal of Social Work, 35*(4), 353–357.

Hampton, M. (n.d.). *Reflective writing: A basic introduction*. Retrieved April 21, 2018, from www.port.ac.uk/media/contacts-and-departments/student-support-services/ask/downloads/Reflective-writing – a-basic-introduction.pdf

Hyland, K. (2008). Writing theories and writing pedagogies. *Indonesian Journal of English Language Teaching, 4*(2), 91–110. Retrieved April 29, 2018, from www.researchgate.net/publication/288842506_Writing_theories_and_writing_pedagogies

Kapoor, J. M. (1961). The role of field work in modern social work education. *The Indian Journal of Social Work, 22*(2), 113–119.

Mailick, M. D. (1977). A situational perspective in casework theory. *Social Casework, 58,* 401–411. Cited from Fook, J. (2012). *Social work: A critical approach to practice* (2nd ed.). London: Sage Publications Ltd.

Mallick, A. (2007). Field work training in social work curriculum: Reflections on learning and teaching. *The Indian Journal of Social Work, 68*(4), 573–580.

Maurya, M. R. (1962). Field work training in social work. *The Indian Journal of Social Work, 23*(1), 9–14.

Mehta, V. D. (1975). Integrated methods approach: A challenging possibility in field work instruction. *The Indian Journal of Social Work, 35*(4), 335–344.

Mullaly, B. (2007). *The new structural social work* (3rd ed.). Canada: Oxford University Press.

Nasreen, A., & Singh, A. K. (2018). Competency development: Fieldwork for culturally diverse students. *The Indian Journal of Social Work, 79*(1), 55–63.

Nigudkar, M. (2017). Monitoring, assessment, and evaluation in fieldwork. Retrieved January 8, 2018, from http://epgp.inflibnet.ac.in/epgpdata/uploads/epgp_content/

Ross, E., & Ncube, M. (2018). Student social workers' experience of supervision. *The Indian Journal of Social Work, 79*(1), 31–53.

Thangavelu, R. (1975). Field work supervision: Its place in social work education. *The Indian Journal of Social Work, 35*(4), 53–65.

7
SUPERVISION USING CONFERENCES IN SOCIAL WORK PRACTICUM

Kalyani Talvelkar

Introduction

Fieldwork in social work is supervised by experienced faculty members or practitioners. The students are provided guided practice opportunities that enable students to acquire the requisite knowledge, skills and professional identity for professional social work practice (Rogers & McDonald, 1992). Conferences in the context of fieldwork refer to planned and regular periods of time the student and supervisor meet to discuss the student's work in the placement agency and review the learning process (Ford & Jones, 1987).

Conferences are mainly of two types – individual conference (IC) and group conference (GC). Individual conferences are meetings between individual students and their fieldwork supervisor, whereas group conferences are meetings between a group of students with their fieldwork supervisor. Though both types of conferences are mainly to discuss, review and plan fieldwork, the specific objectives of individual conference and group conference differ. While individual conferences where the discussions are one-to-one are important for sharing personal thoughts, anxieties and doubts, group conferences can make learning spontaneous and interesting with one idea sparking another

These regular meetings that are held to make sense of the fieldwork experience are the individual and group conferences. They provide a platform for discussion and feedback related to fieldwork. The participation in these conferences is crucial as they are a way of ensuring that learning takes place in the field. Conferences in fieldwork are important for students to:

- Demonstrate accountability for their fieldwork to the fieldwork supervisors
- Inculcate the habit of planned communication and interaction with team mates and supervisors (Wilson, in Cooper & Briggs, 2000).

The importance of conferences is also heightened because of the diverse educational background of student population pursuing Bachelor's or Master's degrees in social work. The graduate and post-graduate programmes in social work can be pursued by students from any stream in India. This means that students of social work are from many different educational backgrounds. In addition, one also finds diversity in terms of age and social backgrounds among students of social work. However, once they enter social work education, for all of them, the coursework begins along with the fieldwork practicum, leaving them little time to acclimatise themselves with the social work culture.

During fieldwork days, students are involved in the daily routine and on-going work of the agency. Additional learning opportunities are created either by the field contact or fieldwork supervisor for the students to get different kinds of practice experiences. The experiences and opportunities students get to learn during fieldwork also differ depending upon the nature of work of the agency and the setting in which it works. The fieldwork placement can be in a government organisation, non-government organisation, people's movements or projects run under Corporate Social Responsibility. The nature and type of fieldwork agency's interventions is determined by its focus area – health, education, livelihood, disability, gender issues, community development, governance, legal advocacy and so on.

While in the classroom, their doubts and questions can be responded to through debates and discussion, in fieldwork they are addressed in individual and group conferences. In these conferences, they would discuss and deliberate about a topic, understand and analyse situations and plan action/s. Conferences are also used to give and get feedback from the supervisor and for evaluation of a student's fieldwork. They give the supervisor opportunities to identify and discuss the learning needs of students. Thus, conferences in fieldwork are a platform for supervisors to:

- Provide support to the students in their immediate concerns
- Discuss surface and hidden implications of decisions and actions of clients/project participants and stakeholders and plan what stand or action the student would take
- Provide concurrent monitoring and assessment of fieldwork so that students can incorporate suggestions in fieldwork immediately
- Identify and consolidate learnings from field practice.

Two kinds of documents that form a basis of meaningful conferences are written reports or fieldwork recordings of students and the agenda prepared either by the supervisor or the student for the conference (Maidment, 2000; Mumm, 2006; Rogers & McDonald, 1995). In ICs, the fieldwork recordings of the student – process recording, case work reports, group work reports and community profiles – will determine the main points to be discussed in the conference. In addition to these, the student can also come prepared with additional agenda points (regarding future course of action or programme plan for instance) to be discussed during individual conference. In GCs, the agenda has to be prepared either by the students together or by the supervisor collating all the issues they need guidance on by the supervisor. Group conferences are rarely used for evaluating an individual student's performance.

Discussion and interaction during a conference is characterised by 'accountable talk', which is one of the features of signature pedagogies (Shulman, 2005). Accountable talk implies that there is a purposeful conversation, arguments in favour of or against a stand, perspective, course of action, data or facts provided to support these arguments and convincing commentary (ibid).

Thus, conferences, individual as well as group, are considered a vital part of the fieldwork process in social work and a critical component of the educational experience (Wijnberg & Schwartz, 1977; Panda & Nayak, 2012). The parallel processes of fieldwork supervision and practice often serve as a model for how social work practice should be conducted.

Stakeholders in fieldwork and conferences

One of the major tools that can be useful in conferences of fieldwork supervision is stakeholder analysis. Stakeholders are those who may be affected by or have an effect on an effort: in the case of social work practicum, it is the activities and interventions done by a social work student (Centre for Community Health and Development, 2018). Stakeholders can be divided into primary, secondary and key stakeholders and their interests might be varied (financial, social, academic, political) depending on how they affect or are affected by the effort or action by the social work student. There are many stakeholders in the whole process of fieldwork supervision; the most important of them being the student, fieldwork supervisor, agency or fieldwork placement, the client system or service users and the department/college of social work.

1   **Students**: Individual and group conferences are mainly for the students to be able to learn and contribute in fieldwork to the maximum extent possible. Therefore, student characteristics determine the importance and nature of conferences. Students apply for a Bachelor's degree in social work after junior college and Master's degree in social work after graduation in any stream in India. While the multi-disciplinary aspect of social work as a profession is fortified when students come from different backgrounds, it also means that students who come from streams such as science or commerce will find it difficult initially to understand the concepts and theories of social work, most of which have come from subjects like sociology, psychology and politics. This highlights the need for an orientation to social work as well as fieldwork to all the students before they start their practicum.

    In the social work practicum students come across disturbing situations as well as extraordinary resilience of people. They also see lived realities which are very different from their own and feel lost or overwhelmed. At such times, it is the supervisor who needs to play a crucial role in ensuring that they are asking questions when in doubt and expressing feelings and views to understand the context and people better.

2 **Supervisor:** When it comes to social work practicum or fieldwork, the supervisor cannot always be on the site to observe the student, therefore the supervision is done with the help of written and verbal records, fieldwork recordings, individual conferences and group conferences. It is through these 'tools' the supervisor maximises the learning opportunities of students within the context of the placement setting, provides guidance, ensures professional conduct of students, puts down certain guidelines both for the students as well as the agency to ensure safety of the students and monitors the progress of professional practice skills of the student.

Certain aspects of supervision differ when the supervision is by an agency supervisor that is a fieldwork supervisor who is a social worker or field practitioner in the agency, or a social work educator or a college faculty. This also has implications for the frequency and structure of conferences:

- Recognition of added workload of fieldwork supervision: There is a need to have a common understanding about what tasks and responsibilities are included in the role of the fieldwork supervisor. In India, the agency supervisors do not get financial remuneration for supervision. While most of the social workers or field practitioners willingly take on the duty to supervise fieldwork of social work students, it adds to an already heavy workload that they have. Though most of the agencies do recognise the need to devote time for fieldwork supervision, very rarely is it possible to reduce the other responsibilities of the agency supervisor so that they can devote separate structured time for supervision. This has implications for the structured schedule of conferences as well as planning and guiding fieldwork tasks.
- When a faculty member in the college supervises fieldwork of a student, on the other hand, it is recognised as part of their workload with the expectation that they would keep time aside to plan and guide fieldwork of students through individual and group conferences.
- Opportunities to share and obtain inputs from other supervisors: When colleges and departments of social work have a fieldwork manual or a policy document detailing the content and process of fieldwork, it acts as a guide or framework within which the student and fieldwork supervisor are expected to plan, implement, monitor and evaluate fieldwork. When such a manual or policy document is not available, the conferences, individual as well as group, are decided and determined by individual fieldwork supervisors. Absence of certain guidelines in terms of expected frequency and outcomes of conferences might lead to too much subjectivity in the practices followed by individual supervisors. Organising team or group meetings of faculty and fieldwork supervisors to discuss common parameters and evaluation criteria for fieldwork might reduce this

subjectivity and ambiguity about what is expected in terms of conferences from the supervisors.
- Fieldwork workshops or meetings arranged at the beginning of the fieldwork for agency supervisors as well as faculty supervisors might not be adequate to develop strategies to transform universal standards of supervision into practice due to unique characteristics and work demands of different settings and agencies, nor are they sufficient to plan proactively in case of different and difficult supervisory situations. This makes it challenging to supervise fieldwork as a social worker working in the agency.
- Structured schedule of conferences: Conferences – meeting the student individually or in a group with the agenda related to fieldwork is the main method of structuring and monitoring fieldwork or social work practicum. In any type of fieldwork, concurrent as well as block, it is imperative that the students get time and opportunity to discuss matters related to fieldwork with their supervisors. As mentioned earlier, the college or department of social work structures the conferences within its time table, whereas in case of agency supervisors, it is not a universal norm. In spite of difficulties, however, agency supervisors manage to structure at least a tentative schedule into their work routine to get feedback and update on the tasks assigned to fieldwork students and help them understand the field realities. Many times, the group conferences would also include other team members who are staff members in the agency in which students are placed for fieldwork. This also gives an opportunity to the students to have a simulated experience of staff meetings in an organisation.
- Ease of assigning tasks: One advantage of having the field professional or agency social worker supervising the students in social work practicum is that there is greater ease of identifying suitable tasks for the students in daily work of the agency. The agency supervisor, however, needs to ensure that the students have enough capacity and training to take up the assigned tasks. There is a risk of agency personnel giving the tasks that a professional would be able to do rather than a social work student and regular conferences with the students are also important to prevent such risks.
- Feasibility of parallel monitoring: When the supervision is done by the faculty member, the monitoring mainly happens during the structured individual and group conferences. On the other hand, when it is done by the social worker or field practitioner in the agency, there is a possibility of concurrent or continuous monitoring of the tasks and learning of the student. Conferences can also be commenced at times other than their structured timings if the situations demand it. When the supervision is done by the faculty member, this role of on-site monitoring is taken up by the field contact, but as their role is not of supervision, there might be limitations to which they can guide and review the work of the student. For instance, as field contact is not involved in teaching the theory to the

students, they might not be able to identify the tasks suitable or in sync with what the student is learning in the class. However, this limitation can be overcome by collaborative efforts by both the faculty supervisor and field contact.

Supervisors need to be proficient in practice; they also need to have certain abilities like ability to evaluate each student's learning needs, capacity to design a progression of learning experiences, skills to facilitate student centred learning, competency in different teaching strategies as well as ability to work with students with different capabilities and limitations.

3. **Fieldwork Placement**: Every aspect of human life – health, education, employment, housing, family life, political participation, recreation, natural environment, agriculture and food security, birth to childhood to old age to death – has opportunities and may need social work intervention. Therefore, the variety of fieldwork placements are also myriad for social work students. The placement can be in a government setting or it can be in a non-governmental organisation or in a corporate social responsibility project of a company. Students can also be placed in an 'open community', i.e. in a community setting where there is no agency working but the college wishes to start an intervention or social work project.

 With so much diversity in fieldwork placements, there is a huge difference also in what students will see, what they will do and, therefore, how their own learning and performance will have to be monitored and guided (Shulman, 2005). This is also one of the challenges for supervisors who might be supervising students in different fieldwork agencies or placements with different kinds of work, different learning styles of students and, therefore, different pedagogical models of practice.

4. **Client System**: People with whom social workers work are called clients or service users. A group of clients is usually called a client system. The members of a client system of an agency often share some common characteristics and therefore, the interventions also might share certain common features.

 Social Work is often divided into three broad practice categories: macro, mezzo, micro. Social work interventions at the macro level are on a large scale that affect entire communities and systems. Mezzo social work happens on an intermediate scale, involving neighbourhoods, institutions or other smaller groups. Micro social work is done at the level of an individual or family (Greene, 2008). As is the case with fieldwork placements, the diversity among client systems is also huge, even larger than the types of placements and the supervision process through its conferences needs to address the students' doubts and learning while working with this diversity.

5. **College or Department of Social Work**: Though there are certain universal standards of social work education, each college or department of social work will have its own fieldwork structure and rules and regulations. The supervisor,

through initial conferences, needs to clarify the college or department's specific rules and procedures related to fieldwork with the students; especially the first year students. Though initially it is the college or department that channels the fieldwork or social work practicum of students, it is not a one-way process. The students also contribute further to strengthen the fieldwork practice of the college or department by bringing in critical thinking, creativity, innovative interventions and identification of new areas or needs for intervention.

Individual conference

Individual conference, a meeting between the social work student and their fieldwork supervisor, is set on specific days and timings in a week or fortnight or a month (depending on the rules and process guidelines of fieldwork of the respective college or department of social work) and is an important process to facilitate learning in and from real life interactions and issues of communities, families, agencies and clients. It channels the students' experiential learning, under the guidance and supervision of experienced social work educators/practitioners in the context of field realities, specific requirements of the college or department of social work, fieldwork agency and the broader framework of social work profession (Cooper & Briggs, 2000).

Individual conferences are vital for both students who have come to the course with some work experience as well as students who are completely new to the social work profession. Experienced or older students need help from the supervisor to cope with the academic or practical learning because they might have come out of their 'student phase', whereas younger students lack the life experiences needed to understand social realities, especially those very different from theirs, and engage with clients in social work.

Fieldwork of a student has three phases based on both process and expected outcomes. The content and process of conferences also changes accordingly. The beginning stage of fieldwork has three clearly identified phases: Planning, building the relationship and clarifying expectations. Middle stage is characterised by consolidation of relationship and goal driven interventions. Closure and final evaluation happen in the final stage of fieldwork. The main content and objectives of each phase also change accordingly. In the middle stage, field educators are expected to consolidate the relationship and take account of issues of oppression. The final stage involves closure and final evaluation (Cooper & Briggs, 2000; Subhedar, 2001).

Initial phase or first phase of fieldwork

The conferences immediately after the beginning of the fieldwork serve to resolve many doubts and questions that the students have about fieldwork, the agency they are placed in and what they are supposed to do. The excerpt of an individual conference shows one of the many ways in which the first few individual conferences would go:

EXCERPTS FROM A TRANSCRIPT OF FIRST INDIVIDUAL CONFERENCE (IC)

SUPERVISOR: The main objective of this IC is to understand from you how your first week of fieldwork has been, your first impressions about the agency, the agency's work and the people with whom the agency works.

STUDENT: It has been a mixed beginning. We reached the agency on time. The social worker was waiting for us and she welcomed us on our first day there. She first introduced herself and then she asked us to introduce ourselves.

SUPERVISOR: Who else were present at the time of introductions? Besides you, your co-students and the social worker.

STUDENT: She called two of the fieldworkers also. The introductions took place in her office. With all of us in there, it was rather crowded. But introductions went fine. She has been working in the organisation for the last 17 years. She was smiling and relaxed while talking. It was not a very formal interaction. Helped me to relax. The fieldworkers – Asha didi and Shabana didi – were also welcoming. They have been working in the agency since the time the agency started. That is more than 25 years! They seem to be well respected by everyone in the agency, including the social worker. Then we all introduced ourselves. She asked whether we had any previous experience in social work. I shared about my experience as a volunteer.

SUPERVISOR: Was your first day as a volunteer in a social work organisation different than your first day as a social work student?

STUDENT: Yes.

SUPERVISOR: How?

STUDENT: First, when I had gone as a volunteer, I did not know much about social work. Now I have some basic information about it. So my expectations from myself – what I would do and learn – are also different. Second, as a social work student, my focus is on learning as much as I can. So I learnt much more as a student of social work on my first day compared to what I had learnt as a volunteer.

SUPERVISOR: What are the most important things that you learnt during your first week of fieldwork? Would you like to share that?

STUDENT: I learnt that the organisation started in 1995 in a very small way. The founder, Ms. Rebecca, had observed that there are many problems in that slum community. As she felt that the priority was health problems as child mortality was quite high in that society, she decided to start with that. She already had built rapport with a group of women who attended the same church that she used to go to and resided in the same community. She

> approached them with the idea of nutrition and health programmes for the children and women were more than happy to help her by connecting her to the other women in the community. Initially, they had to struggle for funding. But they persisted. Health camps were organised regularly. Nutrition awareness programmes were conducted and the organisation started supplementary nutrition programmes for children.
> SUPERVISOR: And what are the programmes that the organisation is implementing at present?
> STUDENT: Oh . . . they have expanded a lot – both in terms of programmes as well as other communities where there was need. Now they are working for child and mother health, they have a counselling centre, they are working with adolescent girls on education and vocational training along with health. The organisation has also started interventions for the senior citizen in the community.
> SUPERVISOR: Were you informed of the programme or interventions in which you would be involved?
> STUDENT: Not yet. She said that for the first month, we will get orientation to all their programmes and centres and then the tasks will be allocated. Actually, that is why I said it was a mixed kind of beginning. I am a little overwhelmed by the amount of work the agency does and also not a little anxious about what would be expected from me.
> (Names in the transcript have been changed for confidentiality)

The earlier excerpt highlights the need of the student to get clear information about what the agency does and the nature and extent of student contribution (and learning) expected.

Thus, the content and objectives of individual conference in the first phase of fieldwork consist of:

1 **Establishing learning objectives and activities**: The fieldwork supervisor must be able to provide students with performance expectations and collaborate with students in establishing learning objectives and activities. ICs in this phase also help the students to gain an insight into their own motivations for training to be a professional social worker. Some students will look at fieldwork as a testing ground to gauge whether that is what they would like to do as a career; some might have come to social work as they have been helped by social workers or social work organisations and want to now help others just as they have been helped and some others might have come with a definite stand on the concepts of social justice and injustice and have a political commitment to change the world for the better (Beddoe, in Cooper & Briggs, 2000).

Individual conferences are crucial for all the students as these motivations are many times latent or not perceived clearly by the students, but they do influence the way they approach the learning tasks (Boud & Walker, 1990). To bring this into their awareness helps them to set targets for their fieldwork based on what they want at present from their social work practicum and how they wish to practice in the future.

2 **Facilitating students to enhance their self-awareness**: Students of social work, as mentioned earlier, come to their fieldwork experiences with an extensive range of prior personal, social and political experiences that impact what they learn and how they approach the task of learning. The students might or might not be aware of this impact. One of the major objectives of individual conference, especially in the initial phase of fieldwork, is assisting students to understand how their subjective experiences and socialisation are impacting their perspective and practice through self-awareness using the strategy and process of individual conferencing (Beddoe, in Cooper & Briggs, 2000).

3 The nature of the field placement/agency and the social problem(s) that the organisation attempts to address: Agency environment; social, political and economic impacts; fieldwork experience of the students in terms of availability of learning and doing opportunities and extent and quality of on-site guidance and network/collaborations with external agencies and stakeholders (Boud & Walker, 1990). Conferences during this time should provide guidance to students to understand the history and context of the organisation, its vision and mission, programmes, operations and the goals and objectives of the organisation's social service delivery system. The conferences and recordings should also cover topics such as organisational structure, types of personnel employed, leadership, the strengths and needs of the client system being served by the agency, problems handled, sources and funding (Subhedar, 2001).

4 **Teamwork and establishing group norms**: The fieldwork supervisor has to facilitate three different types of teams – students placed with the same fieldwork agency, students placed in different agencies but under the same supervisor and multi-disciplinary teams at the agency of which the student is a part, at least for the duration of their fieldwork. Discussing what each student in the group feels about certain rules and norms is very important at the beginning of fieldwork. This clarifies the expectations of students from each other and from the supervisor as well as from the team as a whole.

Middle phase of fieldwork and individual conference

Once the student is 'settled' in fieldwork, i.e. they have obtained a clarity of what and how they would contribute in the agency's work and learn in the process, they start planning concrete action plans with the help of the supervisor during conferences.

The main content and objectives of the individual conference in the middle phase of fieldwork:

1 **Plan fieldwork interventions and activities**: Ability to facilitate planning, which is rational in diverse and complex contexts is very crucial for a fieldwork supervisor to have. Depending on the agency profile (its vision, objectives, client system and programmes) and also what the agency management thinks are appropriate tasks, fieldwork is planned with the help of the fieldwork supervisor. The supervisor, in collaboration with the agency, should try to the extent possible to plan activities and interventions that would help the student hone different skills and develop proficiency over application of different methods of social work, casework, group work, community work, agency administration and research.

Fieldwork planning in individual conference needs to include six components as given in Figure 7.1.

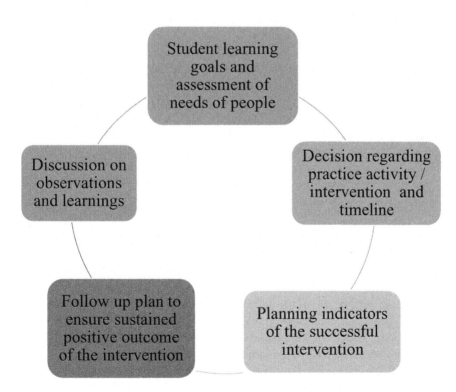

FIGURE 7.1 Components of fieldwork planning

Source: Adapted from Hadgson & Walford, 2007 *Basic components of a learning plan*

A learning plan, including that related to fieldwork, needs to encompass all three dimensions of knowledge, values and skills of the social work profession (Garthwait, 2005 in Hodgson & Walford, 2007). Individual conference helps the student to integrate theory and practice through facilitating four processes (Bogo & Vayda, 1987):

- Retrieval (of observations and learnings during fieldwork as well as classroom teaching)
- Reflection (of choices made, progress made in fieldwork, on knowledge gained, values and attitudinal assumptions made)
- Linkage (fieldwork experiences and observations to relevant theoretical literature) and
- Decision making (about future plans).

2 **Review of the fieldwork**: Review and suggestions for improvement in fieldwork performance continues throughout their fieldwork experience but in the middle phase it is important to ensure timely and need-based planning of interventions and learning experiences. The fieldwork supervisor can also explore autonomy and dependence of the student on the supervisor during this phase.

Fieldwork supervisors can also suggest to the students to read and analyse laws and government programmes relevant to their fieldwork, i.e. relevant to the client groups the agency is working with or relevant to the work of the agency. Individual conferences play an important role in helping students understand how such knowledge would help them in fieldwork.

The excerpt given shows one of the ways in which a supervisor can facilitate this process in individual conference:

SUPERVISOR: Good afternoon! Have you brought the agenda for today's conference?

STUDENT: Yes, ma'am. Today's agenda is to learn how to make 'sense' of the laws relevant to my fieldwork and how to use it in fieldwork.

SUPERVISOR: So . . . have you found out which are the laws which are relevant to your fieldwork?

STUDENT: Yes, ma'am. As the organisation is working on the issue of disability organisation, I feel disability legislations are very relevant to my fieldwork. I have, in fact, obtained copies of both – Persons with Disability Act, 1995 as well as the Rights of Persons with Disabilities Act, 2016.

SUPERVISOR: Very good. Have you started reading them? You should also try to analyse it after reading it.

STUDENT: I am finding it difficult to comprehend and also a little boring because of the legal language.

SUPERVISOR: Yes, sometimes it does become too verbose, but it helps if you formulate a framework of a few questions before reading it. This framework will provide you a focus and it will make reading interesting because you are trying to find answers to the questions in that legal text and not reading it aimlessly.

STUDENT: What kind of questions?

SUPERVISOR: For instance, which are the bodies constituted to implement the Persons with Disabilities (Equal Opportunities, Protection of Rights and Full Participation) Act, 1995? Do you feel the title of the Act is well justified by the provisions given in the Act? Is the Act powerful enough, i.e. does it include strong measures or punitive actions against those who violate the provisions given in the Act? Also, as you have got copies of both the disability legislations – one passed in 1995 as well as the recent Act passed in 2016 – you can compare the two. What are the additions and modifications suggested in the Rights of Persons with Disabilities Act, 2016 which are not there in the earlier Act?

STUDENT: Okay. Can you explain how such laws can also be made useful in fieldwork?

SUPERVISOR: Law plays a number of important roles in the practice of social work. As you must have learnt ecological perspective, you would know that the legal system is a vital part of a client's social environment. For some of the clients, it becomes obvious only when problems surface. For instance, it is only when a child might be denied admission into the school because of their disability, you would need to take recourse of either disability legislation or Right to Education Act to ensure their admission. The knowledge of Sarva Shiksha Abhiyan would also prove useful. Second, analysis of the Act and its implementation would also help you to identify loopholes or weaknesses in the Act after comparing its 'goodness of fit' to the socio-economic contexts of the people with whom you are working. Third, organisations such as hospitals, schools and civil society organisations such as the one in which you are placed are also regulated by these laws. Social workers need to understand these laws in order to ensure that their agency complys with these laws.

STUDENT: Thank you ma'am for clarifying the role of laws. I was finding it difficult to understand as I am an outsider to the agency and so also a stranger to its functioning, at least at present. I have the decision making power regarding my own fieldwork, but it is not absolute. Decision needs to be taken in conjunction/discussion with all the other stakeholders who would be directly/indirectly involved in the process or would be affected by it or both. The decision is never made by one person. So it is an important lesson that along with other stakeholders, legal framework also influences the decision making or policy making in an organisation.

Fieldwork supervisors need to focus on all three areas – thinking, feeling and doing – of the student related to fieldwork and point out if there are inconsistencies between these three. This is especially important as learning occurs when these three areas of response are seen as congruent. According to Tomm (1988, quoted in Cooper & Briggs, 2000) fieldwork supervisors can apply four styles of questions during conferences to achieve the previously mentioned goals:

- Lineal questions that elicit information about situations in the field as well as questions related to the student's actions and observations. Examples of lineal questions are 'Can you explain the problem you plan to work on with the client to me?' or 'What difficulties are you having while assessing the needs of the community?'
- Circular questions, as the name suggests, link the people, ideas, feelings and beliefs. For instance, 'How do the others respond when he becomes aggressive during meetings?' or 'What happened when you confronted the government official for not taking any action?'
- Strategic questions are questions that ensure students are on the right track in fieldwork and that all the necessary components of fieldwork are fulfilled. For instance, 'When are you going to submit the community profile?' or 'Are you completing the tasks as per plan?'
- Reflexive questions facilitate students' learnings from the practicum as well as move ahead in their field interventions. For instance, 'Who do you think can provide support to the client from their informal network?' or 'Which strategies you feel would ensure success of this programme?'

3 **Explore environmental stressors**: Social work is a stressful profession. The work environment of social workers is often characterised by poverty, deprivation, violence and/or conflicts (Lewin, 1948). As stakeholder analysis is an important content component of individual conference, so is the external environmental analysis. Exploring environmental stressors with students also helps him/her to plan for any eventualities (Madsen, 2012).

The face-to-face interactions that social work students have to do with service users/clients require empathy and sensitivity to their emotions and situations which might put tremendous demands on the patience and overall mental health of the students. During the individual conference, the supervisor needs to identify the effects of environmental stressors on the student and help them deal with it positively.

4 **Counselling**: As fieldwork progresses, learning new skills, practices and tasks can be overwhelming for the students. Individual conferences also help students when they are struggling in an unfamiliar environment with demanding work schedules and expected outcomes and balancing the academic assignments and fieldwork action plans. As fieldwork progresses, students realise that learning practice is more than mere application of social work theories taught in the class (Cooper & Briggs, 2000). The fieldwork supervisor can identify

if any kind of transference or counter-transference is occurring between the social work student and the client and discuss it in the individual conference.
5   **Conflict resolution and troubleshooting**: The Supervisor needs to be an effective communicator who is able to resolve conflict and get students to open up, use a variety of supervisory strategies, and collaborate with the student and academic fieldwork coordinator if the student experiences difficulty.

The second phase of individual as well as group conferencing also includes two important functions of the supervisor: Providing information and giving encouragement as well as reassurance. Information can be provided through various techniques such as paraphrasing (to ensure that the student's experiences and observations have been understood the way they were meant to be), offering a range of reasons for the situation as it exists or progresses (to ensure the student develops analytical skills) and providing knowledge (about various relevant policies, programmes and interventions of other NGOs).

Closing or termination phase of fieldwork and individual conference

In fieldwork, the 'ending' or 'closing' is as important as the 'beginning' because social work is a human service profession and change oriented relationships need to be managed properly in order to achieve its objectives. The main content and objectives of individual conference in the closing or termination phase of fieldwork consist of:

1   **Tie loose ends in interactions and interventions**: Students may have started different types of interactions – formal, informal – with different stakeholders during fieldwork and during the last phase of fieldwork; they need to give these interactions and interventions a meaningful fruition. This conclusion might not be final as the student or others may plan to continue to be in touch even after the last date of fieldwork. However, it is important for the supervisor to ensure that the student informs everyone concerned of the last day of fieldwork as it signals the end of formal relationships in the fieldwork context.

    Monitoring in the last phase becomes outcome oriented and picks up the pace so that the planned indicators of successful completion of interventions are met by the student.

2   **Inputs on preparing clients for the student's departure from the fieldwork agency**: The supervisor needs to give guidance to students during conferences on informing the agency and clients well in advance about conclusion of their fieldwork. The termination phase also highlights the supervisor's role in guiding students to discuss with their client/s, individuals or groups or communities how to anticipate and resolve future problems and how to find additional resources. The individual conference during this phase will also address issues related to transference or counter-transference and documentation of the whole year's fieldwork learning.

A final review and assessment meeting is many times planned with the agency personnel. The final session has to be conducted face-to-face with the agency personnel (and sometimes with clients or service users) rather than an email, a phone call or message.

3 **Final assessment and evaluation**: One of the important aspects of supervisory process is assessing student's readiness to progress to the next stage of their professional training or enter the workforce. It is also perhaps the most difficult and conflict ridden area of professional education that is conducted during individual conferences.

Discussing and reaching consensus during individual and group conferences regarding the standards for fieldwork and students' assessment is essential to prevent future misunderstandings and complaints (Cooper, 1994). Such discussion ensures clarity around what is assessed, how it is assessed and the criteria against which the student's performance is judged. The assessment process is based on a clear set of principles and, most importantly, evidence of performance (ibid).

Regular feedback to the students during the whole process of fieldwork helps to make this assessment meaningful and fair to the student. The way evaluation and assessment are conducted by the fieldwork supervisor during conferences also provides opportunity to the student to learn the skills of receiving and managing feedback.

Group conference

Individual conference has been a primary model for teaching and learning in fieldwork for a considerable period of time in the history of social work education. However, group conference emerged as a strong alternative or additional strategy to enhance student learning in the complex social work environment (Maywald, in Cooper & Briggs, 2000). Group conference is a meeting between fieldwork supervisor and the group of students who are under his/her supervision on a regular basis during the course of their fieldwork.

The main purpose of the group conference is similar to that of individual conference, providing guidance and review of students' work and learnings, but in addition to this, it also serves many purposes unique to it being supervision in a 'group' (Panda & Nayak, 2012; Valentino, LeBlanc, & Sellers, 2016):

- Group conference allows much more for the task-centred planning of fieldwork as many more and different kinds of suggestions pour in from the other members of the group, leading to new ideas and help in bringing them together.
- Group conference has the scope of peer feedback and review.
- The student gets first hand opportunity to experience and deal constructively with group dynamics and develop interpersonal skills.
- Group conference has the scope of creating a safe and creative environment for students to brainstorm on new and novel solutions or ideas.

- Students can discover opportunities for collaborating with their peers placed in other agencies for fieldwork programmes or interventions.
- Group conference provides an economical use of the fieldwork supervisor's time.

There have been specific models of group supervision proposed by social work educators and theorists which govern the nature and process of group conference. Kadushin (1985, in Cooper & Briggs, 2000) adapted his model for individual supervision for group supervision with emphasis on the supervisor's role in administration, education and support (Tebb & Kalumann, 1996). Some of the prominent models/theories that guide group supervision or instruction are given in Figure 7.2.

Group conference can have different types of compositions:

1 All the students placed in different types of organisations but under the same fieldwork supervisor participate in the group conference.
2 Students who are engaged in similar fields of practice but not necessarily the same organisation are called together for the group conference.
3 Students who are placed in the same agency participate in the group conference.

Each type of composition has both advantages and disadvantages. The advantage in conferencing with students from different types of organisations is that they learn about varied issues, client systems and interventions, but sometimes the discussion may become too scattered or fragmented for the supervisor to identify similarities and differences in the settings and corresponding strategies. It might become difficult to consolidate learnings, too.

Organising a conference with students placed in the same or similar agencies has advantage in that students learn how same or similar issues can be responded to in different ways, through different programmes. There would be more scope of comparison and learning best practices. However, sometimes the information

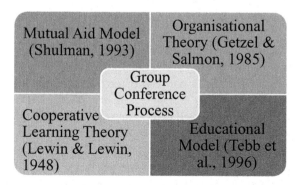

FIGURE 7.2 Models/theories that guide group supervision and group conference

Source: Author

144 Kalyani Talvelkar

shared might seem repetitive or focused on one or two issues on which the fieldwork agencies are working.

The process of group conference

The phases of fieldwork are not as sharply represented in group conferences as they are in individual conferences, though they follow a similar pattern. The first few group conferences would cover the introduction of members, i.e. students and agencies, laying down group norms and protocols and expressing learning expectations from fieldwork. It is a good practice to outline the fieldwork objectives and assessment criteria during the first few group conferences so that students can plan their fieldwork accordingly.

As fieldwork progresses, group conferences become more focused on planned interventions, issues and problems of the vulnerable groups with which the agencies are working; the fieldwork agency's vision; programmes and structure as well as linkages between practice and theory taught in the class. Group dynamics will emerge (Panda & Nayak, 2012). Though group conference might start with a clear agenda, issues might crop up during the conference which the supervisor needs to address. The excerpt of a group conference shows the way it can be used to obtain suggestions on the planned interventions/activities, resolve conflicts and obtain consensus on certain group norms.

TRANSCRIPT OF A GROUP CONFERENCE

SUPERVISOR: Okay. Well, I think we should start as only two more students are yet to join us. They have just messaged me that they are on the way and would reach here in 15 minutes.

SHINY: Yes, ma'am. We can start. Even last time, they were late.

SUPERVISOR: Hmm . . . probably once they come, we can discuss this with them. Let's first hear from them if they have any valid reason for being late.

SHABNAM: Yes, let's not jump to conclusions.

SHINY: I was not jumping to conclusions. It is a fact that they are always late.

SUPERVISOR: Okay. As I said, it is a valid concern and we can discuss it afterwards in the group. Let's start with an update of your work so far in the agency. As you all are placed in three different organisations, it would be interesting and helpful for all of us to know what each one is doing.

SHABNAM: May I and my co-student, Ajit, start first?

SUPERVISOR: Go ahead.

SHABNAM: We two are placed in the centre of the organisation. They have a school and self-help groups (SHGs) of women there with whom we work.

AJIT: We arrive by 9.00 am as that is the time the school starts. It has both primary and secondary sections.

SHABNAM: Initially when we started we were a little frustrated as the structured activities of the school left very little time for us to do anything else.

AJIT: However, after discussing it with you, we decided to start helping the children in their studies. This helped in getting opportunities to interact with the students. While chatting with them, we identified a major issue of bullying.

SUPERVISOR: Yes, you discussed these with me . . . Did you read on buddy programmes worldwide for prevention of bullying?

SHABNAM: Yes. We read and felt that it would be very relevant for this group also. Especially for street children, creating a support system through friends seems a good idea. We have written a concept note with the programme objectives and outline. We would like you to give your feedback on it.

SUPERVISOR: Okay. I will do that.(Two students enter the office where the group conference is taking place.)

SUPERVISOR: Come Maya and Sunaina. We started the group conference without you as you were late. We are listening to what all you students have been doing in fieldwork so far. Ajit and Shabnam were sharing their fieldwork experiences. (to Ajit and Shabnam) So . . . what are your immediate plans?

AJIT: At present, we have planned a few recreational activities with children, after which we are going to plan a session on friendship. We will also discuss individually with students to get to know more about them and their lives. We have attended a few meetings of the self-help groups.

SHINY: We two are working with self-help groups of women in the tribal *padas* where we are placed. Our work consists of facilitating work of the SHGs and registering new SHGs.

JASMIT: Actually, we are facing a few difficulties there as nearly all women in the tribal *padas* are illiterate. So they rely on the fieldworker of the organisation to update the registers. That is the main hurdle.

SUPERVISOR: Hmm . . . actually, during the first meeting the social worker of the organisation had commented on the illiteracy and influence of superstitions among people in these *padas* . . . remember? Have you thought of probable solutions or interventions that would address this issue?

JASMIT: Yes, ma'am. The fieldworker actually suggested the idea of starting a literacy class with these women. But these women are working the whole day in the fields.

SUPERVISOR: Can anyone in the group give any suggestions for this problem?

MAYA: (Addressing Shiny and Jasmit) You will have to sit with them at night, after their daily work is over. When I was placed in rural placement last year, that is what we used to do.

JASMIT: Yes, that's true. We thought of that. But the problem is we don't stay at the tribal *pada*. We stay at the girl students' hostel of the organisation which is at a village nearly 20 kms from these tribal *padas* and there are no buses that are from there to these tribal *padas* even during day time. We travel by jeeps which take money per seat. And it is very dangerous to travel after 7.00 pm in these areas.

SUPERVISOR: What are the other options? Can you stay at the tribal *pada* in someone's house?

SHINY: That might be a possibility. The people there are welcoming and we can pay for our stay. But we will have to check with the fieldworker.

SUPERVISOR: Yes, there are many considerations before such a decision can be made – financial, safety and cultural. Please fix a meeting with the fieldworker and social worker to discuss this issue. I would also come for the meeting.

JASMIT: Yes, ma'am.

SUPERVISOR: Now only Maya and Sunaina's sharing remains. But before that, we would like to know why you two were late.

MAYA: Ma'am, actually we had planned a session at the agency today and it concluded later than planned.

SUNAINA: Yes ma'am. Actually people started coming after only 12.00 pm . . . We couldn't leave sooner as we were the main planners of today's health camp.

SHINY: Last time also you were late.

MAYA: No, we were not late last time.

SHINY: Yes, you were. We had waited for nearly 20 minutes for you two to start the G.C. Remember?

SUPERVISOR: The reason you two gave last time was that the trains were running late.

MAYA: Ma'am, sorry. We will be on time next time.

SUPERVISOR: Our plans need to take into consideration all these factors so that we can be punctual. Some things are not in our control – like a traffic jam or trains being late. But if we decide on the time we need to leave to reach a place taking into consideration these possibilities, it helps. Probably it was not a good idea to plan a health camp this morning if we had G.C. planned for this afternoon. Or you can share your programme plans in the group much in advance so that group conference can be planned accordingly. And this is not only for you two. This is for the whole group. If we are even 5 minutes late, you are wasting not only 5 minutes, you are wasting 5 minutes of each person in the group who had arrived on time. For this group, it means, 25 minutes.

SUNAINA: Yes, ma'am. We will keep this in mind.

JASMIT: Yes, ma'am.

> SUPERVISOR: Does anyone want to add or reiterate any group norm?
> AJIT: Ma'am, I would also like to emphasize the principle of confidentiality of whatever is discussed during this group conference. Whatever we discuss in G.C., should not be told or discussed with anyone outside this group, except perhaps with field contact with whom we need to collaborate in fieldwork.
> (Names in the transcript have been changed for confidentiality)

It is important that the supervisor ensures that all students participate openly and meaningfully during group conferences to maximise the benefits of cooperative learning. In group conference, there are certain ethical guidelines that have to be followed such as confidentiality, accountability and non-judgmental attitude.

Group conference should be a process that encourages collaboration, debate, dialogue and reflection. The fieldwork supervisor can plan specific activities or tasks for the students to do during group conference to give structured learning opportunities to fieldwork students (Getzel & Salmon, 1985; Fernandez, 1997).

Maywald (in Cooper & Briggs, 2000) has given a number of strategies and activities for group conference such as:

- Giving information about the organisation, resources and policy developments
- Case presentations and discussions
- Didactic presentations on theory
- Brainstorming on a particular difficult problem faced in the fieldwork agency
- Identifying ethical dilemmas in practice and discussing possible courses of action in a group
- Sharing stories and listening to others
- Role playing different situations related to fieldwork
- Discussing possibilities of collaborations across fieldwork agencies.

The learning that occurs in group conference is not only from supervisor to the students but also peer to peer. It offers a safe environment for the students to express their views and difficulties and learn from others' experiences. Group conference, when ably moderated and managed by supervisor as well as students, facilitates development of certain skills and qualities in students such as:

- Leadership skills
- Commitment to group processes by allowing others to talk, respecting different views, listening to each individual's contribution
- Sharing ideas and opinions
- Asking for clarification
- Paraphrasing

- Probing and questioning
- Describing feelings
- Guiding, offering suggestions
- Empathising
- Conflict management.

Group conferences can also be used to give opportunities to students to share roles within the group, thus learning and practising different roles as leaders, mediators, planners and minute-takers. Group conference is an active process of students' learning about team work and professional social work practice.

Challenges and dilemmas

Individual and group conferences are the most important processes as well as strategies to ensure quality fieldwork learning of the students. Though they are well structured and supported by the framework of fieldwork policy, sometimes the supervisor has to face challenges and resolve dilemmas that emerge in either planning (and conducting) a conference or during the sharing in the conference. Some of the common difficulties or challenges are:

1. Differences in the social/cultural backgrounds: Indigenous students struggle with agency values and beliefs that differ from their cultural orientation. The fieldwork supervisor needs to have the necessary counselling and moderation skills to ensure open and free expression of their feelings and anxieties. Within the group, there might emerge negative dynamics based on class, caste, cultural or linguistic differences which need to be dealt with by the supervisor before it escalates into hostility or other negative effects.
2. Ethical dilemmas: Students of social work soon discover in their fieldwork that seldom are there clear cut right or wrong answers for any situation in the field. They will need to use a plethora of approaches, all of which are acceptable, but none give a completely satisfying solution.
3. Work load: Fieldwork supervisors or educators may be busy with additional work and unintentionally neglect the students and their need for guidance and support. Conferences, if not conducted for a long period of time, lose their effectiveness in providing learning opportunities, improving fieldwork performance and building team work among students.
4. Difficulties to get sufficient guidance or work at the agency: Some novice students may not receive an adequate orientation by the fieldwork agency. Some students may be given too little work. Sometimes, as most of the agencies are shorthanded, they forget that students are *in training* to be a professional social worker and use them as an extra pair of hands, thus providing little mentoring or administrative support. Such a situation generally occurs with the students who have prior experience in voluntary work and who themselves also tend to welcome being regarded as one of the staff members of the agency.

5 Assessment and evaluation during individual conferences can be difficult if the performance standards were not made clear to the students in the beginning of fieldwork or when students do not make use of conferences to understand and review their work. Generally, the relationship between a fieldwork supervisor and student relies on the development of trust as a way of negotiating these structural issues. Potential conflicts become more overt when a student is seen as marginal between a pass and fail, or when the relationship between student and fieldwork supervisor become strained.
6 Balance between guidance and fostering self-reliance: One challenge the supervisor might face, especially with new students, is balancing the student's need for constant guidance and importance of giving the student opportunity to find out their own answers. Talking too much during the conferences can either result in the student not learning self-reliance or getting bored.

Ensuring quality of supervision through conferences

Fieldwork in any discipline, including social work, needs supervision that would ensure:

1 Knowledge acquisition
2 Development of critical reasoning
3 Development of interpersonal skills
4 Building a skills repertoire for performance in the field
5 Inculcating professional ethical code of practice and conduct.

Fieldwork supervisors should be able to balance student learning needs with the needs of the social work agencies to deliver a service or programme, implement a policy or initiate an advocacy campaign. There are three levels of learning interactions (Gardiner, 1989, in Cooper & Briggs, 2000) during conferences:

1 Content of learning
2 Process of learning
3 Learning to learn.

Learning happens best when the student's thinking, feeling and doing are in sync with each other. Conferences should offer enough opportunities for the student to explore all dimensions over time. Adequate work needs to be given to students on which to base feedback. One of the most important conditions for satisfactory fieldwork performance is maintaining regular contact with the students throughout fieldwork through conferences.

The qualities of the supervisor for quality interaction during conferences and their effectiveness to bring about desired results are:

- Genuineness
- Capacity for growth

- Courage
- Sense of humour
- Respect
- Professional expertise.

Supervisor needs to role model the following competences for the conferences to be effective and efficient strategies for achieving the objectives of fieldwork supervision:

- Relevant knowledge and information: The way supervisors conduct conferences and guide students reflects the extent of knowledge and information they have. Conferences are also platforms on which the transfer of knowledge happens. It is important that the supervisor is knowledgeable about different learning styles so that they can formulate such activities or assignments during conferences that would maximise the student's learning from fieldwork.
- Critical reasoning: The supervisor should be acquainted with theories and literature not only on fieldwork but also on the social work methods and strategies used by the fieldwork agencies. This would ensure that the students get enough guidance to integrate and apply theory to practice.
- Interpersonal skills: Students learn from the way interactions are facilitated and managed during conferences, how to establish rapport, reflect acceptance of diversity and differences, identify one's own and others' strengths as well as areas for improvement and how to resolve any interpersonal conflicts that may develop.
- Practice skills: During conferences, students ask for guidance for helping the clients in the resolution of a particular problem, dealing with group dynamics, working with a government agency or any other challenge that social workers face in their daily work. The supervisors need to give either helpful suggestions based on their own experience as practitioners or direct them to other people or resources which would be helpful to them.
- Ethical reasoning: As mentioned earlier, students may bring ethical dilemmas to the conferences, especially individual conferences, to get some help in deciding the most ethical option available. Though many of these dilemmas do not have clear cut right or wrong answers, supervisors can provide them the way of examining pros and cons of each available option and selecting that which has the least negative outcome. Research (Hughes & Heycox, 1996; Ife, 1997) has shown that supervisors who focus more on positives and strengths of students and who are seen as 'impartial' in their conduct towards all students are seen as most helpful.

Conclusion

Conferences facilitate learning in fieldwork, ensure accountability of the student and provide opportunities for proper planning, monitoring and evaluation. Conferences are the bridge between classroom teaching-learning and fieldwork. Students come to placement with or without any idea of what to expect. If they are new to social work, they do not have clarity about what their role is going to be in fieldwork. They might be scared and anxious while going into this 'unknown'. At the same time, there is also an excitement for the opportunity to do some 'real' work and learn in action. That is why, from the first conference, the quality and transparency in the interaction between the supervisor and student is very crucial.

The reason for fieldwork or practicum being the part of social work curriculum is that students get an opportunity to apply the classroom teaching in the field. This reason is made attainable by the conferences, as they are used to orient the students to social work, clarify their doubts, guide their fieldwork and build their attitude, knowledge and skills. The objectives and content of both individual and group conferences change and develop as the fieldwork progresses. The faculty or fieldwork supervisors need to have the required skills to guide the students ably in each phase.

Able use of conferences by students as well as supervisors have the potential to bring about positive changes not only related to the client groups the fieldwork agency is working with but also related to personal skills, motivation, commitment and core competencies of the students. It is great to witness students gaining in confidence as they progress through their placement.

Conferences have the potential to bring out into the open the student's enthusiasm, passion for social work and an enquiring mind. If students feel free to express their doubts and ask questions in the conferences, they can also develop the capacity for critical analysis of the agency. This in turn can cause the agency to keep looking at the relevancy of how and why they do things. They are able bring a vibrancy to the agency.

Conferences are also used for final evaluations of students' fieldwork. If the fieldwork supervisor or student or both of them have not used conferences to monitor, review and give/receive feedback on a regular basis during conferences, students might get surprised and agitated during the evaluation, especially when negative feedback is given.

When the students feel that supervisors are listening to what they have to say, they are receptive; they feel motivated to put in their best in fieldwork. Conferences can be very empowering when the supervisor reflects unconditional acceptance and regard for the student, attentive listening and mentoring skills.

With the advancement of technologies and newer pedagogical approaches, the nature of conferences is changing. In the near future virtual conferencing may become the common method of discussing, reviewing and guiding fieldwork of students. Whether it offers equal opportunities (or more) to learn and facilitate critical reflectivity during fieldwork remains to be seen.

References

Bogo, M., & Vayda, E. (1987). *The practice of field instruction in social work: Theory and process*. Toronto: University of Toronto Press.

Boud, D., & Walker, D. (1990). Making the most of experience. *Studies in Continuing Education, 12*, 61–80.

Center for Community Health and Development. (2018). Section 8: Identifying and analyzing stakeholders and their interests. In *The community tool box*. Lawrence, KS: University of Kansas. Retrieved from https://ctb.ku.edu/en/table-of-contents/participation/encouraging-involvement/identify-stakeholders/main

Cooper, L. (1994). Improved assessment practices in field education. In *Advances in social work and welfare education: Conference proceedings* (pp. 110–124). Canberra: Australian Association of Social Work and Welfare Education.

Cooper, L., & Briggs, L. (Eds.). (2000). *Fieldwork in the human services: Theory and practice for field educators, practice teachers and supervisors*. St. Leonards, NSW: Allen & Unwin.

Fernandez, E. (1997). 'Effective teaching and learning in practicum education: Perceptions of student social workers and student teachers' in A. Yarrow and J. Millwater (eds). *Practical Experiences in Professional Education Research Monograph no. 2*. PEPE Inc., QUT Publications and Printery, Brisbane, pp. 67-107).

Ford, K., & Jones, A. (1987). *Student supervision*. London: BASW Macmillan.

Getzel, G. S., & Salmon, R. (1985). Group supervision: An organizational approach. *The Clinical Supervisor, 3*(1), Spring, 27–43.

Greene, R. R. (2008). General systems theory. In R. R. Greene (Ed.), *Human behavior theory and social work practice* (3rd ed., pp. 173–200). London: Routledge.

Hodgson, D., & Walford, H. (2007). Planning for learning and learning about planning in social work fieldwork. *Journal of Practice Teaching & Learning, 7*(1), 50–66.

Hughes, L., & Heycox, K. (1996). Three perspectives on assessment in practice learning. In M. Doel & S. Shardlow (Eds.), *Social work in a changing world: An international perspective on practice learning* (pp. 85–102). Aldershot: Arena.

Ife, J. (1997). *Rethinking social work*. Melbourne: Longman.

Lewin, K. (1948). *Resolving social conflicts*. New York, NY: Harper.

Madsen, I. (2012). Social work environment and mental health. Report submitted in fulfillment of Doctorate degree in Social Work. Copenhagen: Faculty of Health and Medical Sciences, University of Copenhagen and National Research Centre for the Working Environment.

Maidment, J. (2000). Methods used to teach social work students in the field: A research report from New Zealand. *Social Work Education, 19*, 145–154.

Mumm, A. M. (2006). Teaching social work students practice skills. *Journal of Teaching in Social Work, 26*(34), 71–89.

Panda, B., & Nayak, L. M. (2012). Strengthening field work practicum in social work education. *Social Work Chronicle, 1*(2), 14–30.

Rogers, G., & McDonald, P. L. (1992). Thinking critically: An approach to field instructor training. *Journal of Social Work Education, 28*(2), 166–177. doi:10.1080/10437797.1992.10778770

Rogers, G., & McDonald, P. L. (1995). Expedience over education: Teaching methods used by field instructors. *Clinical Supervisor, 13*(2), 41–65.

Shulman, L. (1993). *International supervision*. Washington, DC: National Association of Social Workers Press.

Shulman, L. (2005). Signature pedagogies in the professions. *Daedalus, 134*(3), 52–59.

Subhedar, I. S. (2001). *Fieldwork training in social work*. New Delhi: Rawat Publications.

Tebb, S., & Kalumann, T. (1996). A renaissance of group supervision in the practicum. *The Clinical Supervisor, 14*(2), 39–51.

Valentino, A. L., LeBlanc, L. A., & Sellers, T. P. (2016). The benefits of group supervision and a recommended structure for implementation. *Behaviour Analysis Practice, 9*, 320–328.

Wijnberg, M. H., & Schwartz, M. C. (1977). Models of student supervision: The apprentice, growth and role systems models. *Journal of Education for Social Work, 13*(3), 107–113.

8
CONCURRENT FIELDWORK TRAINING AND SUPERVISION IN SOCIAL WORK

Challenges and solutions in the context of Barak Valley, Assam

Kaivalya T. Desai

Introduction

Fieldwork training is often referred to as the hallmark of social work education that distinguishes it from other social science disciplines. Many social workers clearly demarcate the difference between 'knowledge for itself' and 'knowledge for application', with the latter taking primacy in social work. Social work students are expected to apply theories learnt in the classroom using different intervention strategies and methods of social work practice in the field. In doing so, when the social work trainee engages with the field, s/he needs to capture the field dynamics and bring them back to the knowledge base of social work through classroom interactions, research or individual and group conferences. Therefore, fieldwork has been historically considered as the most essential feature of social work education. The following words by late Prof. M.S. Gore aptly highlight the importance of fieldwork:

> Essentially social work skills are concerned with problem solving and as such they rest upon knowledge contained in the social and biological sciences pertaining to man and society. This knowledge is gained partly in the didactic sessions of the curriculum but it becomes meaningful only when the student has to test it in situation after situation in the field. Thus it can be seen that the practical experience must be closely integrated at every step of the way with what the student learns in the classroom.
>
> *(Gore, 1957, p. 3)*

Fieldwork training, usually referred to as 'fieldwork practicum' in social work curricula, consists of many components such as orientation programme, rural camps, study tours, block fieldwork placements, inter-agency meets and concurrent fieldwork placements. Out of these, concurrent fieldwork placements are the longest in duration as well as a continuous process in most social work education institutions. The other components such as rural camps and block placements play a supportive role in providing additional field exposure to students. Moreover, concurrent fieldwork is most closely supervised with weekly reports and supervisory conferences.

It includes placements of students with government and non-government organisations working on welfare and development issues, or in communities directly. The institutional settings include: organisations working with homeless and street children, disabled, elderly etc. and settings such as hospitals and schools. The community-based placements include urban slums, tea plantations, underdeveloped or backward villages etc. The placement in communities (urban or rural) for concurrent fieldwork also depends upon the geographical location of the institution of social work.

For concurrent fieldwork, students visit the agency or the community where they are placed twice a week and spend a minimum of eight hours per visit. Following are some broad objectives of concurrent fieldwork training (Desai, 2013):

- To provide purposeful learning experiences of working in real life situations in which social work interventions may be required by individuals, groups and communities
- To develop attitudes and values in the students that commensurate with the requirements of social work profession, increasing self-awareness and appreciating both the capacities and limitations of social work practice
- To understand and make a commitment to humanistic values and principles of social work practice
- To develop a holistic view of social work and related interventions in the community, with special emphasis on the agency's role in human services
- To develop an understanding of the problems and opportunities in working with diverse populations
- To develop necessary skills in social work methods to help people in need
- To enable students to develop and enhance the capacity to translate theory into practice and vice-versa
- To develop the professional self of the students for providing leadership in developmental pursuits.

Concurrent fieldwork is continuously supervised by the educators who perform the twin role of academic tutors and fieldwork supervisors in social work discipline. Fieldwork supervision teaches the students to integrate theory and practice in the field. It creates an environment in which professional skills for social work practice can be learnt (Kapoor, 1961; Khinduka, 1963; Banerjee, 1975; Subhedar, 2001). In addition, mostly in the case of agency settings, fieldwork is also supervised by agency supervisors.

Having introduced the broad concept of fieldwork training in social work, the following section highlights the methodology used to collect primary data on specific solutions as well as the challenges of fieldwork training and supervision in Assam University.

Methodology

The primary data for this chapter was generated through in-depth individual interactions with social work educators and focused group discussions (FGDs) with both Bachelor's and Master's level social work students of Assam University, Silchar.

Five educators were purposively selected for individual interactions in order to get a diverse range of responses. The criteria for this selection included: (i) number of years of teaching and supervision experience, (ii) past academic and professional training institution, (iii) direct and indirect past and present field engagement in the valley, (iv) gender and (v) areas of interest and specialisation.

FGDs were conducted batch-wise with three groups including final year Bachelor's level students and both first and final year Master's students. The tools included an unstructured interview guide for educators and an FGD guide for the students.

Fieldwork structure: Department of Social Work, Assam University, Silchar

In contrast to the West, social work education and training in India is largely planned at the post-graduate level. Following administrative reason has been highlighted by Dr Armaity S. Desai as to why there are very few institutions of social work in India that offer a graduate degree in social work:

> It is easier for the universities to start the master's programmes than bachelor's programmes because, in the former, the Vice Chancellor can take the decision as the UGC gives them funds for the first five years to open a new department. Thereafter, it has to be taken over by the State Government. In the latter, the college management has to find the funds and then the university sets up a Board of Studies to develop the curriculum.
>
> *(Desai, Pimple, & Jaswal, 2000, p. 319)*

However, in contrast to the general pattern of social work education in India, Assam University offers social work at both a Bachelor's and Master's level. Moreover, it offers a five-year integrated programme in social work ensuring that all students enrolling at the master's level come from a social work disciplinary background at Bachelor's level. Thus, there is homogeneity among social work students at Assam University in terms of their discipline. Also, although fairly infant as compared to the rest of India, it is the first university to offer professional social work education in the northeast. Besides, it is one of the few departments wherein students are placed in rural community settings for their concurrent fieldwork training. For concurrent fieldwork, students go to the field twice in a week with a minimum of twenty-four visits per semester.

While pursuing the Bachelors of Social Work (BSW) degree, students are placed in rural community settings during second, third and fourth semesters and an agency setting (government and non-government organisations) during the fifth and sixth semesters. However, in the first semester the students go for observation visits to different government and non-government organisations. Table 8.1 highlights the specific semester-wise learning outcomes from concurrent fieldwork at BSW level.

TABLE 8.1 Expected semester-wise learning outcomes at graduate level

Semester	Nature of placement	Expected learning outcomes
BSW 1st	Orientation visits to different government and non-government organisations.	To understand the function of different welfare and development organisations. To get exposure to contemporary social issues and intervention strategies.
BSW 2nd	Rural Community	To learn the process of community profiling and mapping. To develop a basic understanding of social and developmental issues in rural communities of Barak Valley. To learn application of 'social casework' in rural community context.
BSW 3rd	Rural Community	To identify community needs and problems. To develop skills of working with children, families and elderly. To learn application of 'social group work' in a rural community context.
BSW 4th	Rural Community	To identify specific challenges of working with the rural populace of Barak Valley. To develop skills of working with differently-abled persons and in the area of community health. To practise 'social action' vis-à-vis a developmental issue faced by marginalised sections of the community.
BSW 5th	Agency	To learn application of theoretical knowledge of administration and law. To learn the use of programme media in implementation of social welfare schemes/projects. To understand the importance of gender mainstreaming in welfare schemes and projects.
BSW 6th	Agency	To learn the importance of integrated social work practice. To develop life skills essential for social workers in practise. To understand the issues of the working class (if possible in the context of the particular agency) To develop basic research skills.

Source: Author

While pursuing the Masters of Social Work (MSW) degree, students are placed in rural community settings during the first and second semesters and an agency setting (government and non-government organisations) during the third and fourth semesters. Table 8.2 highlights the specific year-wise learning outcomes from concurrent fieldwork at MSW level.

Having highlighted the basic structure of concurrent fieldwork and expected learning outcomes, let us now discuss the unique context of 'Barak Valley' wherein concurrent fieldwork training takes place.

The context of Barak Valley

Barak Valley, named after the river Barak in the southern part of Assam, consists of three districts, namely Cachar, Hailakandi and Karimganj. This part of Assam has a unique and strategic location as it shares borders with not only neighbouring northeastern states of Mizoram, Manipur and Tripura in India but also shares an international border with Bangladesh. Before the partition of 1947, Hailakandi and Karimganj were a part of the Sylhet district of East Bengal (later East Pakistan and now Bangladesh) and the majority population in these two districts are Bengali Muslims. In Cachar, the majority population is Bengali Hindus.

The Bengali speaking people of this valley are often referred to as *Sylhetis* as they speak the *Sylheti* dialect of Bengali. Silchar is the biggest and most well-connected town of this valley. Most of the educational institutions, medical services and transport services are concentrated in Silchar. Thus, with regard to basic services, Silchar is the most strategic and important town, for people both in Barak Valley and the neighbouring states of Mizoram and Manipur. Besides the dominant *Sylheti* population, Barak Valley is also home to *Dimasas, Bishnupriya* and *Meitei Manipuris, Rongmei*

TABLE 8.2 Expected year-wise learning outcomes at post graduate level

Semester	Nature of placement	Expected learning outcomes
MSW 1st	Rural Community	To develop the ability to critically analyse different socio-economic issues and challenges faced by the rural populace of Barak Valley.
		To organise capacity building camps for rural people in areas such as education, health, disaster management etc.
		To further develop a practical understanding of social work methods.
MSW 2nd	Agency	To further develop research skills and NGO management.
		To understand the importance of a rights-based approach in contemporary social work practice.

Nagas, and *Deshwalis/Hindustanis* (the ex-tea and tea tribes). Thus, the valley is home to many diverse tribes and ethnic communities predominantly residing in rural areas. Moreover, within the Bengali Hindu community there are numerous caste groups having distinct characteristics, needs and problems. It is in this kind of a diverse context that social work students undergo their concurrent fieldwork training.

Social work students of Assam University develop an understanding of diverse cultures, issues and problems of these diverse communities, and relationship between different communities, some of which are strenuous to say the least. Macro issues such as issues of ethnic identity, migration, immigration, communal polarisation, unorganised labour, geographical isolation and poverty are often encountered by students in their concurrent fieldwork placements. These structural issues also result in specific problems that different communities face which need social work intervention at both a micro and macro level. For example, a social work educator expressed,

> Within the Bengali Hindu community there is a specific caste group called the Koibortos, who are basically involved in fishing business. The other Bengalis (both Hindus and Muslims) call them Bangladeshis as they came to this part of the valley after they were displaced from Bangladesh. They struggle to get social acceptance from other communities in the valley and need to struggle a lot in not just continuing their traditional occupation of fishing but also to sell their catch in the market. In addition, they have extreme anger against the Muslims. As a result although they do enter into economic exchanges with other communities, socially they remain isolated. This also affects the education of their children and child marriage is common in this community.

A community which has a substantial population in this valley are the tea garden labourers who are often referred to as the *Deshwalis/Hindustanis/Baghanis*.

> Baghanis are those labourers who were forcefully displaced – from states such as Orissa, Chota Nagpur Region, Bihar, West Bengal – and brought to this valley around three generations back to work in the tea gardens. Initially they were isolated from the rest of communities in the valley because they were forcefully confined within the gardens by the managers of the plantations. However, as the nature of work became more seasonal in the tea gardens many Deshwalis came out and started to settle in areas near the gardens. When they started to compete for daily wage labour jobs and petty self-employment options with other communities, they started to face resistance from them. Therefore, even after coming out of tea gardens they have again lived in isolation.
>
> *(Personal communication with a social work educator)*

In addition, there are intricacies of changing cultures and languages which need to be grasped to understand the *Deshwali* community. According to another social work educator,

As the Deshwalis (coming from different states) have settled in this valley for the past three generations, a new language has developed among them which the locals call as the Baghani language. This language is a mixture of Bhojpuri, Sylheti, Oriya, Jharkhandi, Assamese, etc.

Again, the Baghanis are referred to as the 'others' and the isolation continues between the Baghanis and the non-Baghanis. Also, from the side of the Baghanis, a conscious attempt is made to retain certain traits of their own identity like following their traditional calendar, celebrating *chhath puja* etc. Interestingly, in recent times, Baghanis are trying to establish a unique identity for themselves containing some cultural traits and using media to assert their political identity. This gives them a sense of security as they do not want to get labelled as 'Bangladeshis', which is a pressing concern among different communities in this valley.

The trend of asserting a Baghani identity even if it isolates them from the Bengali community has increased further in recent times due to the strong initiatives taken by this government to prepare the National Register of Citizens (NRC). This Baghani identity gives them more security to get identified as Indian citizens.

(Reflection of a first year MSW student during FGD)

However, isolated existence and lack of human interactions among different communities is a common phenomenon across rural areas here. Many students reflected from their fieldwork experience that each community here lives in isolation either on ethnic or religious lines. For example, many villages are organised sporadically as *tillas*. Each *tilla* is more or less ethnically homogenous, whether *Bishnupriya Manipuris*, or *Meitei Manipuris* or *Dimasas* or *Rongmei Nagas* or *Bengali Hindus* or *Bengali Muslims* or *Deshwalis*. These *tillas* are located sporadically and the houses of the residents are in closer proximity to their fields, but geographically they are isolated, resulting in lesser human interaction. As the Bengalis are in majority, the influence of their language and culture is evident on other communities, but the assimilation is not complete. Even in villages where one finds more than one ethnic community, the hamlets of each community are clearly demarcated and the interaction between them is minimal.

On the economic front, the major occupations in which different communities are engaged include farming, fishing, tea plantation labour work, daily-wage labour work in brick industries and construction sites, drivers, mechanics, housemaids and petty self-employed businesses. Most of the lucrative businesses are captured by the Marwari community and the salaried government jobs are mostly saturated in the Silchar town, which is dominated by the Bengali Hindu community. Absence of an organised industrial sector is a major impediment to generating employment in this valley. Moreover, the tea plantation is an organised sector, but the majority of the labour force in reality is unorganised in the tea plantations. Thus, the majority of the people, especially those in rural areas, are facing acute problems of poverty.

Even the agricultural sector is underdeveloped (only single cropping pattern) and most of the communities that engage in agriculture practice farming for self-consumption only. Thus, the problems of poverty, low literacy levels and unemployment are not only real but acute here. Also, due to ambiguity with respect to immigration issues, many people are unable to take advantage of welfare schemes as well. A social work educator reflected that implementation of welfare schemes becomes problematic in the wake of preparation of National Register of Citizens (NRC) as well as non-issuance of below poverty line (BPL) cards. It is in the light of such a challenging socio-economic context that social work students undergo their concurrent fieldwork training in rural community settings and agency settings.

Challenges of concurrent fieldwork training and supervision in Barak Valley

Specific contextual challenges in Barak Valley (rural community settings)

There are nineteen rural community settings in which students are placed for concurrent fieldwork training. A striking feature of most of these communities is that they are geographically isolated. As a result, access to basic services whether infrastructural or health related services is remote to say the least. From the students' point of view as well, reaching these communities/villages on fieldwork days itself is a challenge and travelling itself consumes two to three hours, which results in lesser time being spent in the communities on fieldwork days. Table 8.3 highlights the ethnic composition of these communities.

Occupationally in most of these communities people are engaged in subsistence farming, daily-wage labour work or petty self-employed work. Besides, there are few communities where people are engaged in other occupations including fisheries and cattle-rearing. The previously mentioned socio-economic context poses a number of challenges for the students when they visit their respective fieldwork settings.

TABLE 8.3 Ethnic composition of communities

Sr. no.	Ethnic composition	Number of communities
1.	Bengali (both Hindus and Muslims), Deshwalis (each living in separate hamlets)	4
2.	Deshwalis (outside tea estates)	7
3.	Deshwalis (within tea estates)	3
4.	Bengali Hindu	2
5.	Bengali Muslim	1
6.	*Meitei Manipuris*	1
7.	*Rongmei Nagas*	1

Source: Author

For the students placed in communities located in tea estates, the foremost challenge is dealing with the tea estate managers. These managers exercise full administrative control, making it difficult for the labourers to discuss their problems with students. Some of the students have faced threats from the managers as well, when they create awareness on issues such as minimum wages and disbursement of welfare scheme funds in the plantations. A final year BSW student reflected that,

> Any micro-level social work intervention will only be useful with tea plantation labourers when policy level issues are addressed there. With such low income levels it becomes difficult to convince the people to engage with us on individual family related issues or other social concerns such as literacy levels and health related issues. In addition, the manager of the tea plantation keeps a continuous watch on the work that we are doing. He just expects us to work with primary school students in the community through teaching and recreational activities. Even if we try to intervene on issues of high school drop-out rate with district administration or local panchayat members, the manager threatens that he will not allow us to visit the plantation again. In such an environment we feel that no substantial learning takes place with regard to social work interventions. Even when this is discussed with the supervisor during group conferences he/she is unable to convince the tea garden management!

Another unique challenge that students face in tea plantations is the language of the labourers. The *Dehswalis* speak the *Baghani* language which is unique and difficult to understand both for Bengali and Non-Bengali students. This acts as a major barrier in working with this population. However, this problem is not that grave with the *Deshwali* population that now resides outside the tea gardens as they understand Bengali well.

For the students placed in other communities as well, most issues that require social work intervention are structural in nature and thus need application of macro-methods such as community organisation or social action and advocacy. But to garner support of community people is difficult as most of them are daily-wage earners and to find them on fieldwork days and organise them is difficult. This contextual challenge is coupled with the issue of generating resources within the community. While teaching macro-methods in the classroom as well as during fieldwork supervision, students are told to identify needs of the community and first generate resources within the community to meet these needs and then turn to outside government and NGO support. However, the field reality is far more complex and problematic as is reflected in the following deliberation of the first year MSW students.

> A major task that we undertake in fieldwork is to organise resources to meet certain basic needs of the community such as addressing health concerns, education of children, employment opportunities for the youth, etc. As most

> of the communities we are placed in are living in acute poverty therefore to generate resources [*sic*] within the community is not feasible. Naturally, we try to mobilise resources from outside. One such source is government welfare schemes such as: National Rural Livelihood Mission, Mahatma Gandhi National Rural Employment Guarantee Act, Integrated Child Development Scheme, National Health Mission, etc. But there are huge discrepancies in the data provided by the government officials and elected representatives at the village level on the one hand and the responses of actual beneficiaries on the other. When we try to organise people and register a protest after conducting awareness camps on provisions of these schemes we are not successful. These people are daily-wage earners and do not have time to engage in such activities and fight for their entitlements. As a result, we feel demoralised as practising community organisation gets limited only to awareness camps. In such a context, we feel that models of community organisation and social action are artificial and suited more for urban communities probably! Moreover, individualised methods which we are told to practise such as casework and group work seem even more irrelevant as the coping capacity of our prospective clients seems to be negligible.

Such a context coupled with the fieldwork structure poses a lot of challenges for fieldwork supervision.

> The most marginalised /critical cases are found by students in the community (at least twenty per cent of the people in most of the communities). Such cases require immediate services, but these services can't reach them due to geographical as well as socio-economic reasons. Some amount of financial assistance is required by students to connect these people with services and resources, and subsequently continued support is required which is not available. Again, this is not possible within the professional fieldwork training structure. This demoralises the students and creates a dilemma for supervision as well. If such cases are limited then individual supervisors and students can do the needful, but a number of such cases exist in the rural communities here and there seems to be no government or non-government organisation addressing the needs of such people on a sustained basis. Therefore, networking skills to generate resources also get a setback.
> *(Interview with a Social Work Educator)*

Another contextual challenge in rural communities of Barak Valley is the issue of migrant identity. This has become even more critical with the NRC process. Many communities are labelled as Bangladeshis and are living in a constant threat of deportation. The issue is complex and requires social work intervention, but it is difficult to engage with this sensitive issue at the fieldwork training level. At the pedagogical level one can engage students in the classroom on these issues but to connect it with fieldwork is a challenge.

Specific contextual challenges in Barak Valley (agency settings)

The previously mentioned contextual challenges of Barak Valley have an indirect bearing on concurrent fieldwork training in agency settings as well. Most of the agencies where students are placed for concurrent fieldwork training are working with people in the same rural communities. There are sixteen agencies across which concurrent fieldwork placements are made. These include both government funded organisations and welfare agencies and non-government organisations. The major areas of intervention include: public health, education, violence against women, children in difficult circumstances, vocational training for generating employment, SHGs and microfinance, human rights, drug de-addiction, empowerment of differently abled persons, trafficking of women and children, disaster management and human rights.

A general challenge that students face in agency settings is the difference in expectations between the agencies and department. There is a glaring discrepancy between the agency staff and the school supervisors, which often creates confusion and cynicism in the minds of social work students (Pathak, 1975). This seems to be a perennial problem of social work departments across India; however, the problem is graver for newly established departments, especially those located in remote areas. The agencies in the remote areas are fewer in number; they do not recognise the idea of professional social work education and also lack trained social workers.

The students pointed out that agencies mostly want them to work as administrative staff in the organisation. This is even more pertinent in most of the government organisations such as Silchar Municipal Corporation, District Rural Development Authority etc. Therefore, many agencies do not entertain the learning requirements that the department fieldwork supervisors expect from the students. A social work educator highlighted the following reason for this gap,

> The social work department in Assam University is just twenty years old. Thus, the idea of professional social work and concurrent fieldwork training is still in its infancy in Barak Valley. Many people in the organisations where students go for concurrent fieldwork training do not understand the methods of social work practice and their relevance as they are not trained social workers. Also, the regular contact points through whom they are getting slowly accustomed to professional social work education are students. The students themselves are still under training and are not able to clearly articulate the idea of professional social work and its unique ability to intervene on different issues. Thus, a gap remains between the expectations of agencies on the one hand and social work department [sic] on the other.

This concern was also raised by students as they complain that people are not aware of the idea of professional social work. In case of NGOs, lack of funds is also an issue. Therefore, many clients that students refer to these organisations are not entertained by them.

> When I used to take clients from different communities for drug de-addiction process to the agency where I was placed, they used to refuse as the clients did not have the money to pay for the process. I even tried to approach individuals for donations to help these clients financially but could not generate enough resources as the number of cases were more. Thus, I was under the ethical dilemma as to which case should be given priority. After a point I stopped making efforts in this direction and limited myself to only doing awareness campaigns on drug de-addiction in rural communities which was expected of me by the agency. After a point, people stopped coming for awareness camps as the critical cases which came forward for undergoing drug de-addiction were not entertained by the agency. People in the communities observed this and also complained that these camps might only be used by the agency to generate their own funds and not helping people who come forward.
>
> *(Narrated by a final year MSW student)*

When this challenge was discussed with the educators, few opined that the agency should be dropped from the concurrent fieldwork placement list. However, a few insisted on continuing the agency placement as drug abuse is a major issue in the valley and students need practical exposure on different strategies of drug de-addiction. This poses a serious challenge for the fieldwork supervisor in convincing the students about such limitations of the agency.

Generic administrative and structural issues of fieldwork training and supervision

Besides these challenges faced by the students and supervisors in community and agency settings, there are dilemmas with regard to concurrent fieldwork training and supervision due to the overall academic environment within which social work discipline is situated. Social work academics perform the dual role of classroom teachers and fieldwork supervisors in most departments of social work in India. Shankar A. Yelaja highlighted this overall work burden of social work academics as early as 1969:

> Practically all the schools of social work in India depend on the school faculty members for fieldwork supervision. With rare exceptions, the field work supervisor is a member of the school faculty, engaged in classroom teaching, thesis supervision and many other duties that fall on a member of any faculty in addition to his field of instruction.
>
> *(Yelaja, 1969, p. 14)*

The overall academic structure based on evaluation of teachers through academic performance indicators does not recognise the importance of fieldwork training in the social work discipline. This is true for most departments of social work in the country. But for the social work department of Assam university, it is even more pertinent as fieldwork supervision is only limited to department supervisors in community settings. Even in most of the agency settings there is a lack of trained social workers who can effectively supervise the students. As a result, department supervisors (who are academic tutors as well) need to invest a lot of time in fieldwork supervision. But the non-recognition of this important role is demotivating for social work educators who are in a dilemma whether to do research and write papers for promotion or invest time and energy in fieldwork supervision. Whatever may be the reasons, many university administrators are inclined to classify social work programmes as pre-professional and view the field instruction component as a form of vocational training (Jones, 1984).

Also, each social work educator has to supervise at least thirteen to fifteen students each semester in two settings (one community and one agency). This makes the important concept of individual conferences totally impractical. As a result, fieldwork supervision needs to be channeled only through group conferences that further lead to many gaps in learning of students. Students from both BSW and MSW during FGDs highlighted,

> We require continuous individual and group conferences from our supervisors, preferably every subsequent day of our fieldwork, so that we are able to not just concretely plan continuity in our fieldwork but also implement the ideas that are generated from our interactions with community people in the field.

Since students are unable to get individual attention from their fieldwork supervisors, a different kind of group dynamics emerges in the field. Junior students rely on their seniors, and only a few seniors respond. Moreover, if senior students are not regular, it automatically affects the junior students. Also, the fieldwork instructions and expectations as laid down in the fieldwork guidelines of the department are different for each semester. So this problem also contradicts the fieldwork guidelines. A 6th semester BSW student reflected,

> When I was in second semester I was initially hesitant in going to the field. Therefore, I relied on my seniors. But my seniors were not regular and because of the hierarchy between seniors and juniors I was scared to express this in front of my supervisor during group conferences. Also, my supervisor had clearly instructed me to follow the seniors in the field. During one group conference I hesitantly pointed out that according to guidelines in second semester we have to do home visits to understand the problems of the community, but the same is not mentioned for 4th and 8th semester students as

they do that in 3rd and 7th semester. Therefore, my seniors are not doing home visits. Still the supervisor instructed me to follow the seniors only. At the end of the semester I was worried if the external examiner asks me in viva-voce about home visits then what reply will I give and therefore I might get poor marks in fieldwork! This was highly demotivating. This made me think if I would have had individual conferences with my supervisor I would have been able to discuss this problem with her.

All the interviewed social work educators highlighted this as a challenge of supervision. Connecting this with other administrative challenges of supervision, one educator highlighted how, taken together, these administrative challenges become a vicious cycle that continuously affects supervision. According to him,

High supervisor – supervisee ratio of 1:15 leads to three important challenges in fieldwork supervision. Firstly, it is impossible to conduct individual conferences which are essential. Secondly, the challenge of checking their weekly fieldwork reports in detail due to paucity of time. Thirdly, to choose between checking reports and doing other research work on fieldwork days or regularly visiting the communities and agencies on these days. In addition, inability to conduct individual conferences also limits the idea of understanding the heterogeneous background of students in depth so that each supervisee's fieldwork can be planned according to her/his strengths and weaknesses. Even the senior–junior hierarchy is difficult to address in group conferences because juniors are scared to speak up in front of their seniors. Again, looking at the context of community settings collective effort is required by students in the field especially as they are only trainees. In case of agency settings students are again placed in groups due to limited number of agencies in the valley where they can be placed. All this becomes a vicious cycle and gets repeated batch after batch. In the process junior students also develop a casual attitude towards fieldwork and eventually repeat the same mistakes when they become seniors.

Another structural issue that affects concurrent fieldwork training in Assam University is that although curriculum undergoes revision from time to time, fieldwork guidelines do not. This sometimes creates the challenge of relating semester-wise curriculum and pedagogy with fieldwork. This in turn further problematises the theory – practice relationship, the testing ground of which is supposedly concurrent fieldwork training. Students continuously complain that there is a huge gap between what is taught in the classroom and what they practice in the field. They expect that fieldwork supervision should help them to fill this gap. However, as tutors, supervisors are teaching limited papers and it is not possible to bring in aspects from all the different courses in supervision especially given the challenge of supervising fifteen students across five different semesters together.

The objective-subjective dilemma in fieldwork supervision and evaluation

Finally, I would like to highlight the 'objective-subjective' challenge that fieldwork supervision poses to social work students of Assam University. Most of the students are placed under five different supervisors during three years of BSW and two years of MSW concurrent fieldwork placement. Supervisors have different areas of specialisation and expertise. All supervisors have unique supervisory styles, probably based on their previous fieldwork training in the institutions from where they studied social work. Besides, different supervisors have different experience vis-à-vis number of years of teaching and supervision. Although this can become a strength of concurrent fieldwork training, it also poses a challenge for students.

Students deliberated that some supervisors expect concrete individualised interventions in the field such as awareness camps whereas some expect them to understand macro issues in the community. Some supervisors focus more on skills whereas some focus more on how to approach the people in the community. Some supervisors expect detailed records whereas some expect only conceptual records in reports. Some supervisors focus more on observation and analysis in the reports whereas some focus more on work done in the community. Some supervisors want the students to spend a minimum of six hours in the field whereas some are fine with spending lesser time but doing more qualitative work. Taken together all this confuses the students as semester-wise fieldwork guidelines structurally are same for all the students, but supervisory styles are different.

Thus, the challenge is to determine how much subjectivity can be built into fieldwork supervision by each supervisor. This in turn also creates contradictions vis-à-vis fieldwork evaluation as well. Seventy per cent of the evaluation marks of fieldwork are given by an external expert through a viva voce examination. Thirty per cent of evaluation is done by the fieldwork supervisors as part of internal assessment. Thus, internal assessment has more subjective element built into it whereas external assessment is more based on objective fieldwork guidelines. Again, this also worries the students. Especially if the students want to challenge application of Westernised social work methods and some theoretical concepts based on experiential knowledge gained in the field, they are reluctant to express it as they feel that it might affect their evaluation. Many students experience this contradiction, but then they are unable to deliberate further on it and therefore the critical thinking ability of students becomes limited. For example, an 8th semester MSW student reflected,

> Mostly it appears that we are evaluated on the basis of concrete interventions that we make in the field such as doing casework or organising awareness camps or doing group work with school students. In reality we know that outcomes of these interventions are hardly effective. This is problematic as we want to get evaluated on the basis of learning we drew from the field. Also,

observations of each student are unique, even this needs to be a strong criterion for evaluation. However, mostly I feel that this does not get reflected in our fieldwork evaluation. Especially being critical of the agency is viewed negatively.

These words of the student were echoed by others during the same FGD. Most of them agreed that they feel the same about fieldwork evaluation.

> When I practised casework through structured interviewing sessions with the client in the field, I could not see any concrete outcome of that. Therefore, I decided to be creative and thought that I will have a more informal approach with the client and record her case history like a story, at least that way the client might be more responsive to me, even if I don't make any intervention vis-à-vis the problems she is facing in her everyday life. At least this way her problems will come out and later I can think of some interventions. However, this was discouraged by the supervisor who wanted the strict professional approach as taught to us in casework classes. I feel both innovative and critical ways of working in the field are not entertained in the strict professional practice of social work methods.
>
> *(semester student)*

Thus, maintenance of the 'objective-subjective' balance in fieldwork supervision and evaluation is a challenge that needs continuous deliberation as concurrent fieldwork training is a dynamic and evolving process. Having highlighted the challenges of concurrent fieldwork training, in the next section proposed solutions as deliberated on by both educators and students are discussed.

Moving from challenges to solutions addressing specific contextual challenges in Barak Valley (rural community settings)

As far as the challenge of working in rural communities having unique macro socio-economic issues is concerned; a social work educator deliberated on the following solution,

> At the departmental level social work educators should design a format for community profiles that clearly demarcates not just the demographic and social–economic characteristics of each of the communities but also clearly delineates the macro and micro issues that are prevalent in the communities. In addition, together they should deliberate on feasibility of making interventions on different issues and prepare short-term and long-term action plans. These can then be introduced as 'Field Action Projects' (FAPs) of the department in the communities with support of different agencies (which also need to be clearly profiled).

This will have multiple effects on concurrent fieldwork training and supervision. First, it will increase direct field engagement of the educators. This will positively impact both fieldwork supervision and pedagogy, enabling students to better understand the theory-practice relationship through local examples from their own fieldwork settings. Through FAPs community people will also witness concrete interventions and the idea of professional social work will get better acceptance among them. Slowly, the community people might accept and appreciate the initiatives that students undertake during their concurrent fieldwork placements. Also, continuous monitoring of the FAPs will keep the experiential knowledge base updated.

Another educator shared similar views and further deliberated,

> This will also help in maintaining continuity of work with every new batch of social work trainees placed in the same communities year after year. More importantly, it will avoid repetition of work by the trainees year after year, which has made the people in the communities even more non-responsive.

Another major challenge which is highlighted in the community context of Barak Valley is lack of resources in the community. However, some students and one educator highlighted the presence of 'clubs' (mostly involving youth of the community). These clubs can become a major resource for the community. Currently, most of these clubs are engaged in organising cultural activities and sports in their respective communities. If students, through concurrent fieldwork training, start developing these clubs into non-government organisations that work on welfare and developmental issues in these communities then they will become important resources within the community. Moreover, it will empower the youth of the community and will offer employment to them. Again, through this process social work students would gain more credibility in the community. Besides, this will have a positive impact on the motivational level of the students.

Another challenge with regard to community settings is recognition of the understanding that students develop vis-à-vis different macro issues. This can be done by integrating them with their MSW research dissertations (newly introduced in the latest curriculum). Macro-issues require a prolonged engagement with communities for direct intervention. This scope is not there in a concurrent fieldwork training model of two days a week. Therefore, use of social work research method and later using the findings of these studies for social policy advocacy is a more feasible solution. In addition, for channelising students' frustration vis-à-vis the inability to make direct interventions on macro-issues, supervisors should guide them to move from a non-threatening to threatening developmental approach in the communities. Following the example as highlighted by an educator/supervisor provides an alternative way of channelising students' frustrations in a demanding context:

> *My students discovered that in a particular community funds for MGNREGA were being wrongfully utilised by the local government officials and Panchayat members, they started to make people aware of the same. Soon they got threats from the local goons who also told them that if they continue with this then they will not be allowed to visit the community. The students were frustrated, scared and demoralised. Eventually I advised them to carry out a research silently and collect the data, both the official data as manipulated by the concerned authorities and the actual implementation, rather than organising people for social action, as currently it is not the felt need of the people due to lack of awareness. I asked them to prepare a research report at the end of the semester which was then submitted to the district magistrate. This helped the students to realise that they did make an intervention.*
>
> *Also, I made them understand the importance of working around the limitations. The idea was to explain that practising social action required long-term continuous engagement with the communities, and that too after raising awareness about the importance of welfare schemes instead of jumping to confrontation with the authorities. Once people feel the need and get organised and choose their leaders, only then social action bears fruit. This is not possible through 24 days of field engagement, and that too only twice a week. Still small interventions as the one I suggested motivated the students. Thus, they felt that not only did they learn about concepts such as limitations, felt needs, ethical dilemmas, etc. in social work practice but also felt that they made some concrete intervention. Moreover, it helped them to understand the importance of organising awareness camps on different developmental issues to mobilise people, which the students were extremely critical of earlier.*

Addressing specific contextual challenges in Barak Valley (agency settings)

With regard to agency settings the most prominent challenge that emerged was the gap in expectations of the supervisors at departmental level and the expectations of the agency. For this all the educators and students collectively opined that individual supervisors need to increase their interface with the agencies and fill this gap. In addition, the department should take efforts to bring together different stakeholders and agencies together in the university from time to time on different issues. Ideally, if there is sufficient provision of resources, then a 'field instruction centre' can be developed wherein continuous interface between faculty, agency staff and community leaders on different issues can take place (Gangrade, 1975; Henry, 1975; Lawrence, 2016). This will enable each stakeholder to understand their roles clearly as well as interdependence between roles of all stakeholders leading to improvement in fieldwork training and social work practice. This is one of the ways to impart a common understanding among students as to how expectations of agencies (both government and NGOs) as well as expectations of department supervisors (in consonance with each other) can help build their capacities as social workers. However, this is only one possible way to build students capacities along with countering the challenge of the agency-department gap vis-à-vis expectations from students. Besides, inter-agency cultural and sports meets can be organised in the university once a year to celebrate the idea of collectively working in the valley.

Possible solutions for generic administrative and structural issues of fieldwork training and supervision

As far as structural (administrative) issues beginning with the high supervisor-supervisee issue are concerned, again all the research participants opined that somehow space for individual conferences with students has to be revived despite all limitations. But, more importantly, some structural solutions emerged both at the BSW and MSW level. At the BSW level, to provide an objective understanding of fieldwork training, a paper should be introduced as part of the curriculum. This paper should focus on both theoretical orientation to the idea of fieldwork training and practical exposure to different fieldwork settings.

In addition, at the Master's level, during the 1st year of MSW, a three to five-day-long fieldwork seminar should be organised for students. The objective of this seminar would be to provide a platform where they can together deliberate on different aspects of concurrent fieldwork training using a 'case method' approach. The case method approach will permit the students to bring their own fieldwork experiences into play, that is, gathering their own data, making their own construction and proposing future courses of action to deal with the particular problems that they engage with in the field. Basically, the case method approach focuses on building critical and ethical problem-solving skills in future practitioners (Morris, 2008). Moreover, here a case can mean an individual client, a group or a community. For example, if a student engages with the issue of domestic violence in the community, then h/she can investigate this problem in the community, collect data, record her/his observations on domestic violence (different aspects related to manifestations of domestic violence and the micro-macro reasons), interventions attempted by the students and her/his reflections on the success/failure of interventions. Together all this can be presented as a case in the seminar.

TABLE 8.4 BSW 1st semester: contents for paper on fieldwork

Unit	Contents
1.	Fieldwork in social work: importance, structure, fieldwork settings
2.	Fieldwork supervision and evaluation
3.	Skill labs
4.	Application of techniques, tools and methods
5.	Observation visits (both agency and community settings)

Source: Author

During this seminar both educators and students can collectively deliberate on each of the presentations made by the students and come up with tentative models of intervention (either enhancing the interventions already made by the students or developing new ones). These models can then be tested by the students in their concurrent fieldwork placements.

Subsequently, another fieldwork seminar can be organised in the final year of MSW where students can present their reflections on the results of applying the tentative models that were developed in the previous year. They can highlight both the success stories as well as challenges faced in the application of these models.

However, this might require concurrent fieldwork placement of students in the same community or agency setting for both the years of MSW programme. Alternatively, if the students are placed in a community setting in 1st year then while placing them in an agency setting during 2nd year it should be ensured that either the agency is working in that community or on the issue on which the student worked in the previous year. This way continuity can be maintained in their concurrent fieldwork training and they will get an opportunity to apply the models developed through a case method approach.

Maintaining the objective-subjective balance in fieldwork supervision and evaluation

Lastly, let us highlight a few possible solutions to address the challenge of maintaining the 'objective-subjective' balance in fieldwork supervision and evaluation. First, detailed guidelines in sync with the updated curriculum should be designed. A social work educator opined that,

> Fieldwork guidelines should clearly state the objectives for each semester of concurrent fieldwork training, and this should match with the theory and methods papers that students are studying in that particular semester. Only this way the challenge of relating classroom teaching with the field is possible at the structural level. Tacitly each fieldwork supervisor in the department might be doing this, but this needs to be made explicit so that each student can objectively understand the guidelines. This can be one solution towards also balancing the 'objective-subjective' confusions among students with regard to fieldwork supervision.

Another educator further deliberated, 'Within this objective and detailed structure of fieldwork guidelines, the term plans for concurrent fieldwork supervision should be designed by individual supervisors'. Another educator suggested,

> Primarily the guidelines should detail how classroom teaching helps them in understanding the field realities as well as implementation of different

methods of social work practice. Also, these guidelines should state the skills that can be developed through experiential learning of concurrent fieldwork training. Moreover, while supervising we should monitor how the students are interpreting these guidelines during different semesters of concurrent fieldwork placements.

In order to protect the subjectivity of each supervisory style, within the broad objective guidelines, space can be created by ensuring that each supervisor has the liberty to channelise her/his supervision in her/his areas of interest within the concurrent fieldwork settings. In addition, supervision can include all the elements for students' professional development, but a supervisor based on her/his strengths as a social worker can prioritise those aspects of students' learning in fieldwork a bit more than other aspects.

In other words, conceptual learning, skill building, ethical practice etc., all should be included as part of supervision, but which ones to prioritise should be the prerogative of the individual supervisors. Commonly, all supervisors can deliberate and decide on this scope of flexibility within fieldwork supervision. However, this should be made explicit to the students by the supervisors during the beginning of concurrent fieldwork training each year.

At the Master's level students' areas of interests should also be taken into consideration before allotting fieldwork settings to them. This concern was continuously echoed by MSW students during FGDs.

Another important aspect of fieldwork supervision is the recording of concurrent fieldwork training through fieldwork reports. Recording is an indispensable tool of dynamic communication between the student and the supervisor and reflects the student's interests and aptitude at every stage of educational progress (Desai, 1975). However, there needs to be a certain degree of objectivity in recording fieldwork experiences across different supervisory styles with some components that provide subjective space to the students to express themselves critically and innovatively. Students collectively expressed that reporting styles change every year with new supervisors, therefore consolidated reporting writing skills are not developed, rather, it creates confusion for them. Moreover, students deliberated that space for creative style of reporting should be provided within this broad framework. Based on the interactions with educators and students, the following framework (see Table 8.5) is suggested for concurrent fieldwork reporting.

Finally, for addressing the concerns of students with regard to fieldwork evaluation, again one needs to balance the 'objective-subjective' axis. Thus, broad objective criteria can be designed within which a certain scope of subjectivity can be reserved for supervisors for internal assessment of concurrent fieldwork training. To address the students' apprehensions, the students can also evaluate themselves on the same criteria. Moreover, in participation in the evaluation experience, not only does the student become involved in his own learning, but h/she also has an

TABLE 8.5 Framework for concurrent fieldwork reports

Sr. no.	Section	Features
1.	Plan for the day	1. To be stated in clear points 2. Minimum of 1 and maximum of 5 points based on the fieldwork setting 3. Should match with term plan
2.	Work done	1. To be divided into sections on the basis of plan for the day 2. Objectively in brief stating what they did actually with regard to each plan in the field
3.	Observations	1. Subjective depending on the strengths, skills and interest areas of the student 2. Should explain the importance of this observation
4.	Analysis	1. Explaining the understanding developed on the observations made in the field
5.	Self-assessment	1. Learning drawn about the community/agency and the people the student interacted with 2. Mistakes committed 3. Limitations of the context 4. Ability to relate theory with practice and vice versa as well as the challenges faced in doing the same (critical thinking) 5. Methods of social work practice used and critical analysis of the same
6.	Future plan	1. To be stated in clear points 2. Minimum of 1 and maximum of 5 points based on the fieldwork setting 3. Should match with term plan 4. Becomes plan for the day for next report

Source: Author

experience in analysing her/his own performance objectively on the evidence at hand (Thangavelu, 1975). The students' self-evaluation can be given a weightage of 30 per cent and supervisors' evaluation 70 per cent weightage. Again, based on the deliberations of both educators and students, the following model (see Table 8.6) was suggested.

Table 8.6 mentions the weightage as tentative for each of the components of evaluation. This is because here subjectivity can be ensured for both educators and students. The supervisors can divide the weightage based on their individual strengths and interest areas. Moreover, the expectation from students at different levels of concurrent fieldwork training (across different semesters in BSW and MSW) might vary with regard to the previously mentioned criteria. Also, the weightage can vary based on the limitations of the fieldwork setting.

TABLE 8.6 Criteria for internal assessment of concurrent fieldwork placements

Sr. no.	Criterion	Indicators	Tentative weightage (in percentage)
1.	Regularity	Regularity in field Regularity in individual and group conferences Regularity in submission of reports	BSW: 20% MSW: 20%
2.	Attitude	Self-initiative taken in the field Attention to supervisory inputs Ethical considerations towards self, community, agency, social work profession and the issues Conscious attempt to follow principles of the methods of social work practice as well as the principles of the profession	BSW: 30% MSW: 20%
3.	Experiential knowledge and understanding	Knowledge developed from the field vis-à-vis both micro and macro aspects of issues Understanding of the needs of the community/agency Identification of resources to meet the needs	BSW: 20% MSW: 20%
4.	Application of theory to practice	Contextualising theoretical knowledge in the field Application of social work methods	BSW: 10%* MSW: 30%
5.	Techniques and skills	Conscious application of techniques such as observation, interviewing, home visits etc. in identifying needs and understanding of community/agency Skills developed such as rapport building, communication, networking, resource mobilisation etc.	BSW: 20% MSW: 10%

Source: Author

Notes: * At the BSW level students are exposed to different theoretical concepts and social work methods only by the time they reach the last semester, therefore this component has been accorded a low weightage at BSW level.

As far as external evaluation apprehensions of students are concerned, it is assumed that once comprehensive and updated fieldwork guidelines are shared with external experts then certain uniformity can be achieved there as well. In addition, before external evaluation together all internal supervisors can share the criteria that have been followed for internal assessment of the students. Having discussed the possible strategies to meet the challenges of concurrent fieldwork training and solutions, the last section summarises the highlights of the chapter and concludes it with some possible best practices to address the challenges of fieldwork training and supervision.

Conclusion

Overall this chapter has attempted to highlight the structure, challenges and possible solutions to meet the challenges of concurrent fieldwork training and supervision process in Department of Social Work, Assam University, Silchar. In the process, some of the challenges and solutions that arose were generic in nature and thus might be related to the fieldwork training process of other institutions of social work as well. Also, there are certain challenges which are unique to the context of Barak Valley, which highlights the importance of indigenous social work practice and thus having the flexibility to incorporate indigenous models into fieldwork training of the students. Although the chapter highlights the solutions and strategies in the previous section, let us conclude with some best practices which can help resolve dilemmas of fieldwork training and supervision.

Creating a space for case method pedagogy in overall fieldwork training structure through seminars as well as individual supervision and teaching can go a long way in developing indigenous models of social work practice that are relevant in particular contexts. Moreover, this may also result in better acceptance of the work done by students in their concurrent fieldwork placements as it will better suit the local needs of the communities. For example, promoting the youth clubs to become sites of not just promoting local culture but also undertaking developmental activities in the communities of Barak Valley can go a long way in both constructing and sustaining indigenous models of social work practice.

Noble (2001) argues that field instructors should replace the traditional authoritarian method of instilling knowledge with an approach that encourages reflection upon the actual learning that takes place for students engaged in practice. In particular, the curriculum should be designed to highlight the students' growing experience in the 'professional world' (Philipson, Richards, & Sawdon, 1988; Fook, Ryan, & Hawkins, 2000). Such an approach would democratise student learning and celebrate differences (Lam, Wong, & Leung, 2007). Focusing on students' learning from 'the inside' encourages students to speak from their own individual and collective positions (Giroux, 1990). A key aspect of this process is to view students' knowledge in the context of their engagement with practice issues (Noble, 2001). This exposition of practice to reflection allows for inquiry, criticism, changes and accountability (Fook, 1999) and is imperative to a critical learning process (Lam et al., 2007).

Thus, fieldwork supervision should encourage and harness innovative ways of practicing social work methods. In other words, rather than asking the students to apply Westernised methods in a structured way, contextualisation of methods should be encouraged. Fieldwork supervision should continuously aim at developing critical thinking skills among students, especially in challenging and remote contexts such as Barak Valley and give a space to the students for critical reflection and expression on their fieldwork training in the specific context in which they are practicing.

Finally, at the more formal level, collective efforts need to be taken by social work institutions across the country to make UGC and university authorities recognise the unique component of fieldwork training in social work. Accordingly, the need for creating a different criterion to understand and recognise the contribution of academicians as fieldwork supervisors in case of social work discipline needs a strong echo. This might also help social work educators to increase their interface with the field as a part of their regular work rather than continuously struggling to create a separate space for it.

References

Banerjee, G. R. (1975). Professional self and supervision in social work. *The Indian Journal of Social Work*, 35(4), 309–316.

Desai, K. T. (2013). *Paradigms of social work praxis: The case of street children*. Doctoral Thesis, Tata Institute of Social Sciences, Mumbai (mimeo).

Desai, M. M. (1975). Student recording in fieldwork supervision. *The Indian Journal of Social Work*, 35(4), 342–352.

Desai, M. M., Pimple, M., & Jaswal, S. (2000). Social work education and its application to general university system: An interview with Prof. Armaity S. Desai. *The Indian Journal of Social Work*, 61(2), 313–339.

Fook, J. (1999). Critical reflectivity in education and practice. In B. Pease & J. Fook (Eds.), *Transforming social work practice: Postmodern critical perspectives*. St Leonards, NSW: Allen and Unwin.

Fook, J., Ryan, M., & Hawkins, L. (2000). *Professional expertise: Practice, theory and education for working in uncertainty*. London: Whiting and Birch.

Gangrade, K. D. (1975). School of social work: Fieldwork agency liaison. *The Indian Journal of Social Work*, 35(4), 353–357.

Giroux, H. (1990). *Curriculum discourse as postmodernist critical practice*. Geelong, VA: Deakin University Press.

Gore, M. S. (1957). *Fieldwork supervision in an Indian school of social work*. Delhi: Delhi School of Social Work.

Henry, C. S. G. (1975). An examination of fieldwork models at Adelphi university school of social work. *Journal of Education for Social Work*, 11(3), 62–68.

Jones, E. F. (1984). Round hole: The dilemma of the undergraduate social work field coordinator. *Journal of Education for Social Work*, 20(3), 45–50.

Kapoor, J. M. (1961). The role of fieldwork in modern social work education. *The Indian Journal of Social Work*, 22(2), 113–119.

Khinduka, S. K. (1963). The role of supervision in social work education. *The Indian Journal of Social Work*, 24(3), 169–180.

Lam, C. M., Wong, H., & Leung, T. T. F. (2007). An unfinished reflexive journey: Social work students' reflection on their placement experiences. *British Journal of Social Work*, 37, 91–105. doi:10.1093/bjsw/bcl320

Lawrence, R. J. (2016). *Professional social work in Australia*. Australia: ANU Press.

Morris, P. M. (2008). Reinterpreting Abraham Flexner's speech, 'Is social work a profession?' It's meaning and influence on the field's early professional development. *Social Service Review*, 82(1), 29–60.

Noble, C. (2001). Research field practice in social work education, integrating theory and practice through the use of narratives. *Journal of Social Work, 1*(3), 347–360.

Pathak, S. H. (1975). Supervision in social work: Historical development and current trends. *The Indian Journal of Social Work*, 317–323.

Philipson, J., Richards, M., & Sawdon, D. (Eds.). (1988). *Towards a practice-led curriculum*. London: National Institute for Social Work.

Subhedar, I. S. (2001). *Fieldwork training in social work*. Jaipur: Rawat Publications.

Thangavelu, R. (1975). Field work supervision: It's place in social work education. *The Indian Journal of Social Work, 35*(4), 359–366.

Yelaja, S. A. (1969). Schools of social work in India: An overview of their present status. *The Indian Journal of Social Work, 30*(1), 9–21.

9
THE ADAPTIVE SUPERVISOR

Helen Joseph

Introduction

Fieldwork is a crucial component in the development of a social work professional. The "National Assessment and Accreditation Council (2005) describes it as a closely supervised educational internship in a social work setting that provides planned opportunities to apply theory taught in classrooms to field situations, which, in turn, enhances classroom learning" (cited in Paracka, 2014, p. 195). Fieldwork is the backbone of social work education, and the responsibility of providing a meaningful and guided experience to the students falls on the shoulders of the fieldwork supervisor, who through her/his skills and maturity leads the student to synthesise and internalise the knowledge, skills and attitudes/values taught in class.

However, in trying to fulfil this guidance responsibility the fieldwork supervisor in today's world comes face to face with a variety of difficulties. For one, no more are teachers considered the prime repositories of information and knowledge. Information accessibility, through on-line searches, has led to a levelling out of the earlier hierarchical relationship, at least as far as information availability goes. Almost any information that the teacher shares can be checked out by students online, with the result that the educator's earlier claim to superior information and knowledge is constantly being challenged by bright and industrious students. In addition, there are areas that the educator her/himself has not explored but which students, who are increasingly more comfortable with searching through scores of sites on any topic of their interest, may have actually explored.

This overturning of the earlier information differential is even more pronounced in situations where students/supervisees come from the same socio-economic-political-cultural milieu in which they are placed for fieldwork. A good example of this was found in an evaluation study that explored the nature of social work supervision in Shenzhen, China and the constraints of cross-border supervision faced by fieldwork supervisors who hailed from Hong Kong. Here the supervisors had to be oriented by the supervisees about the situation in mainland China, and supervision became an interactive process whereby supervisees brought the supervisors up to speed on the social and political culture of Shenzhen, a process that one supervisor named 'reverse supervision' (Hung, Ng, & Fung, 2010, p. 372). Here was a situation where some of these students were more aware and knowledgeable about the situation on the ground, as compared to the fieldwork supervisor who came from outside that milieu. In such situations it is incumbent on the supervisor to be open to learning from the student/supervisee. The chapter thus raises a fundamental issue of the 'universalised versus contextualised' nature of social work knowledge and skills. Clearly then, in India, where there is so much diversity and disparity within the country itself, this further confirms the insight that supervisors do not necessarily always have the advantage of greater information and knowledge.

Again, even though the experience of the educator cannot be underestimated, the dynamic nature of social work as a subject and its inter-connectedness with various disciplines offer a lot of scope for differing perspectives, leading to a questioning of whether the educator's perspective is really the more appropriate one in all situations. Thus, the 'guidance' that a teacher offers could be questioned and challenged by a host of alternative perspectives. To take an example, an educator who subscribes to the clinical approach (*casework*) which normally focuses on getting an individual or family to fit into accepted social norms of society, may be challenged by the perspective of a student who suggests that it is society (*which the student sees as being built on patriarchy, or on economically unjust structures or on oppressive caste realities*) which has to change to accommodate the individual, rather than the other way around. An example of this could be found if the student is placed for fieldwork in an extremely patriarchal society/community where the daughter is seen as the property of the father and where honour killings are acceptable. In such a situation, a student may be more interested in fighting the system rather than in helping individuals adjust to the social norms within which they live. Of course, this is an easy example since the example of extreme patriarchy given earlier is not subscribed to by any social work college/university. A more serious dilemma would arise, for instance, if the student believed that a highly pressurizing pro-choice abortion-supporting social milieu is ethically repugnant and felt that the individual client should oppose it, rather than adjust to it. These are only examples that highlight some of the difficulties faced by supervisors in today's world.

Observing the changes in the understanding of what the main functions of fieldwork supervision have been over the years, Jeanne Marie Hughes (2010) noted that Kadushin (1992) and much later Morrison (2003) focused on the '*supervisor*' when talking about the main function of supervision and that they believed that the supervisor's role was to be educative, supportive and managerial. On the other hand, Inskipp and Proctor (1995, cited in Hughes, 2010) focused on the '*benefits for the supervisee*', while describing the main functions of supervision as being formative, restorative and normative. Later on, Hawkins and Shohet (2006, cited in Hughes, 2010) focused on '*the process*', where the function of supervision in social work was perceived to be developmental, resourcing and qualitative (Hughes, 2010). These varying views seem to suggest that the function of supervision has evolved over the years.

In this regard, Moffat made an interesting observation when he stated that the debate about what is the ideal supervision relationship, "ranges between authoritarian – democratic, formal – informal, detached objectivity – warm personalisation, reserve about one's own professional problems – freely showing them, adopting the role of instructor – providing the student with opportunities to draw his own conclusions and learn from his own experiences." He then goes on to assert that "unfortunately there is little objective evidence to support one view or another since most of the literature is descriptive and speculative" (Moffat, 1969, p. 32).

So clearly, there is no agreement among writers on the subject as to how best to supervise students during fieldwork. Furthermore, modern realities, some of which are indicated earlier, seem to make it difficult, if not impossible, for any one supervisor to really have the knowledge and skills required to deal with these multiple realities and different contexts. What seems to emerge quite clearly, however, is that the nature of guidance offered by the fieldwork supervisor needs to be more interactive, so that it becomes a two-way process, where both the supervisor and the supervisee are open to learning and sharing their knowledge, experiences and perspectives.

In this context, then, it might be necessary for social work educators to reflect first of all on whether the term 'supervision' adequately represents or describes this changing understanding of fieldwork guidance.

Supervisor or facilitator?

The word 'supervision' comes from the Latin word **'super'** which means 'over' and **'videre'** which means 'to see' – in other words "to oversee and superintend the work or performance of others" (Harper, 2001–2018). According to the *Merriam-Webster Dictionary* (2018), supervision means the "action, process, or occupation of supervising;" especially "a critical watching and directing (as of activities or a course of action)". According to the Cambridge Dictionary (2018b), supervision is "the act of watching a person or activity and making certain that everything is done correctly, safely". The word 'supervision' in all these definitions seems to imply a superior role that the supervisor assumes vis a vis her/his supervisee/student. It appears to be more directive and critical in its execution. However, what emerges from all the reflections earlier, is that in social work education, a completely or purely hierarchical relationship between a social work educator and student is no more appropriate in today's context.

Would it be better, then, to use the term "facilitator" instead of "supervisor"? According to the Cambridge Dictionary (2018a), the term "facilitator" means "someone who helps a person or organisation do something more easily or find the answer to a problem, by discussing things and suggesting ways of doing things". Thus, even though in "facilitation" there is admittedly a slightly hierarchical relationship, the environment of learning that the facilitating relationship offers is completely different from that of the more hierarchical supervisor-supervisee relationship. In my understanding, inbuilt into the facilitating relationship is the concept of a joint pilgrimage, for the facilitator too is actually also walking this journey. Thus, 'facilitating', according to me, appears to be a more collaborative kind of leadership, because it is a relationship that often leads to the mutual development of both persons involved – that is the facilitator and the facilitated. It is a relationship that is clearly based on the principle that both have something to learn from each other, and both have to find solutions together. In this context a comment by Lowy is instructive when he says: "Learners should be viewed as resource persons and teachers as facilitators". He elaborates: "Learners reflect upon their experiences and these become subject matter. The supervisor focuses on such experiences of the student and nurtures insights drawn from them, allowing the learner to develop and to grow by providing optimal conditions for such growth" (Lowly, 1983, p. 57). Bruner (1966, cited in Saari, 1986) notes something similar when he suggests that "too much dependence upon a supervisor is not desirable, but a poor prognosticator for long-term learning. The learner capable of true creativity has to learn through discovery" (p. 69).

The 'facilitative' approach is therefore quite a different one from the 'supervisory' approach, and changing the term used to describe the function of the fieldwork supervisor could constitute the first step in discovering a response to the question regarding how to guide students in fieldwork today. This is because language often controls the way we think,[1] and subsequently how we act. Therefore, the use of an alternative term to 'supervisor' may help the social work educator to understand her/his role differently and then to function accordingly.

This change in the understanding of the role of the fieldwork educator from supervisor to facilitator is even more necessary because, even though students may come from the same socio-economic-political and cultural milieu and share other similarities, each student/supervisee is unique and different from every other student. This is because there are also differences among students/supervisees in the way they think, the way they interact, differences in their intelligence, their interests, aspirations etcetera. Thus, for example, while educational institutions do recognise different **'levels'** or degrees of intelligence among students, most still do not recognise that there are different **'types'** of intelligences among them – some of whose intelligences fit snugly into the requirements of the academic system, while other types of intelligences are not really appreciated or recognised in the same way. In this context a reflection of the well-known science fiction writer, Isaac Asimov, can be very instructive. Noting that he himself got a score of 160 (genius) in IQ tests, he questions the validity of these intelligence tests in the following manner:

> "Don't such scores simply mean that I am very good at answering the type of academic questions that are considered worthy of answers by people who make up the intelligence tests – people with intellectual bents similar to mine? [He then speaks of his auto repair man who could repair his car while

he himself was completely at sea. He then goes on to ask] "Well then suppose my auto-repair man devised questions for an intelligence test. Or suppose a carpenter did, or a farmer, or indeed almost anyone but an academician. By every one of those tests I'd prove myself a moron."

(Asimov)

Thus besides the commonly accepted differences between IQ and EQ (emotional intelligence) that was popularised by the American developmental psychologist Goleman (1995), Howard Gardener had much earlier described nine different types of intelligence (i) Naturalist (nature smart), (ii) Musical (sound smart), (iii) Logical-mathematical (number/reasoning smart), (iv) Existential (life smart), (v) Interpersonal (people smart), (vi) Bodily-kinaesthetic (body smart) (vii) Linguistic (word smart), (viii) Intra-personal and (ix) Spatial (Gardener, 1983).

These differences in types of intelligences are also clearly on display when social work students are placed in different fieldwork agencies. For example, some social work students have great potential in working with people at an individual or family level where they show a keen understanding of human and family dynamics. Another student may be extremely gifted at interacting with small groups, while still another may have the aptitude and interest in working with larger communities, based on a keen understanding the socio-political complexities impacting them. Then there are those who are good at research in social work, some being particularly good at research of a quantitative kind and some of a qualitative kind. And so on and so forth. Each of these areas of social work intervention requires some specific skill sets and knowledge, in addition to the generic skill sets and knowledge required of all social workers.

In addition to the differences in types of intelligences among students, differences in learning styles is another factor that fieldwork supervisors/facilitators need to contend with vis a vis their students. As Raymond Fox and Pat Guild put it, learners "*see the world through the windows of their own personality. . . . They perceive certain elements and not others because their experience* is filtered through the screens of cognitive processes, preferences, values, experiences, etc." (Fox & Guild, 1987, p. 66) that are specific to them. The authors discuss how research in learning styles confirms that individuals have their own way of perceiving or gaining knowledge, processing it, valuing/judging and reacting to information and ideas, and finally behaving. They believe that "these dimensions, when taken into careful consideration lead to a supervisory programme which is at the same time more individualised and rational" (Fox & Guild, 1987, p. 72).

Davenport and Davenport (1988) in their article on "Individualizing Student Supervision – The use of Andragogical-Pedagogical Orientation Questionnaires", point out that sometimes even older supervisees prefer heavily structured arrangements (i.e. a pedagogical approach) while others prefer self-directed experiences (i.e. an andragogical approach). The same is true of the younger learners. Similarly, they note that many students, including both younger and older ones, fall into a middle range, apparently preferring a combination of approaches. Therefore, one cannot assume that all adult learners prefer an andragogical approach to learning. According to Schulz (1977, cited in Fox & Guild, 1987), a student's "preferred environment, emotion and social setting, need for structure, cultural influences, preferred sensory modalities, reasoning patterns and memory factors" (p. 68) all play an important role in the way an individual learns.

To add to this mix of variables of which some elements have been listed earlier, the supervisor her/himself comes with her/his own 'background', as well as her/his own biases, intelligences, interests and capacities. These add to the complexities of the relationship between the supervisor and the supervisees.

All this makes the task of the fieldwork supervisors/facilitators a very daunting one. Therefore, the need for supervisors/facilitators to recognise and understand these variables in the students and in themselves is critical, in order to offer guidance that is meaningful to the teaching-learning needs of the student. Unfortunately, at times, fieldwork supervisors tend to fit all students into pre-set 'boxes' based on the specific ideology/focus of the particular college or university in which the social work programme is being offered. This is because, in a university setting, there is an attempt to treat all students equally and so it is difficult to take their diversity and uniqueness into account when it comes to assessment patterns. However, given that one of the key principles of the social work profession is to respect the uniqueness and differences in each individual, it would be more meaningful and worthwhile for a fieldwork supervisor not just to be a facilitator but move towards becoming an **adaptive facilitator**.

Becoming an adaptive facilitator

How does one become an adaptive facilitator? In the context of social work education in India, most reputed schools/colleges of social work have developed a fieldwork curriculum where the goals that have to be achieved through the fieldwork programme are clearly enunciated. These goals generally spell out the expectations from students with regard to developing their knowledge and their skills, as well as the attitudes and value systems they need to internalise in order to become well-rounded social work professionals. Whereas the expectations of 'knowledge' would include the student's ability to understand the philosophy, goals, structure and services of the agency and her/his ability to link theory taught in class to field situations, 'skills' would refer to the interpersonal, interventional, organisational, research, analytical and other such skills that will help them to act in the best interest of the people or groups they engage with. As for attitudes and values, social workers already have in their professional codes an articulation of the attitudes and values they must bring to their professional work. All these elements then become the criteria to evaluate the performance of the students.

While the exigencies of a university system may demand that, in the interest of 'fairness', one cannot have different sets of criteria for different students in judging their performance, it is also true that a blanket application of the same criteria for all may be extremely unfair to students who come from 'alternative' backgrounds and who, for instance, have other types of intelligence than the IQ/academic intelligence that is given a premium in our universities.

Therefore, when working out the criteria for evaluating performance, care must be taken to see that the criteria are not unfairly weighted in favour of one kind of student. To ensure this, fieldwork supervisors would do well to take time to understand and gauge a student's **'potential'**, before evaluating her/his **'performance'**. In this context 'potential' refers to the mental, emotional/psychological, intellectual and social capacity inherent in the student. Identifying this potential is crucial for both the student and the supervisor, for it is this which will give the latter an understanding of where and how much to push the boundaries, in order to help the student attain a performance that is commensurate with her/his own potential. Subsequently, after a reasonable period of time (perhaps at the end of a semester of fieldwork), a perceptive fieldwork supervisor could more fairly gauge the student's potential and then could use the same to push the student to perform better. This means that the supervisor needs to focus, initially at least, on 'performance' matching 'potential', rather than on performance alone, which latter would be based on the criteria that are enunciated in the fieldwork curriculum of the specific social work college to which they belong.

This actually means that the earlier 'scoring' of the fieldwork supervisor would be tentative, and it is only at the end of the first year (at least) that the scoring for the entire year should be finalised, with the willingness to revise earlier impressions if necessary. If this is done, then even though the social work educational programme cannot be individualised for every student, every student can be individualised, so as to gradually help him/her to adjust to the educational programme (Mathew, 1975).

An approach to individualising the student

Kadushin and Harkness categorise the research findings on characteristics associated with effective supervision and leadership in two clusters of factors – one which relates to the **task-centred**, instrumental considerations of supervision and the second to the **people-centred** expressive considerations of supervision. This, they say, is similar to the two variables Blake and Mouton described when they talked about the development of their Managerial grid – **'concern for production'** (the instrumental consideration) and **'concern for people'** (the expressive consideration). Fiedler's (1967, cited in Kadushin & Harkness, 2004) research on leadership too suggests an optimum mix of these two major dimensions and a judgement as to which jobs or situations require a greater focus on task-orientation and which require a greater focus on the human relations aspect. Kadushin and Harkness therefore conclude that "the best managerial style, both psychologically satisfying and economically productive, is an optimum combination of the two concerns" (Kadushin & Harkness, 2004, p. 218).

If the social work supervisor's role is primarily a managerial one, then such a conclusion may be valid. However, in social work education, which is concerned with preparing social workers, who will be eventually working within a very dynamic socio-economic and political reality, it would not be enough to discuss task-orientation versus person-centred approaches, because the **task** *is* the development of the full potential of the **person** (student). This challenges the task-person duality. Consequently, the fieldwork supervisor needs to move a step further towards learning how to individualise each student, so that, based on the background, strengths, weaknesses, concerns, personalities, learning style etcetera, the supervisor carves out a fieldwork experience that allows the student to explore her/his own full potential. This is possible because the social work arena is vast, and there is room for different students to hone their skills in the areas that best suit their personality and/or interests. The primary task of the supervisor would then be to gauge the needs of individual students and their potential and then find out the best fit for each. As Mathew writes: "Students have not yet become, but they are in the process of becoming. That is, their personalities are at different stages of development. The supervisor is at an advantageous position in that she is able to observe students while they are learning by doing, and thus come to see their personalities functioning at various levels" (Mathew, 1975, p. 327).

It is in this dynamic context that a 9-box **Facilitating Matrix**[2] is proposed (see Figure 9.1) in an attempt to help supervisors as they work to identify the **'potential'** of each student, even while looking at their **'performance'**. The matrix proposed is only indicative and does not intend to claim that all variables of all students' possible learning journeys are included. Nor does it claim that all students' learning journeys will follow the same trajectory. However, the matrix could help the supervisor to adapt her/his facilitating role, keeping in mind the context, the curriculum and the student and thus grow into becoming an adaptive facilitator.

The use of this matrix is based on the assumption that a supervisor would attempt to try to identify where the student is coming from, what is her/his background, history, her/his capacity to conceptualise, her/his learning style etcetera. The supervisor will then be in a position to provide for the student a fieldwork experience that will help her/him discover and enhance her/his own potential and performance, so that s/he develops the knowledge, skills and attitudes that are considered necessary for a professional social worker As explained earlier, a supervisor who learns to function as an adaptive facilitator could use this Matrix to help her/him to change his or her style vis a vis a particular student, based first on the 'perceived potential' that the student shows and on how the student 'performs' in the tasks assigned to him/her within that perceived potential.

Given later is an explanation of each of the boxes that together constitute the 9-box matrix shown earlier.

However, before explaining each 'box' in the matrix, it is important to first clarify that the different boxes shown in the matrix are actually part of two continuums. The vertical axis indicates the 'perceived potential' of the student, that is, the potential of the individual student as perceived by the supervisor/facilitator, while the horizontal axis indicates the level of 'performance' of the student as judged by the supervisor/facilitator.

The adaptive supervisor **187**

	C	**B**	**A**
HIGH	Supervisor/Facilitator attempts to understand reasons for lack of performance Reassigns task/roles based on aptitude and interest areas	Supervisor/Facilitator provides the student scope for independent assignments and responsibilities. Facilitator is a sounding board – supports and questions appropriately, and nudges to perform to full potential	Supervisor/Facilitator provides the student scope for independent assignments and responsibilities. Facilitator is a sounding board – supports and questions appropriately
	F	**E**	**D**
PERCEIVED POTENTIAL	Supervisor/Facilitator attempts to understand reasons for lack of performance. Reassigns task/roles based on aptitude and interest areas	Supervisor/Facilitator encourages and sustains interest in the student, while nudging him/her to explore more creative and better ways to improve potential and performance	Supervisor/Facilitator encourages and sustains interest in the student, while nudging him/her to explore ways to discover one's own full potential
	I	**H**	**G**
	Supervisor/Facilitator is more directive. Provides structured tasks. More hand holding so as to help student realize fuller potential and better performance	Supervisor/Facilitator encourages and sustains interest in the student, while nudging him/her to explore more creative and better ways to improve potential and performance	Supervisor/Facilitator encourages and sustains interest in the student, while nudging him/her to explore ways to discover one's own further potential
LOW		**PERFORMANCE**	
	LOW		**HIGH**

FIGURE 9.1 Facilitation matrix

Source: Author

And though some boxes seem almost exactly the same, (shown in the diagram in the same colours) they are yet shown as different boxes because these differences are only meant to help the supervisor/facilitator decide which aspect (potential or performance) needs to be immediately focused upon to bring about incremental changes. For example, if the perceived potential is low (e.g. Box H) then the adaptive supervisor/facilitator might want to focus on trying to understand the student's background more and work on enhancing potential, and if both potential and performance are at the middle or sub-optimal level (e.g. Box E), then the adaptive supervisor/facilitator needs to judge which of the two needs to be worked on first. However, it must be remembered that these boxes are not isolated silos and the matrix is not to be used to place students in a particular box, especially since the dynamic nature of human growth and activity means that a student could move from one 'position' to another and back again, depending on a variety of circumstances.

Box A: Indicates a student who is self-actualised. Such a student has probably come with some experience and knowledge of the field and shows a lot of capacity and maturity for self-learning, reflection and a good understanding of field realities. In such a situation, it is imperative for the supervisor who desires to function as an adaptive facilitator to respect the student's knowledge and experience and form a collaborative relationship with her/him. The student here needs to be stimulated through discussions and assignments, and the tasks assigned or agreed upon should be in keeping with the interest, potential and capacity of the student. In such a situation, as Saari puts it: "The learner offers observation of what has taken place in the interactions with the client (system) while the supervisor offers supplementary observations which may be slightly more differentiated or complex based on a wider range of experience. Together the two participants in the process may contemplate or speculate about possibilities which the student may not have previously considered" (Saari, 1986, p. 76).

I am reminded of a student who joined the social work programme with much experience of working with youth and carrying with him a vision of making the youth a very important stakeholder in the transformation of society. He already had the vision, the drive, the energy and some amount of knowledge to give shape to his dream. What he probably was seeking from a training in social work was help to enhance his search for knowledge and hone his skills so that he would be able to realise his dream. A student such as this would need a different kind of a facilitator – one who would be able to challenge and question him yet respect his individuality and understand his dream; a facilitator who would guide yet be a learner with him.

Box B: Refers to a student who is quite similar to the one described in Box A, in that the student shows a lot of potential but for some reason s/he is not performing up to her/his full potential. It could be a temporary phase – something in her/his personal or professional life which in all probability would correct itself over a period of time. In such a situation, it might be necessary for an adaptive facilitator to allow the student some time and space to get her/his act together. The supervisor/facilitator could offer her/his time to the student, help the student discover/identify for her/himself the possible restraining factors, so as to help her/him to move out of the performance predicament that s/he is in. In short, s/he can help the student to deal with some of the hindering factors. However, if the student is not willing to take the responsibility to work on the issue, then the supervisor/facilitator would have to push or nudge the student a little to get her/him to realise her/his full potential.

Boxes C and F: These boxes represent those students whose potential, as perceived by the supervisor/facilitator at least, is either high or medium but whose performance does not match that potential. This could be because of some inner block within the student or some external factors. For example, a student may find it difficult to deal with a case of domestic violence or child sexual abuse, because of the trauma that s/he experienced in her/his own childhood. Here it would be important for the supervisor/facilitator to find out the reasons for the lack of performance. On the basis of what the problem is, s/he either works out a different task/assignment for the student, or helps the student to deal with some of the blocks that the latter is experiencing which prevents optimal functioning. In some cases it might also be necessary to refer such a student to a counsellor for further help.

Boxes D and G: These boxes represent those students who are performing to their potential but where their potential itself needs to be enhanced. Here the supervisor/facilitator can encourage and sustain the efforts made by the student, while at the same time pushing them to expand their horizons by reading, participating in discussions, questioning etcetera. By doing this the supervisor/facilitator helps the student to explore areas where s/he can develop her/his own potential further.

Boxes E and H: Students who 'fit' into this box are those who do not show much potential and also perform only at an average level. What the supervisor-facilitator could do here is to first find a way of developing or creating an interest in the student for the work s/he is doing, perhaps by giving the student tasks that are simple and more structured, so that successful completion of such tasks create an affinity for the same. Assistance to such a student could also include altering guidance styles depending on the style that the student is more comfortable with, so that the student feels challenged to discover her/his potential and perform better.

Box I: This box indicates those students who, at least for the time being, do not show much potential and neither do they perform up to minimal expectations.

I remember a time about 25 years ago when a tribal student was placed under my guidance for field work. During the course of her work, she was expected to make phone calls to an agency for referral of her client, which she kept delaying inordinately. This seemed like laziness or a lack of professionalism, as the student had been reminded of this multiple times. It was only on further exploration that I discovered that she did not know how to use the telephone and was too embarrassed to acknowledge this publicly.

This was before the time of the ubiquitous mobile phone, and perhaps in today's age one would not find such cases in most schools of social work, but it is illustrative of how there could be hidden reasons as to why a student could be seen as belonging to Box I.

There would be many other such examples not only in India but in other parts of the world as well. Fieldwork supervisors need to remember this, because the lack of performance in particular cases could be due to various reasons. Either the concepts are too new, or the environment is too threatening, or the language is something that the student is not familiar with, or myriad other reasons. Many students who come to city colleges from remote villages or from tribal belts in India may fall within this category at first. For such students, the hugeness of the concrete jungle that is the city, the alienation they experience because of the diverse cultures and the surroundings that they are thrust into, are all a source of great stress and frustration. The role of the supervisor/facilitator here is to invest time and effort in making such students feel at ease, helping them to familiarise themselves with the new environment and navigate through this difficult phase. Since, in reality, it is for this set of vulnerable communities found in villages that much of social work in India is directed, the ability of the fieldwork supervisor to empathise with students coming from these backgrounds is put to the test, and the fieldwork supervisor becomes a model for her/his student. In this context, it is important to appreciate the value of frustration in the educational process, so that the supervisor/facilitator works to ensure that frustrations do not hinder but actually are used as spurs to growth.

In general then, over the span of the two to three years of the social work degree programme, a supervisor/facilitator could, using the ideas expressed in this Matrix, help the students discover for themselves their own individual interests, capacities and skills – and guide them to develop that potential to the fullest, while at the same time making sure that the knowledge, skills and attitudes that are minimally necessary for all social workers are not compromised. This will be possible only if the fieldwork supervisor is able to adapt her/his own style of facilitating to the individual reality of each student. In other words, the supervisor would need to become an 'adaptive facilitator'.

The adaptive facilitator as a model – fostering appropriate attitudes and values

Finally and most importantly, a crucial element in the facilitating role is the supervisor/ facilitator her/himself, who by **'being'**, or **'demonstrating'**, offers great opportunities to the student to learn by osmosis as it were. As Kolb (1974, cited in Fox & Guild, 1987) puts it, "*successful learning [is] a constant tension between action and observation, and involvement and reflection*" (p. 70). This is a very effective method of teaching, because the supervisor/facilitator's knowledge, ways of functioning, maturity, contribution and dedication to her/his work as a social work professional, can contribute greatly to the student's learning. This kind of learning, though subliminal, plays a crucial role in the formation of a professional. Here too there is need for the supervisor/facilitator to have the ability to adapt to real life situations as will be explained further later.

A fieldwork supervisor imparts knowledge and helps to develop skills in her/his students not only by what s/he communicates by way of sharing and instruction but also by the way s/he conducts her/himself. Just like children learn more from the actions of their parents rather than from their instructions, so too students imbibe a lot from the actions of a teacher. What a fieldwork supervisor demonstrates by her/his actions and interactions with students and in her/his dealings with others in the institute or fieldwork agency become lessons that the student can learn from. Such demonstrations happen in real life situations, where the supervisor/facilitator responds effectively to changing situations. This kind of modelling calls for a highly adaptive ability in the supervisor/facilitator, because, as Schubert (1965) points out, making use of real-life situations as opportunities to teach is an important aspect of fieldwork supervision (cited in Mathew, 1975).

> A good example of this was seen during an educational work camp where a conflict arose among a group of students. In this particular instance, the students had split into two factions, with each accusing the other of inappropriate and disrespectful behaviour towards the villagers with whom they were engaging at the camp. The social work educator who was present felt the conflict was spiraling into a bitter spat which would affect the entire experience of the camp. Hence she decided to bring up the issue openly in the evaluation session at the end of the day. At this meeting, she asked a representative of each of the two groups to present their own perception of what had happened. The others from each of the groups were then given a chance to add whatever they felt needed to be added. By listening respectfully to each student and not allowing any other student to interrupt, the educator demonstrated a certain initial step in dealing with conflict, that of listening. Then the educator told the students that she would not sit in judgement of all that had happened because each group was naturally giving their own side of the story – their own perspective. And since there appeared to be some truth on both sides, it would be difficult to come to any conclusion. However, she said that in order to move forward, she invited each student to reflect and come up with any one or more actions that they themselves could have individually taken at any point to change the trajectory of the conflict as it spiraled. This approach changed the entire environment, as now the focus was not on what wrong the 'other' had done, but to reflect on what 'I' could have done so that the conflict would not have spiraled the way it did. The sharing that followed helped each student to reflect on their own behaviour (without any finger-pointing being allowed) and how they could have probably taken the initiative to change the flow of the conflict that could have led to a more positive outcome. The educator then ended the exercise by pointing out to the students that they themselves had come up with ways by which they could have solved the issue. She then asked them to suggest what they could now do to resolve the issue in a manner that would not spoil their remaining village experience. The result was that the rest of the camp went off without a constant harking back to the conflict, and the students learnt one way of handling conflicts.

Conflict management situations are very helpful opportunities in this regard, because they help bring a host of human dynamics into the open. As the example illustrates, the way the social work educator dealt with the issue can become an important learning moment for the student(s) concerned. It may also be pointed out that the process used by the educator could ideally be re-visited and reflected upon by both student(s) and the educator at a later stage, and lessons drawn could be further strengthened or refined. In the process, the educator too learns something new.

In a similar way, 'group conferences' too can be a very potent way for the fieldwork supervisor/facilitator to model the behaviour and attitudes that are expected of the students. In group conferences, for example, the manner in which a fieldwork supervisor helps students handle specific ethical dilemmas they face is something that could be an effective learning moment for students. This is particularly important, because it would seem that the ability to reflect and to act ethically is an aspect that is not given very serious thought to when assessing a student's 'performance', and yet this must be a constant foundation on which the performance is built.

What then can be done to ensure that the ethical dimension is taken care of? In India we are fortunate to have certain Social Work Codes of Ethics that are prepared by various associations of social workers. There is also the International Code of Social Work Ethics. These codes can be used as the touchstone to judge a course of action.

However, it is incumbent on the fieldwork supervisor to make sure to bring up matters of ethics when exploring with the student(s) the kind of interventions that are being considered or being made in the process of the field placement. This would mean that the supervisor must ensure that some fieldwork conferences include sufficient time to reflect on the ethical aspects of some of the interventions.

> For example, in a particular case, a student came to the supervisor worried about what she should do as the HIV patient (male) who she was counselling was refusing to give his consent to revealing his HIV status to his engaged partner even though she had made every effort to discuss with the client the pros and cons of not sharing the information with his partner. She felt it was more important to protect the unsuspecting partner from a life-threatening situation than to honour the principle of confidentiality. Here, the field work supervisor helped the student to see that this was an ethical dilemma, where there was a clash between different values. On the one hand there was the value of self-determination and confidentiality and on the other hand the value of doing all in one's legitimate power to protect the life of an unsuspecting and vulnerable partner (which is an obligation that all human beings ought to have). And like in many ethical dilemmas, the unfortunate fact was that not making a choice was also a choice.
>
> In this case the supervisor/facilitator first of all acknowledged that it was a difficult situation and worked together with the student to explore all the dimensions of the situation. However, since there was merit on both sides, it was difficult to make a choice. It was then that the Social Work Code of Ethics was brought into the discussion to find out whether there was any clear

guideline to decide on what was most appropriate. In the medical profession the Hippocratic oath offers a clear guideline, namely that a doctor must always try to save life rather than destroy it, which is why euthanasia has been proscribed for so long. In the Social Work Codes of Ethics drawn up by the different associations in India, however, there is no clear guideline or hierarchy of values offered. The question then was what should form the basis for the decision. It was then decided to go by the ideological stance of the institute/agency in which they were both functioning, which was to honour the confidentiality and self-determination that was promised to the HIV person.

Thus, through this process, the supervisor/facilitator helped the student(s) to develop the ability to enquire ethically into an issue, rather than take the easy and ethically unacceptable way out of 'just do what you think is right' (whether the 'you' is the student or the social work educator).

In this manner, the supervisor/facilitator models for the student the way to deal with an ethical dilemma, rather than just 'teaching' her/him what is ethically right or wrong. In doing this the supervisor/facilitator not only demonstrates how to make ethical decisions but also shows by her/his actions that s/he too is open to new ideas and perceptions. This calls for a highly adaptive ability in the fieldwork supervisor so that s/he does not impose but uses the Socratic method to push the student to think and reflect and grow.

Conclusion

In conclusion one can say that for a fieldwork supervisor the learning process is never over. While not downplaying his or her own expertise and experience, the fieldwork supervisor must learn to adapt her/his supervisory style to the type of intelligence, the learning pace and the perceived potential and performance of the individual student. Furthermore, as cues for learning will keep coming from students who bring fresh insights through their interactions and work, the supervisor/facilitator can and must use these to stimulate fresh thinking so that things can be seen in a new light, both intellectually and emotionally. Additionally, the supervisor/facilitator needs to have an understanding of the diverse socio-economic-political and cultural backgrounds that students come from and tailor her/his guidance accordingly. Such a supervisor/facilitator would also need to be alert to latch on to real life learning opportunities and use these to model the attitudes and ethical principles that are currently articulated in various Codes of Social Work Ethics. S/he would thus be walking with the students to help them develop such an ethical approach within themselves – always remembering that this too is a mutually educative experience. In this manner, spurred by the students and her/his own experiences and knowledge, the fieldwork supervisor will be able to function as a facilitator who will continually evolve and adapt to different students' needs and changing situations.

It is this dynamic nature of the social work profession that makes the teaching of social work and especially the role of the fieldwork supervisor, very challenging and interesting. The acknowledgement and respect for different perspectives and individual realities will allow for a more meaningful application of social work strategies and skills by the fieldwork supervisor/facilitator in a manner that makes her/him more adaptive to each student, while not losing sight of the goals of the profession.

Notes

1 Studies in labs at Stanford University and MIT by Lera Boroditsky and others have concluded that *people who speak different languages do indeed think differently and that even flukes of grammar can profoundly affect how we see the world.* www.edge.org/conversation/lera_boroditsky-how-does-our-language-shape-the-way-we-think. Linguists like Antonio Benítez-Burraco Ph.D. have argued that the language we speak affects the way we think. Retrieved March 4, 2018, from www.psychologytoday.com/blog/the-biolinguistic-turn/201702/how-the-language-we-speak-affects-the-way-we-think
2 This Matrix is adapted from the performance-potential 9-box matrix that is often used in management studies. However, it is not clear who first introduced the Matrix used in these management studies. Hence no author is given.

References

Asimov, I. (n.d.). What is intelligence, anyway? *Mafiadocs*. Retrieved March 2018, from https://mafiadoc.com/asimov-intelligencepdf_59f4a0721723dd69dda3eb00.html

Cambridge dictionary. (2018a). Cambridge: Cambridge University Press. Retrieved February 1, 2018, from https://dictionary.cambridge.org/dictionary/english/supervision

Cambridge dictionary. (2018b). Cambridge: Cambridge University Press. Retrieved February 1, 2018, from https://dictionary.cambridge.org/dictionary/english/facilitator

Davenport, J. A. (1988). Individualizing student supervision: The use of andragogical: Pedagogical orientation questionnaires. *Journal of Teaching in Social Work, 2*(2), 83–93.

Fox, R., & Guild, P. (1987). Learning styles: Their relevance to clinical supervision. *The Clinical Supervisor, 5*(3), Fall, 65–77.

Gardner, H. (1983). *Frames of mind: The theory of multiple intelligences*. New York, NY: Basic Books.

Goleman, D. (1995). *Emotional intelligence: Why it can matter more than IQ*. New York, NY: Bantam Books.

Harper, D. (2001–2018). *Online dictionary*. Retrieved October 30, 2017, from www.etymonline.com; www.etymonline.com/word/supervise

Hughes, J. M. (2010). The role of supervision in social work: A critical analysis. *Critical Social Thinking: Policy and Practice, 2*, 59–77

Hung, S. L., Ng, S. L., & Fung, K. K. (2010, May). Functions of social work supervision: Insights from the cross-border supervision model. *International Social Work, 53*(3), 366–378.

Kadushin, A., & Harkness, D. (2004). *Supervision in social work*, pp. 217–277. New Delhi: Rawat Publications.

Lowly, L. (1983). Social work supervision: From models towards theory. *Journal of Education for Social Work, 19*(2), Spring, 55–62.

Mathew, G. (1975). Educational and helping aspects of field work supervision. *Indian Journal of Social Work, 35*(4), 325–333.

Merriam Webster dictionary. (2018). Retrieved February 1, 2018, from www.merriam-webster.com: www.merriam-webster.com/dictionary/supervision

Moffat, R. (1969). The student-supervisor relationship in social work education. *Australian Journal of Social Work*, 27–33.

Paracka, S. (2014, January). The venue for competence development on social work. *Indian Journal of Research*, *3*(1), 195–196.

Saari, C. (1986). Concepts of learning through supervision. *The Clinical Supervisor*, *4*(3), Fall, 63–69.

CONCLUSION

Issues for the future of field instruction in social work education

Srilatha Juvva, Vimla V. Nadkarni and Roshni Nair

Social work education is expansive to address emerging social issues, and fieldwork provides the testing ground for knowledge and skill building in social work students. The basic structure of social work education has not radically changed since its inception in 1936 in India. This reiterates that there is something fundamentally right about the way social work education is being offered. While there is a need to modify and adapt to suit the current context, it is unwise to discard what is working for the profession merely to keep abreast with changing times.

The changes that influence the profession are diverse. They range from contrasting ideological perspectives between the fieldwork placement agency or organisation and the educational institution, alternate problem solving mechanisms and addressing and resolving systems and cultural norms that actually require thinking out of the box and which are antithetical to social work values (e.g. gender discrimination, where girls are not sent to school in a family). Further, social issues (e.g. changing family forms, child care services etc.) that were hitherto not a 'problem', influence of media and communication technology and systemic issues in social work education which are mandated by the authorities in higher education also influence the way the profession spans out. Each of these changes will be elaborated later.

Contrasting ideological perspectives between the fieldwork placement agency or organisation and the educational institution create conflict for the students. The only way to resolve this would be for faculty to work closely with the agency to adopt changing perspectives or for the department or college to float its own field action projects where the social work students would be mentored in more human rights and social justice oriented perspectives and approaches. Within this, the practice of the social work methods would be viewed differently: not as the traditional casework, group work and community organisation but with the issue as the starting point. For instance, College of Social Work, Nirmala Niketan, placed students for fieldwork on the issue of child labour. Using their research skills, they collected evidence about the nature of child labour in some of the Mumbai slums, created a report which was shared with the government and media and developed a lobby to influence the government to ban child labour. Similarly, TISS started a field action project to change societal perceptions about 'beggary' and worked on an alternative law. The students thus placed in the Beggar's Home worked differently. For example when the Bombay Prevention of Begging Act (1959) penalised the 'beggars' and brought them into confinement, the students of social work treated them as 'homeless' and tried to understand their social situation in a holistic manner.

Both, the College of Social Work, Nirmala Niketan and TISS were actively involved in placing students for fieldwork in adult education. This also became a precursor for 'floating placements', that is, moving away from fieldwork within a structured setting like a family welfare centre or hospital or school. This led to placing students to work on specific issue-based interventions, such as work with youth or on shelter for children living on the streets and, more recently, the homeless.

Human rights intervention is another area of practice which has evoked a positive response from some departments and colleges of social work in the country. This could be related to the availability of funding from the UGC encouraging universities to set up centres or offer programmes in some of these specialised areas as mentioned before. Again, protecting human rights, for instance of LGBTQ communities or people with disability, may not necessarily be part of the mission of the university or college of social work. The vision and mission of the university or educational institution would influence the nature of university-community-societal collaboration and field practice. The enlightened leadership of the institution would tailor the teaching and practice of social work based on an ethical and enlightened vision and mission. Besides, human rights work is multidisciplinary. There are other professionals providing leadership in innovating courses in human rights, especially, for instance, the law colleges.

The affiliation of the institution is also critical in this regard. Where the funds are mainly from the government, the institution would not encourage students to take any interventions questioning government policy. Thus fieldwork would be planned using a structural-functional approach or a systems perspective where the focus would be on change within the agency or institution, for example, working with the staff of a children's home or hospital to stop discrimination against children and patients living with HIV. The challenge for the social work educational institution would be thus to question and influence government policy by making the polity and people allies in the process of change and transformation. This informs fieldwork. For example, a student would take up cases of burns in the hospital as cases of violence against women and not merely as a case for marital counselling with the goal of 'adjusting with' the husband or perpetrators of this form of violence due to lack of family support. Also placements with organisations that focus on research and activism would re-orient students and faculty to adopt anti-oppressive and feminist perspectives and approaches and not depend purely on the more comfortable 'problem-solving' or functional perspective where most often the exploited or oppressed are persuaded to adapt to the exploitative reality and not attempt to protest and change it.

Some of the reasons probably for the continuation of practice in traditional specialisations like urban and rural community work, medical and psychiatric social work, family and child welfare and industrial social work, may be due to their 'seeming' popularity and their continued imperative need. There remains much more to be done in these fields of practice and one is still dealing with emerging complexities in these sectors. Hence students are taught practice in traditional formats of fieldwork in urban and rural community development (Chougule, 2015). This is supported by Johnson, Bailey, and Padmore (2012) who describe the pattern of fieldwork in undergraduate and graduate social work programmes as having remained consistent, with the mix of observation visits, study tours, concurrent and block fieldwork. According to Ramsey (1989), the combined model is the ideal approach, as students are able to benefit from both the agency/practice orientation of the block model and the classroom/theoretical orientation of the concurrent model.

Given the versatility of social work, the pedagogy of fieldwork is responsive to these changing and newer contexts. There is an imperative need to develop creative and culturally competent strategies to make fieldwork education more responsive and effective in producing results on the ground. There is no 'cookie-cutter' answer to issues. Social justice may be influenced by the funding agency. Interventions in floating placements should be relevant to the sociocultural context.

Challenges in designing fieldwork

The current practice of offering fieldwork in concurrent or block formats is raising further challenges, especially with the curriculum requirements of student involvement in a plethora of activities: classroom learning, research, writing assignments besides maintaining journals and so on. In addition to this, the UGC mandates certain changes in the curriculum, for instance, opening up non-social work courses as a part of the Choice based Credit System (CBCS) to the students. Planning fieldwork thus becomes more challenging unless the different departments offering the CBCS courses are in sync. Most of the departments and colleges of social work have continued with concurrent fieldwork in the first year and block fieldwork in the second year. Some colleges also offer students a choice to change their placement in each semester. This practice has both advantages and disadvantages. The criticism is that this does not provide enough scope for students to adequately test out their social work knowledge and skills learnt during the first year. Students also may not have the opportunity to appreciate the continuity of interventions in some fields of practice. For example, work with police and prisons or grassroots movements requires time to understand the context for concrete outputs. Further, they may not have the opportunity to share and exchange their experiences in the classroom to facilitate peer learning.

The students of social work are often challenged to integrate theory with practice. The two have seemingly become dichotomous, often juxtaposed between on-the-ground practicality and intellectual imperialism. On the one hand, fieldwork supervisors experience discomfort with theoretical frameworks and constructs, and social work teachers are far removed from the reality of comprehending the practical nuances of the field (as, in some colleges, teachers visit the field only once a month or once a semester). Due to the lack of a seamless linkage, the students are caught in an important and indispensable double bind, and they feel pressured to maximise their learning and yet contend with the challenges of these realities. The contributors to this book also reflect on the contestations of social work education and the field of practice that social work students have to deal with. There needs to be a continuous dialogue between practitioners and social work educators so that there is an alignment between theory and practice.

Nuances of field instruction

The contributors to this book share their perspectives of field instruction in their respective school/college of social work. The various perspectives across the country are region specific, taking into account the sociocultural and geographic characteristics of the place in which they are located. What seems to emerge is a common pattern of fieldwork across the programmes – whether based in a rural/tribal or urban setting. The pattern does not seem to have changed over the years since the beginning of social work education in India. Five chapters have discussed very similar components for fieldwork starting from orientations in the first semester to concurrent fieldwork and community settings in the first year of the master's and integrated programmes, leading to placements in more structured agency settings in the final two semesters. The predominant degree programme is at the master's level, a legacy of American social work education.

Dealing with structure

Social work education programmes have remained status quo-ist in most cases; however, as is seen internationally, there is the expressed need for teaching students about social action and policy development, working with structural issues and macro planning, especially in remote areas like the Barak Valley where the students are placed and supervised with highly oppressed and exploited poverty groups. The experience of supervising students on domestic violence and sexual abuse issues is mentioned in two chapters.

The supervisory challenges and coordination across the spectrum also appear to be very similar. The most common of these is matching students with the placements and locating placements with professional social workers, a rarity in the current context and especially in non-government organisations which are being closely monitored for their sources of funding. Many NGOs have closed down; the smaller ones that continue doggedly offer low salaries and do not employ trained social workers.

The lack of 'on-the-spot' supervision and in the field from professional social workers cannot be compensated fully by faculty supervisors who are too busy with teaching and research. The new norms are not always learner-centred but focus on result or performance orientation by the faculty in a statistical format such as teaching hours per week in the classroom, participation and leading research and publications, and presenting papers in national and international conferences.

Fieldwork supervision receives very low priority as many universities tend to apply the same criteria for the social work programme as they do for the social sciences. Thus several authors have described how faculty members are not available for individual conferences and close individual student-based supervision as was traditionally expected. The number of students they have to supervise is large – about 15 to 20 in various settings. Thus they have to depend on senior students for helping the junior students and also find other forms like group supervision as more practical. Reading records and using them as learning tools becomes almost impossible. Junior students (as exemplified in the chapter on Assam University's department of social work) face problems when senior students are not available and do not follow ethical practices. Supervisors may tend to neglect this responsibility and deny the student the freedom to speak freely about these problems.

As witnessed through the book chapters, fieldwork instruction or supervision is a complex process that needs foresight and oversight throughout the process of facilitating learning in social work students. Challenges are contextual, learner and supervisor related, agency/organisation and community related, as well as in interacting with the programme itself, the curriculum, fieldwork objectives and assessment criteria in different semester and different degree levels; in the structuring of fieldwork when there are many students to be placed in single agencies due to the lack of placements or non-availability of professional social workers and committed field staff. Barriers are at the micro and macro levels with the changing norms and curriculum expectations trickling down from national bodies like the UGC and evaluating National Accreditation and Assessment Council.

At the level of curriculum, organising and executing fieldwork in a rural area is challenging given the limited human resources for supervision and discussion. The use of case study method and research on structural and macro issues builds evidence for action. The introduction of a fieldwork course in the first year is useful so that students are aware of the objectives, tasks and assessment criteria and are better able to adjust to the requirements of fieldwork. Creating fieldwork centres, field action projects provides opportunities for greater faculty involvement in the field. It also provides for continuity of community work while students are being supervised on the ground by social work teachers.

Dealing with diversity

Another challenge common across the programmes is the diversity in student background, discipline, personality, intelligence, skills in communication and so on. Similarly there are differences in the supervisors with regard to their commitment, teaching style, personality, attitudes and ethics. How do we find the best match so as to create an ideal environment for students to learn and grow? Some of the authors have proposed having standardised guidelines and assessment criteria for fieldwork and supervision as the only way out for meeting of subjective-objective responses. Do we need external examiners for fieldwork as they are not aware of the context and the difficulties that students face in the field unless they are well oriented before the assessment, which may also be discouraged to maintain 'objectivity'? These are dilemmas that are being dealt with through fieldwork coordinating committees and fieldwork coordinators using variable mechanisms across the different programmes. While these may be speculations, it becomes worthwhile to examine these questions to respond to the changing realities of the profession.

A significant area of diversity pertains to ideological differences between students and the supervisor. Each of them comes with their life experiences, and young students come with their preconceived notions that get challenged during the course of their study. The ideological differences coupled with the generational differences may influence the supervisory relationship. The consequences of such diversity may help the student and the supervisor grow or may lead to a wide gap that needs to be bridged. However, this is a challenge that the supervisor needs to deal with. This is influenced by the age, experience and sociocultural background of the supervisor.

Dealing with field realities

The nuances of understanding the field with all its ramifications influence the relationship between the student and the supervisor; they sometimes blur in the boundaries between a supervisor and teacher. The innovation of 'supportive fieldwork pedagogy' of Karve Institute of Social Sciences, for instance, fosters learning of complex skills through training and synthesis. The relationship between the supervisor and the student contributes significantly to the learning process. The supervisor thus becomes a role model with skills and competencies to navigate the complex system to produce a result. Supervisory discussions serve to enhance this learning. There is a need to transcend the binary way of functioning in the classroom and the field and juxtapose the two through converging classroom teaching with field realities and praxis.

The lack of a unifying model that can hold multiple and intersecting perspectives for theory, practice, policy and research creates an opportunity for supervision. The application of theory to the field can become an important aspect for learning in the supervisory space. The supervisory process has the potential to plug the gap between what is taught in classroom as theory and what is being practiced in the field in reality. When one is able to do this, it becomes the arena for praxis and the potential to create sustainable change that makes the unworkable system workable. Supervision thus has import in transcending the challenges that students face while linking theory to the field realities.

Coordinating fieldwork

With increasing numbers of social work education programmes having opened across the country and an expanding number of students, fieldwork coordination becomes a great challenge. The fieldwork director is expected to work together with colleagues and supervisors to outline clear guidelines for fieldwork and supervision and monitor these processes both in the department/college as well as in the agency/organisation/field. The fieldwork director or coordinator does get frustrated with the changes in the curriculum and performance expectations as the burden of supervision falls more on young faculty with less field experience. Thus the director has to do a balancing act of ensuring that there is fair distribution of fieldwork supervisory workload across the faculty team. The greatest challenge is to ensure quality supervision, with the changing scenario of increased competition for agency placements with mushrooming of schools of social work and increasing faculty workload. How do we reconcile these differential expectations, especially in the current context where faculty are being appointed when they freshly graduate and without adequate field experience? Fieldwork coordination can become a painful process unless the faculty members of the department or school are together in their vision, mission and goals for their department or school.

Roles in supervision

In the current context, supervision is a nurturing rather than a vigilante process. Again we see a repetition of similar challenges relating to the dyad relationship of student-supervisor influenced by factors over which the supervisor or student does not have control. For instance, the introduction of the Choice Based Credit System resulting in reduced contact of supervisor with student, less time for reading recordings and appointment of faculty with doctoral degrees but without the necessary field experience. The roles of the supervisor as mentor, motivator, model, learner and guide may overlap, for example, mentor is a motivator and a model for the social work student.

The change of nomenclature from 'supervisor' to 'adaptive facilitator' or 'adaptive supervisor' challenges the current perspectives on supervision. With the information revolution, students may be better informed than the supervisor who has to be open to a process of 'reverse supervision'. Also, supervision is increasingly seen as being developmental, formative, restorative and subjective and hence focusing more on the process of supervision at an interactive level where the student learns from his/her own experience of fieldwork and draws conclusions. Should we change the title of 'supervisor' to 'adaptive facilitator'? This is a question that has to be handled probably at the level of a national council or national association as it would create a lot of resistance in the existing secure system where the idea of supervising is better understood than merely facilitating. However, this could be experimented with in a school that has some autonomy to innovate rather than in a straitjacketed university system. A well-documented researched experience from both the teacher and learner perspectives could be recommended to the national council or national association for application across the country.

Tools of supervision

Most of the authors mention the importance of recording as a necessary tool in field instruction. It is through student records that supervisors steer the social work student to make the right moves in their fieldwork. Supervisory comments which may be often misinterpreted as criticism by the student are essential to guide the social work student in learning skills, acquiring knowledge, analysing issues and planning interventions, as well as implementing action within a value-based ethical framework of practice. The authors have expressed frustration when faculty and fieldwork supervisors do not use the records productively in the ICs for facilitating students in fieldwork. Also, there are constraints due to lack of time, lack of field experience and indifferent attitude of the supervisor. They also may lack the capacity to show the student the linkages between theory and practice either because they do not read and keep up with social work theory or they are too busy with their own responsibilities and view supervision as an extra burden on their limited time.

How do we deal with these issues where a longstanding and basic teaching-learning tool does not receive the attention required for effective supervision of social work students? Is technology and the use of social media the answer? Audio and video records rather than written process records which often students find a burden to complete especially in today's globalised world where we have forgotten to write as we are more on laptops, iPad and our mobiles? Maybe we need to review our traditional structure and innovate new structures for writing and reflecting on fieldwork so that it becomes an exciting process for students. Encouraging creative styles and methodology of recording and documentation even in a graphic format may enthuse students to learn better in the field. There is a need for students to engage in critical and reflective thinking, synthesis and producing a result on the ground simultaneously through the documentation. Recording is therefore very crucial for praxis in student learning.

Fieldwork conferences are critical sites for learning from the field. The challenges identified range from the large student group who works with one supervisor, thus leading to the contention of a skewed student-supervisor ratio, on-site supervision and related experiences and the content of supervision and its contestations in supervision. The nuances of supervision relate to students' experiences in the field being brought retrospectively into supervisory discussions, introspection and self-awareness. The student's adjustment to the field and its realities influence the planning and executing of fieldwork tasks and working with teams. Further, writing records/fieldwork reports in the medium of instruction can be difficult for some students, especially those who are not comfortable with expressing themselves in writing. Using fieldwork records as learning documents during supervisory discussion for reviewing tasks and the process of fieldwork can pose a challenge too. Students may tend to stretch to relate theory or classroom learning to the field reality. Through individual and group conferences, the students learn to navigate the challenges and dilemmas related to diversity, workload and ideological and ethical concerns. With adequate guidance from the agency and the supervisor, students are able to work with increasing independence, while assuring quality and yet reaching out to the supervisor as an anchor. The role of the supervisor is to model to the student trainees through these conferences and work with them to face and deal with initial anxieties. Further, the supervisor moors the student to face challenges while 'dirtying their hands and feet' in the field. While one may debate the efficacy of individual conferences over group conferences, each has its advantages and can be leveraged to enhance student learning.

Embodying values in supervision

Values and ethics are the foundation of social work practice and need to be taught in the field. This is a difficult arena for supervisors: how do we teach values and ethics through fieldwork; how do we deal with the ethical dilemmas that arise when there are class, gender, regional and caste differences and differential treatment given to clients or students from the backward areas; dilemmas for the student being unable to deal with structural issues or with supervisory biases against a particular practice or community? What is refreshing is to learn a new integrated Indian concept, namely *Samagratā*, which embraces the main values of compassion, social justice and respect for life embedded in spirituality and consciousness, society and social dynamics and ecology (Narayan & Pandit, 2017). This chapter wakes us up to the 'good' and the 'bad' impacts of globalisation and exposure of youth to these influences. Thus, they do not come into the course as 'clean slates' open to learning but as complex beings with baggage from the past and the current changing cultures. Through the roles of mentor, role model, facilitator and educator (mentioned in other chapters also), the supervisor should provide a safe space for assimilation by the student of values and principles of practice and ethical interventions. The core values discussed cannot be divorced from the process of empowerment of all persons. Practices are also described (in the book) which students can be taught to adopt if the values that seem abstract have to be translated in response to field realities. There are areas which need strengthening in supervision: peace and conflict resolution practices, non-violent communication, compassion and love, respect for humanity and the earth through interactions with nature and so on. Besides yoga and meditation, we may need to also study our local indigenous practices through which we convey values and ethics to our students. All religions have certain local cultural practices which we may support or not support but which we need to analyse and integrate into our curriculum if they are beneficial to the community and client system.

The editors attempt to design a broad framework for social work practice and field instruction. Drawing from the *Samagratā* framework of Narayan and Pandit (2017), that exhorts professionals to focus on the juxtaposition of values of the spiritual, social and ecological domains, the authors of the framework locate practice that is rooted in the sociocultural and systemic levels of human existence. This implies that interventions are not only sensitive to human beings but also to nature and values.

Self-system-action focus of social work

Even though the context in which social work is practiced tends to undergo change, the essence of fieldwork does not get altered. This includes the ability of the social work student to source his or her inner power and the values of the profession. It is interesting to note that the aspect of inner power/self of the social worker and the values of the profession do not change drastically with time. However, what changes are the shifts and leverages of the system and the results that we produce commensurate with the changing times.

The dynamic shifts that the context undergoes calls for greater sourcing of values, generation of multiple perspectives, competency development to leverage systems and cultural norms that need to be shifted, and sharpening and practice of skills in order to produce results that are relevant to the profession. Such a shift in systemic and cultural norms and solving problems to produce action or result must occur simultaneously in order to produce an impact in society. In order to do this, the social work educator and supervisor must steward change. 'Successful leaders must learn to: (1) source the power of their inner *wisdom*, anchoring themselves in their values, not just personal interests; (2) seek the *understanding* of the underlying complexities and behaviour patterns that contribute to harmful spirals, and discern and work towards healthier alternatives; and (3) use *knowledge* and know-how to deliver measurable results, offering everyone a way to contribute, to pick up a shovel and dig' (White, 2012, pp. 12–13). The power of wisdom rests in each individual to use and harness.

The first aspect includes the 'being' self, which is manifested as one's wisdom or inner power, the core of a person, which forms the foundation for developing competencies and solving problems for impact. Rodriguez and Juvva (2018) note that while using one's inner power, '[S]he/he is liberated from limiting beliefs, habits and structures and is free to be an authentic human BEING based on universal values. Responsible citizens use intellectual skills such as critical thinking, participatory skills (such as deliberating civilly, monitoring the government, building coalitions, managing conflict fairly, speaking up and speaking out, being in action), source their universal inner values to participate actively in the economy, promoting policies and programs that result in prosperity for all' (p. 128). As White (2012) writes, 'wisdom, born of a deep reverence for life, unleashes our inherent resilience, potential and power, and helps replace fragmentation with unity, short-sightedness with vision, and fear with courage' (p. 13). Any intervention which is born out of this space is bound to be impactful and successful as it is the driving force that initiates change and transformation (Ramanathan & Juvva, 2016, p. 12). This is the space on which ethics of the profession are based. 'The universal values and ethics are the unifying factors that hold us all together, irrespective of nationality, caste, class, race, gender, sexual preference, etc. They form a foundation of principled and ethical leadership for results, where we uphold dignity, equity and respect diversity while holding multiple perspectives; call out unworkable norms in different cultures and organisations, and establish new patterns at home, in community and at work' (Rodriguez & Juvva, 2018, p. 128). For example, social work values of respect for dignity and self-determination of the person would be the foundation with which to shift norms related to inequality or denying agency to a person with mental illness to make decisions for themselves. If dignity and agency are core values, we would alter the spirit-breaking patterns that disempower a person with mental illness to create an enabling environment where s/he would be able to use their agency to make meaningful contributions to society and thus enhance wellbeing.

The second aspect includes understanding, the 'seeing' of (White, 2012) the contexts and their complexities. Typically understanding equips us to design strategies to cater to the systemic issues that need to be addressed. White (2012) says that, 'understanding the root causes of systemic problems is needed to identify strategic pathways, in order to replace destructive patterns with constructive alternatives that will ensure lasting change in thought and behavior' (p. 16). While working with systems that deter optimum human functioning, it is imperative that we understand the complex dynamics and interrelationships operating and influencing a system and design strategies that bring about change on all parts of the system. It also includes that we challenge those parts of the system that oppress, discriminate and exclude. Such characteristics are antithetical to wisdom that typically does not exclude. This is possible only when there is an alignment between wisdom and understanding of self and the system. The third aspect of knowledge or skill sets depicts the 'doing' aspect that produces a result. Interventions that stem from wisdom and help in understanding the context need technical knowledge and skill sets that assist in the process of transformation. White (2012) mentions that, 'knowledge and experience are needed to mobilise the information, people and resources to replace ignorance and inaction with expertise and measurable results' (p. 18). The doing part of self uses skills sets learnt to challenge unworkable systems that are unsustainable and work towards social justice and larger human values that pervade all areas of development.

Critical components of knowledge that are ever-changing, processes of intervention, supervision and skills of intervention also play a key role in determining the content and robustness of fieldwork. Social workers are viewed as system transformers and are called to respond radically. Sharma (2017, p. 24) elucidates seven characteristics of a unique radical response. She urges:

1   Actions and results to be 'sourced from inner power' – this will ground us in the values of social work. While doing this, we will be encouraged to align for congruence between the values we hold as individuals and as professionals.
2   Have the ability to 'transcend social biases and personal positions' – while we hold perspectives we are not attached to our positions, 'isms' and ideologies that exclude and isolate people. When we are not attached to our social profiles, we

are not only able to accept 'as is' and alter it, we do so for alignment with what we stand for and the results we produce.
3. Capitalise on 'innate human understanding of patterns, systems and cultural norms, even without formal education' – it is important to recognise that all human beings can steward change, as they are wired for systems thinking.
4. Have the ability to 'deal with complexity'– we can use our innate understanding of systems to not only comprehend complexities but also simplify it to manage and deal with and resolve problems.
5. Encourage people to 'participate in personal and planetary change' – as human beings we are not only responsible for ourselves but also the environment we live in.
6. Use the 'ability to design responses, take action in a comprehensive manner' – since we have the ability to plug gaps, it is imperative that we design for impact, in alignment with the values of self and the profession.
7. Design for 'fractal (each person's contribution affects the whole), using a set of tools and templates' – given the interlinkage of components and systems we work with, it is important to define our boundary of work, to produce results and let others produce results too. The methods of social work, tools and techniques of intervention provide us a pathway for both outputs and impact. It also means that when we design our interventions in an aligned and holistic manner, we will not only produce results but will also shift policies, systems and cultural norms that can be taken to scale.

The architecture for equitable and sustainable results, as elucidated by Sharma (2017, p. 107) rests on simultaneously dealing with complexity from three domains of solving a problem, shifting systems and cultural norms so that solutions are game changing and sourcing inner capacities and universal values. As social workers, we are constantly dealing with unworkable systems and cultural norms that are entrapping and those that we tend to take for granted. For example, cultural norms of girls not sent to school, only women undertaking care work, disability and mental illness being a curse from above and thus stigmatised and excluded. Other examples pertaining to systems include: the poor will continue to remain poor due to poverty, poverty is a natural phenomenon, development is tokenism, etc. The previously mentioned unworkable norms are reinforced by the notions of exclusion, ableism, scarcity, inequity and a sense of resignation that agency of people will remain dormant.

Field instruction requires us to work while thinking on our feet. This means that it becomes imperative for social workers to source our 'Being', our inner capacities (Sharma, 2017) and compassion (Narayan & Pandit, 2017): 'Synthesising', developing competency or capacity for synthesis that shifts cultural norms and systems (Sharma, 2017) and social justice that addresses the social dimensions of human existence (Narayan & Pandit, 2017); and 'Doing', to solve problems (Sharma, 2017). The BSD Full Spectrum Praxis framework for field instruction is represented as follows in Figure 10.1.

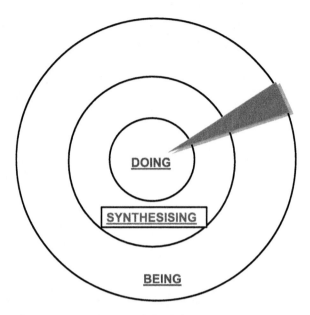

FIGURE 10.1 The BSD Praxis framework for field instruction

This framework allows for 'Being', 'Synthesising' and 'Doing' simultaneously so that results are produced by the student to facilitate the agency of the individuals and groups with whom they work. 'Being' is the foundation on which change can be created. This draws on values of the individual, the profession and the constitution of the country. 'Being' allows for embracing diversity, embodying the values of the individual and the profession, rather than just talking about it. It respects nature and the ecosystem in which we live. 'Synthesising' is the place of designing action, where the structures, cultural norms and ways of functioning are challenged using the ability to draw from the foundational values and ask what is missing. The knowledge, theory, ability to reflect, question and challenge using competencies enrich the design. This is the place for strategy that can leverage change. This informs the action, where we use skill to 'Do' and produce a result. When we design in such a manner that there is an alignment between 'Being', 'Synthesising' and 'Doing', then there is a higher chance of effecting sustainable and equitable change that unleashes individual and collective capacities.

As supervisors and students, it is imperative that we source the fullest potential of both in order to design interventions that tap the same in the people we work with. To illustrate, while undertaking a needs analysis in a tribal village, the student trainees mobilised groups of women and identified needs and ways to address them by enrolling them. The first step they undertook was enquiring about what the women cared for about themselves, their children, their village and the entire ecosystem. The women identified various values that they stood for and embodied in their lives. They identified the shifts they wished to see in their village, the foremost being electricity. They reported that they had depended only on the men in their village, who were bribed with alcohol by the *sarpanch* (village leader) and now they wished to take it forward, for the sake of their children. So the women, with the help of the students, wrote a letter of request to the District Collector for a meeting during which they pitched their request to him. The collector heard them out and instructed the Block Development Officer to ensure that this village got electricity supply in two months, which they did. However, this move of the women unnerved the *sarpanch* and menfolk of the village. The women rationally explained to them that irrespective of the means or the gender, they were able to procure electricity for the village and requested them to see the bigger picture for the future of their children. In doing so, they invited the menfolk into their greatness to be able to transcend the gender differences and solve the problems related to basic needs in their village. The women transcended the unworkable cultural norm that only men should approach the District Collector and solved the problem in their village by using their agency. Who they were 'BEING' enabled the women to synthesise and strategise to be able to solve the problems in the village. The students were able to steward change in the village using this framework.

This book attempts to capture the nuances of field instruction across the country and suggest a framework that is theme agnostic and can be applied to any context. It becomes imperative to address the constantly changing concerns that emerge in fieldwork. The flexibility of this framework enables the students and supervisor to use self-awareness, to be aware of systems and cultural norms by way of challenging them using critical thinking and produce results that reinforce the values of social work and foster dignity in people.

Field instruction is a reflexive process of teaching and learning in a partnership between the supervisor, student trainee, the social work department and the larger educational institution (college or university). This is a continuous growth sustaining process in which we are constantly pushing our boundaries to learn, review, unlearn and introspect so that we renew ourselves and approach fieldwork with an open mind. The continued dialogue, reflection and engaging with the dynamic curriculum helps to bring about alignment required for social workers to produce results that can be scaled. This is possible only if we approach an issue from the position of 'inside-out' recursively to foster praxis in learning and doing in the field.

References

Chougule, M. P. (2015). Social work education in urban and rural community development specialization: An analysis of theory and fieldwork practice in Maharashtra. *Contemporary Research in India*, *5*(2), 153–159. Retrieved May 3, 2017, from www.contemporaryresearchindia.net/Pdf/June-2015/00%20Content%20Page.pdf

Johnson, E. J., Bailey, K.-R., & Padmore, J. (2012, April). Issues and challenges of social work practicum in Trinidad and Tobago and India. *Caribbean Teaching Scholar*, *2*(1), 19–29. Retrieved May 7, 2017, from http://libraries.sta.uwi.edu/journals/ojs/index.php/cts/article/viewFile/28/26

Narayan, L., & Pandit, M. (2017). 'Samagratā' framework for social work. *Indian Journal of Social Work, 78*(3), 533–560.

Ramanathan, C. S., & Juvva, S. (2016). Introduction: Perspectives on development. In C. S. Ramanathan, S. Juvva, S. Dutta, & K. Khaja (Eds.), *Spirituality, culture and development: Implications for social work*. Lanham, MD: Lexington Books.

Ramsey, P. (1989). Practice orientation of students in field instruction. In M. Raskin (Ed.), *Empirical studies in field instruction* (pp. 137–160). Binghamton: Haworth Press.

Rodriguez, S., & Juvva, S. (2018). Embodying universal values and ethical leadership in higher education: Creating change agents for social transformation and wellbeing. In B. Chatterjee, A. Banerji, & P. Arya (Eds.), *Resolution to resolve: Sustainability practices in industry and education*. New Delhi: Bloomsbury.

Sharma, M. (2017). *Radical transformational leadership: Strategic action for change agents*. Berkeley, CA: North Atlantic Books.

White, J. (2012). Explosive wisdom: What landmines teach us about liberation and leadership. *Kosmos: Global Citizens Creating the New Civilizations*, Spring/Summer, 12–20.

INDEX

academic performance indicators 165
acceptance 12, 18, 23, 33, 87, 90, 124, 150, 151, 158, 169, 176
accountability 5, 24, 46, 111, 127, 147, 150, 176
action system 13, 91, 96, 98–100
activist 18, 30, 88
adaptive 7, 184, 186, 187, 188, 190, 191, 193, 194
adaptive ability 191, 193
adivasi 30
administrative 40, 49, 66, 102, 117, 123, 148, 155, 161, 163, 164, 166, 171
agency 40–42, 60–64, 127–139, 141–144, 163–166, 170–172
agency supervisor 8, 40, 41, 49, 50, 52, 62–64, 70, 73, 75, 82, 130, 131
agenda 2, 78, 84, 89, 128, 131, 138, 144
analysis 6, 8, 16, 17, 72, 139, 140, 151, 152, 167, 174, 208
analytical 6, 10, 24, 39, 44, 72, 107, 118, 123, 141, 184
anchor 68, 204, 205
anti-oppressive practice 12
anxieties 33, 45, 66, 127, 148, 204
application 6, 107, 112, 120, 137, 140, 153, 156, 161, 167, 171, 172, 175 184, 194
aspirations 31, 44, 91, 182
assessment 39, 41, 45–47
assimilation 13, 159
assumptions 22, 30, 39, 108, 109, 138
attitudes 3, 5, 31, 32, 34, 40, 42, 44, 45, 49, 73, 138, 154, 179184, 186, 190, 192, 193, 200

attributes 14, 23, 84
authentic 15, 21, 201, 205
autonomy 14, 36, 68, 113, 138, 20

balance 12, 14, 74, 149, 168, 172, 174
Being 7, 20, 74, 80, 190, 205, 207–209
bias 15, 16, 111, 118, 154
block placement 3, 40, 52, 57, 64, 66
boundaries 20, 74, 88, 90, 91, 185, 201, 209
BSD full spectrum praxis framework 207, 208
burnout 23

campaign 29, 37, 117, 118, 149
capacities 14, 32, 37, 40, 121, 154, 171, 184, 190, 207
case study 114, 117, 200
case work reports 128
casework 81 89, 137, 156, 162, 167, 180, 196
challenges 30–32
change 1, 12, 18, 21–24, 30, 31, 32, 35, 43, 46, 49, 58, 62, 63
change agent 96, 97, 98, 99
changing contexts 2, 3, 4, 5, 45, 46
choice based credit system (CBCS) 83, 85, 198, 202
circular 140
classroom theory 41
clinical approach 180
collaborative relationship 3, 188
collective action 90,
college or department of social work 132, 133

conceptual learning 173
community 16, 44, 61, 69, 70, 75, 89, 98, 102, 111, 122, 160, 166
community development 2, 36, 39, 128, 132, 154, 156
community organisation 43, 54, 89, 106, 161, 162, 196
compassion 11, 12, 15–17, 20, 205, 208
competencies, 6, 24, 25, 35, 95, 151, 201, 205, 208
confidentiality 111
conflict 45
connectedness 14, 25
consultation 33
contextualising 25, 175
continuum 92, 107, 186
controlled emotional involvement 30
convergence 5, 31, 42, 43, 46, 105
coordination 49, 56, 60, 61, 64, 67, 121, 199, 201, 202
cope 36, 71, 91, 133
core skills 21
councils 41, 83, 179, 200, 202
creativity 17, 63, 133, 182
critical thinking 24, 107, 111, 113, 118, 119, 133, 167, 174, 176, 205, 209
critique 32, 72
cultural norms 196, 205, 207–209, 200, 202, 204, 209

daily log 114
dalit and tribal communities 88
deep listening 21
Department supervisor 49, 53, 62, 165, 171
design 204, 206–208
development 91–96, 205–207
dialogue 19, 21, 22, 24, 37, 42, 93, 99, 100, 107, 147, 199, 209
dignity 10, 12, 20, 25, 43, 88, 111, 206, 209
dilemmas 5, 23, 24, 43, 75
Director of field work 59, 60
disclosure 33
discovery 93, 99, 121, 182
documentation 6
doing 10, 31, 74, 136, 140, 149, 181, 186, 206–208

Earth 11–12, 16–17, 204
empathy 12, 15, 77, 80, 144
empowerment 6, 14–15, 23, 31, 49, 87, 92–94, 98–100, 111, 124, 163, 204
engagement 20, 30–31, 43, 46, 83, 91, 124, 169

environment 7, 11–12, 14–15, 32–33, 43–44, 105, 132, 136, 140, 184, 207
equity 12, 18, 88, 112, 206
ethics 10, 15, 43, 51, 68, 111, 117, 192, 204–205
evaluation 41, 51, 58–59, 91, 123, 128, 142, 149, 167–168, 172–175
expertise 150, 167, 206

facilitate 6, 15–17, 23–24, 53, 59, 79, 107, 122, 136–139
faculty advisor 13
faculty engagement 43, 46
Field Action Projects (FAPs) 14, 168
feedback 22, 33–34, 43, 45–46, 121–122, 131, 151
feminist perspectives and practice 12
field instruction centre 170
fieldwork coordinator 36, 40, 41, 140–141, 202
fieldwork guidelines 55, 130, 133, 165, 172–173
fieldwork: placement 52–53, 72–73, 174–175; supervisor 110, 140, 148–149, 189; tasks 13, 53, 95, 130–131, 203
format 57–58, 113, 116–117, 124, 168, 203
fractal 207
framework 5, 11–12, 40, 88, 92, 96, 113, 173, 207–209

generic 34, 164, 171
globalisation 1, 12, 204
green social work 12
group conferences 24, 53–54, 58, 127–128, 144–148, 192
group labs 55, 56
group work reports 128
guidance 32, 33, 62, 107, 122, 130, 136, 141, 148, 150, 180, 189, 204
guidelines 24, 55, 84, 130, 133, 165, 167, 172–173

harmony 14, 20
healing 17, 20, 23
hierarchical relationship 33, 179, 181
holistic 10, 11, 23, 41, 57, 154
home visits 76, 165–166, 175
human rights 1, 10–11, 21, 30, 87, 114, 163, 197

IASSW 1, 10, 31, 92
ideologies 10, 88, 206
IFSW 1, 10, 31, 92
indigenous 21, 69, 87–88, 148, 176, 204

individual and group conferenc, 1, 20, 24, 127–131, 151, 203
individual conferences 76, 83, 127, 136, 149–150, 166, 171
inherent worth 10
inquiry 6, 14, 73, 176
insights 30, 39, 44, 112, 114, 116, 120, 193
inspiration 13, 107
integrate 9, 17, 52, 72, 89, 111–112, 121, 123
interlinkage 5, 207
intersectionalities 7, 19
introspection 5, 34, 116, 119, 209

job placements 56, 59
journal keeping 114
justice 10–12, 18–20, 32–33, 66, 198

knowing 30, 73–74
knowledge 3, 13, 17, 31, 36, 54, 63, 71, 80, 90, 112, 149–153, 206

learning: by doing and reflecting 31, 186; cycle 32; environment 7, 32, 69, 186
liaising 106
life skills 102, 156
local language 22
love 15, 18, 22, 204

macro, meso and micro 4, 40, 107
management 25, 32, 60, 121
manual, 66, 106, 123, 130
map 91–100, 156
marginalisation 20, 89
matrix 93, 186–190
mentor 6, 13, 25, 46, 77–79, 84, 196, 202
meso 41, 91
methods 1, 35, 41, 76, 90, 161, 174, 196
micro 4, 132, 161, 168
mid-term reviews 35
mindfulness 15–16, 23
minutes of meetings 106
monitoring 33–34, 43, 77, 107, 121–12, 131, 141
motivation 7, 9, 13, 15, 38, 77–78, 109, 110, 121, 135–136
multi-disciplinary teams 41
multidimensional 72

narrative 66, 75, 105, 111, 114–115
NASW 92
navigate 4, 5, 77, 190, 201, 203
negotiate 24, 40
network 37, 55, 57, 95, 136, 162, 175

non-discriminatory 111
non-government organisations 2, 60, 128, 154, 162, 169, 199
non-graded activity 66
non-judgmental attitude 83, 147
non-labelling 111
non-recognition 165
nurture 23, 58, 68, 182
nurturing 5, 16, 23, 66–67, 83, 202

objective-subjective 167–168, 172, 174
observation 74, 80, 82, 114–115, 117–118, 137–138, 171, 174, 198
official noting 106
openness 6, 33, 43, 81, 100
operationalisation 14, 25
opportunities 9, 20, 25, 46, 82, 110, 128, 130, 136, 148, 154, 191
orientation 32, 34, 40–41, 43, 51–52, 60, 74, 148, 153, 171, 198
orientation visits 1, 34, 156
outcomes 6, 33, 36, 101, 120, 133, 140, 156–157
outputs 36, 40, 91, 207

parameters 16, 41, 46, 57, 61–62, 123, 130–131
participation 11, 24, 87, 118, 127, 174
participatory 34, 41, 93
partners 2, 60, 63
partnership 37, 82, 93, 101, 209
patriarchal 30, 88, 180
patterns 73, 75, 118, 184, 205–207
peace 20, 21, 204
pedagogy 15, 43, 82, 166, 176, 198
peer 32, 33, 45, 142, 143–144, 147, 198
people-centred 11, 185
performance 7, 33, 35, 51, 53, 68, 124, 135, 148–149, 181, 185–189
person-in-environment 90
perspective 6, 11–14, 30–31, 43, 46, 53, 71–72, 90–91, 107–110, 113, 180, 196, 206
phase 23, 59, 67, 93, 133–138, 141, 151
philosophical orientation 43
planning 32, 53, 77, 91, 111, 114, 122, 133, 136–138, 198
policy 31, 42, 46, 53, 69, 71, 81, 117, 130, 147, 199
positive learning environment 32, 82
practicum 31–32, 69, 112, 129–131, 140, 153
practitioner 31, 33, 46, 52, 74, 87, 89, 91, 130, 171
praxis 57, 100, 201, 203, 207–209

process recording 44, 114–117, 120, 128
professional 45, 71, 80, 83, 127, 130, 148–159, 179, 184, 206
professional and personal development 68
project management report 117
project proposal 77, 106, 111

qualifications 68
quality 6, 109

radical response 206
reassurance 77, 141
recordings 6, 24, 53, 105–108, 111, 118, 121, 123
reflect 17, 74, 75, 3, 24, 72
reflexive 71, 35
reports 77, 82, 106, 107, 110, 111, 112, 117, 121, 128, 201
research 137, 153, 165, 166, 169, 183, 197, 200
resilience 14, 16, 129, 205
resource persons 52, 54, 60, 102, 182
review 138, 209, 106, 110, 117, 119, 120, 127, 131, 138, 142, 203
role model 13, 24, 33, 42, 80, 150, 201, 204
rural camp 34, 54, 56, 59, 66, 101, 153

Samagratā 11, 14, 25, 204
self 12, 14, 16, 23, 71, 74, 80, 94, 107, 118, 119, 154, 205–207
self as a student social worker 4
self-awareness 5, 6, 16, 23, 34, 74, 94, 114, 136, 154, 203
self-care 23
self-determination 10, 111, 192
self-esteem 14, 23, 35, 78, 94
self-reliance 94, 149
site of practice 7
skill development 65, 76, 77; laboratory 31, 35, 43; training 34
skills and values 1, 24, 111
social change 1, 12, 31, 49, 105, 111
social justice 18, 25, 32, 112, 135, 198, 204, 206
social transformation 20, 26, 31, 41, 44
social work organisations 2, 3, 135
social work practice 11, 14, 25, 50, 66, 76, 81, 88, 91, 92, 112, 148, 154, 170, 172, 176, 204

socio-economic contexts 139, 160
specialisation 34, 36, 41, 155, 167, 198
spirituality 11, 14, 204
stakeholder analysis 129, 140
stakeholders 41, 45, 49, 50, 56, 67, 121, 128, 129, 140, 141, 170, 188
standards 13, 41, 79, 89, 92, 131, 132, 142, 149
strategic 140, 157, 206
strategies 140, 143, 148, 150, 153, 175, 206
strengths perspective 12
study tour 55, 66, 153, 198
summary record 79, 114
supervisor 3, 4, 6, 7, 130
supervisor-student relationship 6
supervisor–student–agency triad 4
supervisor-supervisee relationship 33, 43, 71, 80, 81, 182
supervisory process 23, 45, 68, 69, 72, 74, 82, 142, 201
synthesis 73, 107, 201, 203
systems 22, 30, 71
systems theory 88, 90, 91, 94, 96, 99

task-centred 23, 142, 185, 82
teaching and learning 142, 209
teamwork 136
termination 91, 141
theory: eco-systems 88, 90–91, 99; empowerment 88, 91–94, 99
time diary 25

UGC 94, 155, 177, 197, 198, 200
UGC model curriculum 55, 80
universal values and ethics 205

values 73, 80, 83, 84, 88, 90, 95 108, 111, 114, 138, 148, 154, 179, 183, 190
vigilantism 68, 83
visits 34, 51, 52, 55, 60, 63, 64, 70, 76, 117, 154
viva voce 55, 58, 64, 166, 167
vulnerability 16, 30, 93

welfare 30, 31, 41, 87, 88, 102, 154, 160, 162
well-being 14, 17, 18, 23, 25
wisdom 32, 68, 88, 205, 206
workload 40, 66, 130, 202, 204
writing 24, 75, 88, 106–108, 111, 113–115